Get The Love You Want

Soul Partners

A Self and Relationship Healing Guide For Singles and Couples

Ra Heter, Ph.D.
Mu Skher Aakhu

Universal Consciousness Publications

Universal Consciousness Publications (UCP)

Nuvo Development, Inc.
Decatur, GA 30034

Copyright © 2017
All rights reserved

ISBN 978-09968000-3-7

www.universalconciousnessinc.org

About the Authors

Dr. Ra Heter *(aka Patricia Dixon)*, educator, author, and dating, relationship and marriage, life, and spiritual wellness coach, served as an associate professor for over 20 years at Georgia State University where she developed and taught courses in numerous subject areas including relationships, marriages, and families. She is the author of several books on relationships. Mu Skher Aakhu *(aka Timothy Spear)*, has a lifetime of experience as a life and spiritual wellness coach, entrepreneur, and musician. They are husband and wife and the founders of Universal Consciousness, Inc (UCI).

In loving memory of
Anna Mae & Genie Dixon

Contents

Introduction	ix

Chapter

1. Seven Aspects of the Self	1
2. Shaping Factors	13
3. The Unfolding Self	29
4. Love and the Wounded Child	41
5. The Seven Chakras	71
6. Healing the Energy Body	95
7. Seven Steps to Healing and Awakening	115
8. Seven Principles of Conscious Dating	139
9. Seven Compatibilities	167
10. Talking and Listening with Care	201
11. Sexual Healing and Bliss	245
12. The Stairway to Heaven	279
References	301

Exercises

Chapter 2. Family Reflections	20
Chapter 3. Identifying Unfinished Tasks	38
Chapter 4. Identifying Childhood Wounds	60
Chapter 5. Identifying Energetic Wounds	85
Chapter 6. Healing the Energy Body	111
Chapter 7. Healing and Awakening	129
Chapter 8. A Plan for Dating	160
Chapter 9. Compatibility Check	182
Chapter 10. Talking and Listening with Care	233
Chapter 11. Towards Sexual Healing & Bliss	273
Chapter 12. Climbing the Stairway to Heaven	296
Attunements	106

Introduction

According to ancient wisdom traditions, your soul was birthed by the Soul of the Universe and took on a physical body to experience life on Earth. The goal was for you to become the highest expression of yourself, and a vehicle through which the Universe Soul could express itself on Earth. Once you achieved this goal, you could then return to the Universe Soul. However, because most of us get lost along the way, we do not become the highest expression of ourselves; nor do we do achieve unity in one lifetime. It may take many lifetimes to learn lessons and/or resolve issues from previous lives as well as this life to achieve the highest expression of ourselves and unity with the Universe Soul.

Wisdom traditions also recognized three primary states of awakening or consciousness. In our earthly conscious state of awakening, there is a primary focus on the temporal material world including the self and material things. When we awaken to Universe Love, we awaken our compassionate selves and our moral obligation to others and to be our best self. Awakening to Universe Consciousness awakens us to the knowledge of our highest potential, and the power we have to access the realms of God's wisdom and power. If we choose the path of Universe Consciousness, we are choosing to continue to grow and evolve deeper into God Consciousness and open the doorway to a happy, healthy, fulfilling, and blissful life. Your soul's partner is the person to help you on this journey.

Like you, your soul's partner left the Universe Soul and assumed an earthly body to experience life on Earth. If you have the good fortune to meet, it is the person (or persons if there are more than one) who will assist you in your soul's evolvement in this lifetime. Your soul's partner serves several functions. First, he or she is the person you will share your life with so you can enjoy earthly things including love, companionship, children, family, etc. He or she is also the person who will support you in the face of life's most difficult challenges. Secondly, he or she provides the opportunity for the mutual learning of lessons in this lifetime so that your souls continue their evolvement toward unity with the Universe Soul. Third, he or she is the person to help you share your gifts to fulfill this earthly life purpose and to facilitate your mutual spiritual cultivation so that you become vehicles through which the Universe Soul can express its will on earth. Finally, if you and your soul's partner can unify with each other and continue your evolvement toward unity with the Universe Soul, then he or she provides the opportunity for your mutual journeys, as *soul partners* to experience a happy, healthy, fulfilling, and blissful life together.

Overview

The first half of this book outlines how our experiences can lead to wounds, and social conventions can lead us away from our true selves with exercises to help recognize how these experiences may have affected us and our interaction patterns in relationships. The second half outlines steps for healing and awakening and tools to get the love you want. In Chapter 1 we outline the seven aspects of the self and the seven chakras. We also introduce two ancient tools - the step pyramid and the Tree of Life that have been used to facilitate awakening to our true selves, and how to become our best selves. In Chapter 2 we explain the role that the physical, emotional, mental, and spiritual communities play in shaping the physical, mental, emotional and spiritual aspects of ourselves. In Chapter 3 we outline the tasks that should be completed and the strengths that should be gained as the self unfolds in the cycle of life after the soul enters the earthly realm. In Chapter 4 we describe how early experiences with our caregivers/families can leave lasting effects that reveal themselves in who we attract, and in our attachment styles and interaction patterns. In Chapter 5 we explain how our wounds can lead to leaks or blocks of vital force (energy) to the seven chakras (life force energy centers) and can contribute to diminished health and well-being.

In Chapter 6 we provide a brief overview of healing modalities that can be used for healing the energy body, including but not limited to: sounds, colors, crystals, meditation, and attunements. In Chapter 7 we outline a seven-step program for healing and awakening. In Chapter 8 we outline seven principles for conscious dating that can lead to a relationship, and in Chapter 9 we provide an overview of seven areas of compatibility that should be considered whether one is choosing a partner or are already in a relationship, and how to reconcile differences. Chapter 10 provides practical tools for communication and conflict resolution. Chapter 11 provides an overview of energy practices from Tantra and Traditional Chinese medicine (TCM) that can be used for sexual healing. Finally, in Chapter 12, using the Tree of Life, we provide a guide for couples to follow, to help each other grow and evolve spiritually.

Chapter Exercises

Each chapter is followed by exercises that are designed to help you explore those factors that have shaped who you are, where you are in terms of your health, well-being, and awakening, and how all of this shapes your relationships interactions, and patterns. The exercises are also designed to help you heal, awaken, and evolve spiritually.

If you are not in a relationship, the exercises can be completed as they apply to yourself and as a guide for attracting your soul's partner, making you better prepared for a relationship. If you are already in a relationship or married, they can be used to strengthen you, your partner, and your relationship.

Finally, this book is a self and relationship healing guide with tools to help you find and keep love, and ultimately, get the love you want.

1

Seven Aspects of the Self

Energy is where religion (which is based on spiritual traditions) and modern scientific approaches to understanding reality converge. When one takes an energy approach to understanding reality, it reveals that science and religion are essentially one and the same thing but with a different focus. Science focuses on the world of matter in physical reality; spirituality focuses on all of reality. In the world of science, the universe was created through a big bang (sound), and all of existence is energy vibrating at different frequencies governed by physical laws. In the world of spirituality, the universe was created through the spoken word (sound), by an intelligence, which we are calling Universal Consciousness; energy repeats itself in patterns and is governed by universal laws put in place through intelligent design. Since all of existence is energy vibrating at different frequencies you are therefore energy vibrating. Because the Universe Soul is the undifferentiated source from which all things originated, and energy can neither be created nor destroyed (it can only be transformed from one form to another) and you were birthed by that source, there is a part of you that is eternal. This part we are referring to is your soul.

SEVEN ASPECTS OF THE SELF & THE FOUR BODIES

We are able to live on Earth through four bodies that make up seven aspects of the self. Although these aspects of the self are referred to by different names and vary in how they are described by different cultures, we are naming and briefly describing them as follows:

1. *The Physical Body*—how we are able to exist on Earth in the physical realm
2. *The Emotional Body*— how we sense and respond to the world and our desires
3. *The Mental Body*—how we cognize the world, our thoughts, and imagination
4. *The Compassionate Self*—our capacity for love and compassion; the aspect of the self that connects to Universe Love
5. *The Conscious Self*—our capacity for rightness and justice; and the aspect of the self that connects to Universe Sound and gives us the ability to hear
6. *The Enlightened Self*—our capacity for wisdom and understanding; the aspect of the self that connects to Universe Light and gives us the ability to know and see
7. *Eternal Self*—the aspect of self that is a part of the Universe Soul (i.e., God)

The physical, emotional, and mental bodies correspond to the physical, emotional, and mental aspects of the self (i.e., the lower self). The compassionate, conscious, enlightened, and eternal aspects of the self correspond to the spiritual body, (i.e., the higher self).

THE SUBTLE ENERGY BODIES

All physical reality has a corresponding subtle energy body through which it receives Divine force. For example, the Earth has its own subtle energy body that expands outward and interacts with the subtle energy bodies of other celestial bodies (e.g., the moon, sun, and other planets that affect its physical body and the life contained therein). Likewise, humans have subtle energy bodies that interact with the subtle energy bodies of those in their physical, emotional, mental and spiritual worlds.

These subtle energy bodies can be found in the spiritual tradition of India in the Upanishads, believed to be composed between 800-400 BC. According to this tradition, there are five sheaths or coverings of the soul, referred to as Koshas. These five layers range from the denser body to the levels of emotions, mind, and spirit. They were later renamed and expanded upon (for Western understanding) in works by members of the Theosophical Society founded by Helena Petrovna Blavatsky and Henry Steel Olcott in 1875.[1] These Koshas include the following:

1. **Physical body** —which is nourished by food (food stuff)
2. **Etheric body**—the energy that vitalizes the physical body and holds it together (vital force)
3. **Astral body**—lower mind along with five sensory organs—also referred to as the sense and emotional bodies (manas or mind stuff)

---

[1] The most prolific writers of the Theosophical Society were Annie Besant, Charles Webster Leadbeater, Alfred Percy Sinnet, and Helena Petrovna Blavatsky herself. Many of the spiritual concepts of the Theosophical society were founded primarily upon the philosophy of ancient India. New Age spirituality seems to have originated from the Theosophical Society. However, the spiritual traditions of the Kemetians, (Black Egypt) and other African and indigenous peoples, Dravidians (Black India), Chinese, (Traditional Chinese Medicine) Japanese (Reiki), mystical Judaism and Christianity, and other Western esoteric traditions (Hermeticism, Rosicrucianism, Freemasonry, etc. which are themselves founded on Kemetic spirituality) seem to form the basis of New Age Spirituality.

4. **Mental body**—intellect—the faculty that discriminates, determines, or wills. It consists of both the lower mind and the higher mind (manas or mind stuff)
5. **Causal body**—supreme bliss state; self-realization unity or oneness with the Divine

The three subtle energy bodies—the etheric, astral, and mental bodies are explained further.

The Etheric Body
The etheric body, the first layer of the aura, and a replica of the physical body (referred to as our double), is a physical heat layer, about 1½ inches wide, that sits around the body. It is the bridge to the core energy body, which consists of the seven major energy centers called chakras (or wheels of light in Sanskrit). The chakras, which are centered around the major glands, organs, and other parts of the physical body, are the channels through which the vital force –which gives us life and is referred to as, Reiki (in Japanese), Chi (in Chinese) and Prana (in India)—is distributed to the body through the 21 minor and 49 minuscule chakras, 72,000 nadis, and 12 meridians. The vital force is what holds the physical body together, making it possible for us to exist in the earthly realm and to be in communication with the other realms.

The Astral Body
The astral body (considered the vehicle of the soul), also referred to as our sense or emotional body is the subtle energy component of the five senses and is thought to be activated by our desires (Powell, 1978)[2] As with the etheric body, the astral body is a replica of the physical body but is composed of finer matter. It is the bridge between the mind and the physical body and allows us to dream, fantasize, and have out-of-body experiences, as well as experience a full range of emotions; sadness, happiness, fear, anger, love, and hate. Since the astral body is thought to be the vehicle of the soul, it is the

medium through which the soul can travel while in the dream state (through lucid dreaming), trance, astral projection, meditation, etc.

Through the astral body we are able to correspond with the astral world (also referred to as the fourth dimension), thought to be the abode of those who have died (including our ancestors) and other beings who exist on different planes within this realm. The astral body is where all our emotions and feelings are stored, and it stores all emotional experiences accumulated throughout all our lifetimes (and the karma attached to them). The astral realm is where the soul goes before it is reincarnated to return to earth or ascend to higher realms. The astral body has an oval aura that extends four to nine feet beyond the body and reflects our emotional state.

The Mental Body

The mental body is the subtle energy body that corresponds to our thoughts. Since our thoughts also have vibrations, and nothing came into the world without thought, they can enter the world as thought-forms. Whenever one thinks a thought, it enters the mental plane. The intensity of a thought or how often it is thought will determine whether that thought takes form.

The mental body is the vehicle of the lower and higher minds. The lower mind corresponds with reason and logic and everyday thinking in the concrete physical world. The higher mind corresponds to abstract ideas and is the part of the mental body that is used in deep states of meditation, contemplation, innovation, and invention. When one focuses primarily on matters in the concrete physical world, this is where their thoughts remain and subsequently their consciousness. When they focus on higher levels of selfless thought,

---

[2] See the work, *The Astral Body* by Arthur E. Powell for a more in-depth understanding of the astral body. This work as well as others authored by him helps to simplify the numerous works authored by other members of the Theosophical Society.

their level of consciousness enters into the world of Universe Love and when they focus on Universe Consciousness, they are able to tap into vibrational frequencies that open them to higher levels of consciousness. Tapping into Universal Consciousness can awaken the causal body, which, unlike the etheric, astral, and mental bodies which are subtle energy bodies, is a *state* of consciousness— the bliss state.

The Seven Chakras

The seven chakras are the vehicles or centers of consciousness through which vital force is distributed throughout the body and connects us to the different dimensions, aspects of ourselves, and levels of consciousness. How the chakras correspond to the different aspects of the self are described below from the bottom to the top and they are shown in *Figure 1.1.* that follows.

1. ***The Root Chakra*** corresponds to our physical body and social survival in the physical world. It is the driver of our instinctive self to survive and thrive.
2. ***The Sacral Chakra*** corresponds to our emotional body and our desires. It is the center of pleasure, sensuality, and our procreative, creative, and expansive capacities.
3. ***The Solar Plexus Chakra*** corresponds to our sense of power to bring into manifestation those things we desire. It also corresponds to our lower mind.
4. ***The Heart Chakra*** corresponds to our capacity for love and compassion at higher levels of consciousness.
5. ***The Throat Chakra*** corresponds to our voice and capacity to hear at higher levels of consciousness.
6. ***The Third Eye Chakra*** corresponds to our higher mind and our capacity to see at higher levels of consciousness.
7. ***The Crown Chakra*** corresponds to the Divine world, allowing us to unify with and become one with the Universe Soul.

Figure 1.1
Seven Chakras

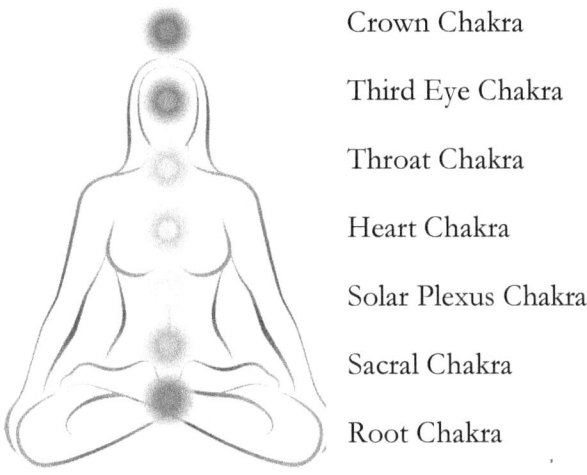

Crown Chakra

Third Eye Chakra

Throat Chakra

Heart Chakra

Solar Plexus Chakra

Sacral Chakra

Root Chakra

SEVEN STEPS TO BLISS

In ancient Egypt, among the Kemetians, the step pyramid was symbolic of the steps to the bliss state, unity with the Universe Soul, and eternal life. It was so to speak, the stairway to heaven. Initiates who were on this path had to gain mastery over lower aspects of the self—the physical body (first step from the bottom of the pyramid) and awaken to higher aspects of the self—unity (step seven on top of the pyramid). This was achieved through spiritual cultivation.

STEPS TO BLISS

1. Mastery over the Physical Body
2. Mastery over the Emotional Body
3. Mastery over the Mental Body
4. Awakening to Universe Love
5. Awakening to Universe Consciousness
6. Awakening to Universal Light
7. Unifying with the Universe Soul

Figure 1.2
Step Pyramid

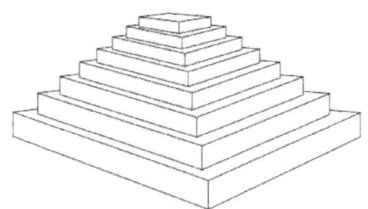

TREE OF LIFE

A tool that is used for spiritual cultivation is the Tree of life. Although it has been used as a symbol to illuminate spiritual ideas among peoples throughout the world, among the ancient Kemetians and represented as the Kabbalah in mystical Judaism, the Tree of Life was used to facilitate mastery and awakening. According to these traditions, when the universe unfolded it did so in 10 emanations resulting in 10 spheres. Spiritual evolvement could be achieved by mastering and awakening faculties that man in the earthly realm possesses and shares with energetic forces in these spheres. In most, if not all traditions, while creating the universe, the Universe Soul also created intelligences which we are referring to as Universe Helpers to help create and have dominion over different aspects of the universe. They are referred to in various ways in different cultures. Below are just a few of the most widely known ones.

- Kemetic/Egyptian—*Neteru*
- Judeo-Christian—*Angles and Archangels*
- Islam—*Angels and Archangels*
- Yoruba—*Orishas*
- India—*Devas*
- New Age—*Angels, Archangels, Ascended Masters* (who once had an earthly body and evolved spiritually and ascended)

The roles of the Universe Helpers are to maintain the universe in both the cosmic and earthly realms, while the role of humanity is to maintain the earthly realm. Thus, the qualities we share with Universe Helpers manifest in our persona (a vehicle of sound) or personality. They also manifest in our special gifts and talents. Not only does spiritual cultivation enable us to awaken these faculties in ourselves, but it awakens the ability to tap into the interdimensional energetic force of the Universe Helpers that have dominion over that sphere.

Through spiritual cultivation of the faculties corresponding to the spheres on the Tree of Life, we have the potential to tap into the neteru, archangel, angel, or genius, and ultimately God within. *Figure 1.3* below shows the Tree of Life that has been adapted with some variations from the Kemetic version articulated by Ra Um Nefer Amen (1990) in his work *Metu Neter*. This is followed by a brief description of each sphere that will be expanded on in chapter 12.

10 Soul Partners

Figure 1.3
Tree of Life

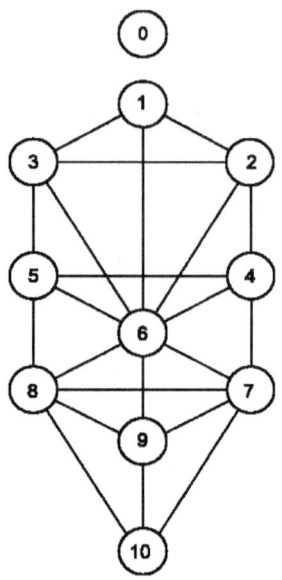

SPHERE
0. Non-being no-thing, no thought
1. Unity—undifferentiated, unlimited potential; infinity
2. Will and Knowledge—to bring things into manifestation
3. Power—to manifest things
4. Law—ruling principles for things manifested; order and oneness
5. Justice—enforcement of order and oneness for the preservation of the whole
6. Love—the binding force; balance between the upper & lower worlds[3]
7. Imagination—coordination of imagery that synthesizes differences
8. Thought—distinguishes and segregates differences between things
9. Emotion—from desire; the driving force and coordinator of all shaping forces in spheres 1-8 to manifest the physical world
10. Physical—the world manifested

Clearing, cleansing, and opening the seven energy centers or chakras, becoming attuned to healing energy, and climbing the seven steps as we cultivate the 10 spheres on the tree of life are necessary to help us heal our wounds, and tap into the best of who we can be. Such work can awaken us to higher levels of consciousness, thereby increasing our energetic vibrations so that we are able to find and attract the right person, our soul's partner and sustain a relationship with him or her. How all of this can be done will be expanded on throughout this book. Let us first begin with the factors that shape who we are.

---

[3] Amen refers to the sixth sphere as the duality of self—and equilibrium between the subjective unconditioned self which we share with the Supreme Being and our conditioned selves. It is also our personal free will choice to live according to Divine laws with unity as the driving force. We have called this sphere love to indicate that Universe Love awakens us to the understanding that everything is connected and therefore awakens our sensitivities to Divine laws and the personal free will choice to live in accordance with them. This leads us to live through our higher selves.

2

Shaping Factors

What are the factors that have shaped who you are? Defining and examining the physical, emotional, mental, and spiritual communities in which you grew up is important to understanding the factors that have shaped you. More importantly, increasing your awareness of how these communities have shaped you is the beginning of unraveling what is necessary to attract your soul's partner and sustain a relationship with him or her.

When your soul left the cosmic realm to come to Earth, it came through a family, which was surrounded by a local, national, and global community. In essence, your soul assumed a physical, emotional, mental, and spiritual body that shares experiences with the physical, emotional, mental, and spiritual communities in which it was born.

COMMUNITY

The national community can be viewed as an all-encompassing community that governs local communities and families. The communities that shape the national community are defined below.

The Physical Community is characterized by land, material resources from that land and elsewhere, and the physical and social structures put in place to protect it.

The Emotional Community is the energy or driving force (e.g., values and corresponding desires and wills) that moves the society forward. These driving forces affect its members including their behaviors and their interaction patterns.

The Mental Community consists of ideas about how the nation governs itself, the values underlying these ideas, and the social structures put in place to carry them out. The social structures include the political (i.e., who determines how the material resources will be distributed); economic (i.e., the actual resources); and social institutions (e.g., family, education, media, and religion) that guide how members are cultivated physically, emotionally, mentally, and spiritually.

The Spiritual Community is the nation's ideas about and practices that connect it to the cosmic realm and the Divine world. The interpenetrating bodies of the various communities are illustrated in *Figure 2.1* below.

Figure 2.1
Four Communities

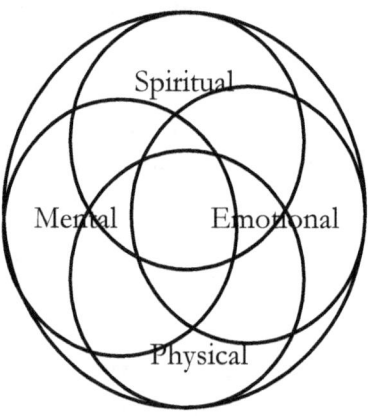

CULTURE

Once your soul enters the earthly realm, it enters into a culture—which means cultivation of the soul. The goal of cultivating people into society is so that they understand the language and rules governing that society. Cultivation is necessary to create healthy, functioning members of that society, who will, ultimately, participate in its evolvement. However, just as there exists an ideal self (i.e., who we would like to be) and a real self (i.e., who we really are) societies have dual personalities. Some societies may express high principles regarding how their citizens should be treated, however, they may not necessarily follow through on them. Such societies may be challenged by conflicting ideas and the values driving them.

For example, in the U.S., a fundamental guiding principle is equality for all. However, because the country's economic system is based on capitalism i.e., free-market competition which is driven by ideologies of materialism, individualism, survival of the fittest, and white supremacy, etc. such ideologies undermine the country's ability to operate by this principle. The result is that it is stratified by race, class, and gender hierarchies, which leaves those who are less protected and more vulnerable (minorities, low income, females, and/or non-conforming gender people) at the bottom. Such vulnerability can profoundly affect individuals' physical, psycho-emotional, and spiritual growth and development; this affects the level to which they can function, who they attract, the state of their relationships, marriages, and families, and how they evolve.

FAMILY

Since the family is a microcosm of the national community, it is greatly influenced by it. Through the family, we learn what it means to be a member of society. Our experiences within families shape our sense of identity and belonging. When examining the family one was born into, one would look at how its structure helped to shape who one is. The traditional idea of a family within the U.S. is a two-parent monogamous, nuclear family. Under this model, the family begins with the marriage of the couple, which is the central unit around which the family unifies and functions. In other cultures, when one marries, one is merely extending one's family and the bloodline is the central unifying force. The U.S. is a multicultural society and, although the monogamous, nuclear family is the ideal type, for some ethnicities, their family practices are more in line with their cultural roots. For example, in African, Asian, and Hispanic American families, the family of origin may play a significant role in the choice of a partner; moreover, there are rules guiding the obligations of family members. In some African American families that have retained their African cultural roots, all family members are obligated to care for children and the elderly.

Boundaries

Boundaries distinguish the family from the local community in which it exists.

External boundaries circumscribe the family and serve to differentiate and protect it from the external environment. It marks the boundaries that indicate who is in the family and who is not.

Open boundaries are boundaries that allow enough input from outside sources to allow the family to grow.

Closed boundaries are those that are too rigid and do not allow enough input from the outside to allow the family to grow.

Diffuse boundaries are those that are too open or loose, which may mean that the family is poorly organized or under-organized, allowing too much input from the outside.

Internal boundaries serve to differentiate one subsystem or dyad from the other within the family, i.e., spousal, parent-child, sibling, as well as dyads that are formed around generations, sexes, interests, and functions (Minuchan, 1974, p 52).

The internal boundaries can also be open, closed, or diffuse. For example, open boundaries in a couple dyad may allow enough information to flow between them and allow for mutual growth and development. Conversely, closed boundaries in a couple dyad may stifle their growth and development, while diffuse boundaries may allow too much input from extended family members and friends and interfere with their growth and development.

Structure and Functioning

The structure has to do with whether the family is a couple without children, two-parent, single-parent, extended (including members of the family of origin, and/or fictive-kin—those who are like family), etc. The family structure can profoundly affect family functioning. For example, a single-parent family may function differently than a two-parent family, mainly because one adult is primarily responsible for meeting all the needs of the family, e.g., provider, protector, nurturer, etc.

A family's structure and functioning are greatly affected by the national and local communities and depend upon the distribution of material and non-material resources and how its members can access them. The family's sense of security and safety are affected by the quality of life of the local community. This includes availability and quality of jobs, material resources (i.e., food, clothing), and social institutions (i.e., schools, churches, municipal, and other human service organizations) surrounding it. For example, if a family lives in a community with few or no jobs or legitimate means to earn a living, poor quality food, low quality social institutions, and high crime and violence, its members may feel insecure and unsafe; as a result, this can profoundly affect the mental and emotional bodies of the family and the interaction patterns of its members. The structure and functioning shape the physical, emotional, mental, and spiritual bodies of the family.

The Physical Body of the family consists of its material resources including safe, affordable, and decent housing, food, clothing, communication, and other material resources for healthy survival in the culture, i.e., computers, access to the Internet, etc.

The Emotional Body of the family is simultaneously shaped by and influences the interaction patterns between the family members. The intensity and degree of connectedness between the family members affect their interaction patterns and may be characterized as being enmeshed where members are tightly knit, but in extreme cases do not allow enough room for independence and autonomy. At the other end of the spectrum, they may be disengaged, where there may not be enough emotional connectedness and members do not receive enough emotional support; this contributes to weak relationships between the members within and between the subsystems. The interaction patterns show in both verbal and non-verbal communication.

The Mental Body of the family is shaped by the family's ideas, values, and beliefs about how the family should be governed. This body is greatly influenced by the social institutions of the national and local communities, and how the adult members have been shaped by the ideas, values, and beliefs of their families of origin. The mental body includes the family's governing structure, which includes the hierarchy, how power is shared, and rules, including who sets and governs these rules. The *spoken* ideas, values, and beliefs, and the governing structure affect the family members and the *unspoken* rules, roles, patterns, and processes that emerge because of them.

The Spiritual Body is a family's ideas about and connections to the cosmic realm and the Divine world through religious and/or spiritual practices. Such connections shape the values and moral principles guiding the family. A family's ideas and practices are generally shaped by the larger society. The religious ideas and beliefs and how they are practiced in the family shape the beliefs, practices, moral principles, and values of its members.

When examining the family that has shaped who you are, several factors should be considered:

- Where was your family in the socio-economic strata and how did its access/lack of access to material and social resources affect its ability to survive and thrive?
- What type of internal and external boundaries characterized your family, and how did they affect its structure and functioning?
- What was your family's governing structure? How was power shared? What were the ideas, values, and beliefs, guiding your family? How did all these factors affect your family's rules, roles, patterns, and processes?

- What was the level of connectedness between family members and how did it affect interaction patterns?
- What were the religious/spiritual beliefs of your family, and how did they shape your family's moral values, principles, and practices?

How did all these factors affect the family and its members? More importantly, how did they shape and affect you?

In summary, your physical, emotional, mental, and spiritual bodies have been shaped by the broader society as well as the family in which you were raised. How did these experiences shape who you are? What role do these shaping factors play in how you interact in relationships? The exercises that follow are designed to explore your family structure and functioning, how they affected your life in both good and bad ways, and how these experiences continue to affect your life. The exercises at the end of the chapters that follow will explore more deeply the effect of your family experiences on your relationship interactions and patterns.

Chapter 2 Exercises

Family Reflections

The purpose of these exercises is to reflect on how your family has shaped who you are.

EXERCISE 2.1. *Your Family Structure*

1. Check the box that best describes the boundaries in your family (and your partner's family if applicable).

You	Your Partner
☐ Closed—rigid, not many people came in or out, and/or we were prohibited from sharing our business with anyone outside our family ☐ Open—fairly balanced, people came in and out of our family in a healthy way ☐ Diffuse—too open, too many people were in and out without structure ☐ Other _____	☐ Closed—rigid, not many people came in or out and/or we were prohibited from sharing our business with anyone outside our family ☐ Open—fairly balanced, people came in and out of our family in a healthy way ☐ Diffuse—too open, too many people were in and out without structure ☐ Other _____

2. Check the box that best describes how your family (and your partner's family if applicable) were structured.

You	Your Partner
☐ Single parent family—was raised by primarily one parent ☐ Dual parent—was raised with primarily two parents who lived	Single parent family—was raised by primarily one parent ☐ Dual parent—was raised with primarily two parents who lived

in the same house ☐ Dual—was raised primarily by two parents who did not live in the same house ☐ Extended—was raised by one or both parents with other family members who lived in the same house ☐ Extended—was raised by one or both parents with other family members who lived in other households ☐ Other_____	in the same house ☐ Dual—was raised primarily by two parents who did not live in the same house ☐ Extended—was raised by one or both parents with other family members who lived in the same house ☐ Extended—was raised by one or both parents with other family members who lived in other households ☐ Other_____

3. Describe who was in your family_____
_____
_____
_____
_____

EXERCISE 2.2. *Your Family Functioning*

Physical Environment

1. Put a circle (and square if you have a partner) around the response that corresponds to your family situations.

I feel/My partner feels I/we ...	Not at all				A Lot
Had what we needed	1	2	3	4	5
Had what we wanted	1	2	3	4	5
Felt safe	1	2	3	4	5
Felt secure	1	2	3	4	5
Felt worried	1	2	3	4	5
Felt afraid	1	2	3	4	5
Felt embarrassed	1	2	3	4	5

2. Describe what you felt and why you felt the way you did when you were a child.

_____
_____
_____
_____

3. Check the box that corresponds to the economic situation of your parents/caregivers.

☐ Parents did well and we pretty much had what we needed and wanted. ☐ Parents really struggled to make ends meet but they were able to get through it peacefully ☐ Parents struggled to make ends meet and it caused a lot of (conflict) ☐ Other _____	☐ Parents did well and we pretty much had what we needed and wanted. ☐ Parents really struggled to make ends meet but they were able to get through it peacefully ☐ Parents struggled to make ends meet and it caused a lot of (conflict) ☐ Other _____

4. Describe how the economic situation, what your parents did for a living, your family's socio-economic status, living conditions, etc. affected your family environment.

_____
_____
_____
_____

5. Describe the community you were raised in and the effect it had on your family.

_____
_____
_____
_____

Emotional Environment

1. Check the box that corresponds to the level of connectedness between family members.

You	Your Partner
☐ Enmeshed—close in a healthy way; had conflict sometimes	☐ Enmeshed—close in a healthy way; had conflict sometimes
☐ Enmeshed—close in an unhealthy way; highly charged, conflicted	☐ Enmeshed—close in an unhealthy way; highly charged, conflicted
☐ Distant—Not close at all; very little communication and family members usually went their own way	☐ Distant—Not close at all; very little communication and family members usually went their own way
☐ Balanced—enough closeness to feel connected, but enough distance to be able to pursue individual interests and be ourselves.	☐ Balanced—enough closeness to feel connected, but enough distance to be able to pursue individual interests and be ourselves.
☐ Other _____	☐ Other _____

2. Put a circle (and square if you have a partner) around the number that corresponds to the predominant emotional environment of your families.

Peaceful	1	2	3	4	5	Conflicted
Good drama	1	2	3	4	5	Bad drama
Quiet & reserved	1	2	3	4	5	Lively & active
Fun & loving	1	2	3	4	5	Miserable
Full of life	1	2	3	4	5	Lonely

3. Describe the relationships between family members including those between parents, stepparents, parents and children, siblings, and extended and non-family members who were involved in your family life.

_____
_____
_____
_____
_____

Mental Environment

1. Check the box for how power was shared among your parents/caregivers.

You	Your Partner
☐ Authoritarian—one parent dominated the other parent and the children ☐ Authoritative—parents discussed matters and shared decision making ☐ Other_____	☐ Authoritarian—one parent dominated the other parent and the children ☐ Authoritative—parents discussed matters and shared decision making ☐ Other_____

2. Put a circle for you and a square for your partner around the number that corresponds to how children were parented /disciplined by the respective parent.

Parenting Styles	Parent/ Caretaker 1 _____	Parent Caretaker 2 _____
Authoritarian—strict and children did what they were instructed to do by parents	1	2
Authoritative—children were disciplined but things		

were explained; children could express themselves	1	2
Permissive—children allowed to do what they wanted to do	1	2
Uninvolved—parent not Involved	1	2

3. Describe the parenting and disciplinary styles of parents/care givers, and the effect they had on the family environment.

_____
_____
_____
_____
_____

4. Put a circle (and square if you have a partner) around the number that corresponds to the flexibility of roles and rules.

	Very Rigid				Very Open & Flexible
Roles	1	2	3	4	5
Rules	1	2	3	4	5

5. Describe how your family was governed, e.g., who set the rules, who enforced them, how they were enforced, and the effect they had on the family environment.

_____
_____
_____
_____
_____

6. What were the gender roles in your family? For example, who worked outside the home, did household chores, provided care and nurturance to children, etc.? How did these gender roles affect the family environment?

___

7. Describe the ideas and values guiding your family, and the effect they had on your family, e.g. work hard, help people, get an education, family comes first, etc.

___

Religious/Spiritual Environment

1. Describe your family's religious beliefs and practices, and how they affected the family environment.

___

2. Describe your family's moral values and principles, and how they affected the family environment.

___

EXERCISE 2.3. *Family Narratives*

1. Describe how your family experiences have affected you (and your partner) in both healthy ways and unhealthy ways. How do these experiences affect your lives today?

___

Additional Notes

3

The Unfolding Self

When you enter the earthly realm, your soul goes through the lifecycle in a succession of awakenings as the self unfolds. However, before delving into the life cycle and the unfolding of the self, it is important to first understand time. At the most fundamental level, there is Earth time and cosmic time. Time on Earth is measured in terms of wavelengths of light. There are approximately 86,400 wavelengths of light (seconds) in a day and 31,536,000 wavelengths of light in a year. Time on Earth is, therefore, measured by the sun. As the light from the sun is the source of life on Earth, one can understand why the ancient Egyptians viewed the sun as a living God. Cosmic time is outside the realm of the cycles of the sun or the solar system. When your soul journeys to Earth, it enters into the domain of Earth time. When you die a physical death, your soul returns to cosmic time.

According to Fu-Kiau (1994), everything goes through a time process under four realms of time. Planets undergo cosmic time, living things undergo vital time, nature undergoes natural time, and social processes undergo social time, activities of human beings. When the soul takes on a physical body as a human being, it undergoes vital time in the earthly realm. How you utilize your vital force will determine your vital time, which dissipates as you go through the cycle of life. How you progress at each stage in the cycle of life will affect how you continue to progress at each successive stage.

Attachment & Detachment

Just as the Universe Soul detached from the watery abyss and differentiated so that it could experience, your soul detached from the womb of the Universe Soul so that it could experience. However, as your soul goes through life cycles, it undergoes a process of attaching and detaching. After it experiences all there is to experience, and it is ready to let go of its attachment to things in the physical world, it will return to the Universe Soul, which is undifferentiated and eternal. Your soul's return may occur in this cycle of life or after many life cycles.

Pre-birth

Although things may have occurred in previous lives before your soul decided to journey to Earth this time, the physical body that it inhabited began when your father's sperm detached from his body and your mother's egg detached from her fallopian tube and they found each other and joined together, and attached in the uterus of your mother so that her body could provide sustenance and vital force to nurture the vehicle (your body) that your soul would inhabit while on Earth. When the egg and sperm joined, they carried all the genetic coding and material from the human family and its evolution from eons ago, as well as the genetic coding and material from your ancestral family line. Your parents also transported their present health conditions and vital forces. If their health and vital forces were weakened by diet and the circumstances surrounding their lives, it would have affected what they passed on genetically and energetically to you. What they passed on in turn, affected not only your physical, emotional, and mental capacities, but your healing capacity as well. In addition, all that happened to your mother physically, psychically, spirituality, and energetically while she was carrying you affected the development of your physical, emotional, and mental vehicles.

Entrance of the Soul

After nine months, your soul detached from the watery abyss. The moment that you exited your mother's womb and entered the physical world, you were given the breath of life—the cord that attaches you to the source: God. The aspect of your soul that was still attached to the cosmic realm detached and entered fully into the earthly realm. At the moment that your physical body detached from your mother's body when the umbilical cord was cut, the cord of the breath of life then attached it to the Universe Soul from where it now receives its vital force directly.

The Unfolding Self

When a soul first enters the earthly realm, it knows that all things are possible. These possibilities particularly show in early childhood in what adults call the "imaginary" world. For the soul, everything is a miracle, including the simple things in life: a bubble, a flower, a butterfly. There are no limits to what the soul can do, who it can become, or what it can transform into. It can fly, change its form, or become something or someone else. At this stage, the soul knows all the possibilities. However, as it becomes more anchored in its physical body and more attached to its earthly existence, it begins to lose memory of the possibilities and becomes more attached to the reality of the limits of its earthly form. Loss of these possibilities may become entrenched, more or less depending upon the culture, family, and various communities in which the soul is nurtured. As the self unfolds, if it is not made aware of the eternal aspect of its soul, it may lead to a disconnect between the self and soul. This can result in the self being lost on many levels, including awareness of the reason that its soul journeyed to Earth this time.

However, no matter the culture, family, or community, as the self unfolds in the earthly realm there are tasks that it must complete in the cycle of life to become a healthy functioning human being.

Although different schools of thought exist on the life cycle, we are using the life cycle as articulated by Erik Erikson as a framework for understanding the strengths at each stage of the unfolding of the self. The different stages include childhood, adolescence, young adulthood, middle adulthood, and old age. Each of these stages has tasks that one completes for successful development. While all the tasks are present at once, different tasks rise to ascendency and become more significant at different stages throughout the life cycle. The tasks during childhood include attachment, exploration, initiation and purpose, and competency. For the adolescent, the developmental task is identity, while for the young adult the tasks are love and intimacy. In the middle of life, the developmental task is the creation of others and for old age, it is wisdom. Completion of tasks at each stage in the life cycle can result in certain strengths. Likewise, incomplete tasks at each stage of the life cycle can become a place of weakness and, potentially, a crisis at that stage, making it difficult for the self to continue through each successive stage successfully. Accumulated failures can lead to a general life crisis which can ultimately lead to a breakdown physically, mentally, emotionally, and/or spiritually. Childhood is the most critical period in shaping how the self will continue to evolve.

Infancy—Trust

During the first 12 to 18 months after birth, the infant begins differentiating from the mother but needs the basics of food, warmth, comfort, sensory stimulation, and the other things necessary to develop a good sense of security. The developmental task for this period is trust and the strength is hope. The consistency with which these needs are met enables the infant to develop trust in and attachment to its caregiver, which subsequently leads to healthy and secure attachment. If the care of the infant is inconsistent, inadequate, or rejecting over a period, then a sense of mistrust can develop and may result in insecure attachment. Not being able to trust that the world is a secure and safe place, can arrest the development of the infant, and task completion at subsequent stages in the life cycle.

Toddler—Autonomy
Between the ages of 18 months and three years, the toddler continues the process of differentiating from the primary caregiver and begins to explore the world to test his/her ability to do things on his/her own. The developmental task is autonomy and the strength is will. The challenge is to be able to explore the world and remain securely attached. This is something that continues throughout the life cycle: to explore the world but return to a secure base. If the boundaries of exploration are too restrictive or too open, where the toddler does not feel safe and secure, he/she may begin to doubt himself/herself and develop feelings of shame.

Preschooler—Initiative
Between the ages of three to six years, a preschooler begins to take initiative and show directed purpose in activities. The task is to develop initiative and the strength is purpose. This is the stage at which the child begins to try new things and identities but needs acceptance as he/she does so. If their initiatives are not recognized or they feel unaccepted as they try new things, then feelings of guilt can arise.

School Age—Industry
From age six to puberty, the child develops competence through industry or attention focused on accomplishments. The developmental tasks are learning skills, using them successfully, and accomplishing goals, while the strength is competency. Here, the child seeks to become an accepted and competent member of the culture. If he/she cannot accomplish such tasks, then feelings of inferiority can arise.

Adolescence—Identity

During adolescence, the adolescent begins the process of differentiating from the family of birth so that he or she can detach and find new expressions in friendships, love, family, and ideas as well as his or her reason for being. Although the search for identity began during preschool, it is in this stage when peer attachments become important and the search for identity becomes significant. The adolescent is seeking answers to the questions: who am I and why am I here? This search for identity may lead him/her to try out different identities and/or something worth committing his/her life to that will give him/her a sense of identity. I am ... because I do... The developmental task at this stage is identity and the strength is commitment. If the adolescent does not have a clear sense of who he/she is, then it can lead to identity confusion and an overall shaky sense of self.

Young Adulthood—Intimacy

As a young adult, the self continues to differentiate from the family of birth and finds new expressions in friendship, love, family, and career. He/she will also become more attached to friends, partners, or spouses (i.e., intimate relationships), children, ideas, and ways of being, and jobs or careers. In this stage, the young adult learns to share love in its many forms, including with a partner, children, friends, etc. Those who unable to share love in one or more of its many forms may become isolated.

Middle Adulthood—Generativity

Middle adulthood is the stage that the self may undergo detachment from the family of birth (the death of family members), children (who are leaving home), divorce (if the marriage dissolves) and cultural ideas, etc., and begins to search for new meaning. The self, now in a more awakened state, may begin to ask other questions, such as: where have I been and where am I going? The person may begin to race against the Earth's time clock to make up for lost time and missed opportunities, creating what has been referred to as the mid-life crisis. They may also be operating at a lower energetic level that has dissipated based on their life experiences and may go in one of two directions. The person may accept their mistakes and begin to regenerate and do their best to repair the damage. Such acceptance may lead to acceptance of others and extension of the self in the creation of others, which is carried out through the psychological giving of self through parenting, teaching, artistic endeavors, etc. Alternatively, they may continue a downward path of self-absorption, over-indulgence, illness, disease, and/or continue to be weighed down by negative karmic weight or soul debt accumulated in this life as well as past lives. If the person finds himself/herself in such a state and is unable to find creative outlets, then psychically, socially, and spiritually, he/she will begin to stagnate.

Old Age—Integrity

In old age, the self may have already experienced different types of loss including but not limited to family members, job, career, etc. However, a new wisdom may set in and he/she may begin to look forward to detachment from Earth life to cosmic life. In this stage of the life cycle, connecting back to the cosmic world becomes significant. The older adult may be able to look back on his/her life and see that he/she did the best they could, given the circumstance surrounding their life, and say, "It has been good." Although mistakes are recognized, they can live with the idea that they did the best they could. Just as the infant learns to trust life, the older adult learns to trust death. Those who cannot trust the idea of death may sink into despair. See a summary of the stages of the life cycle in Table 3.1 below.

Table 3.1 Erik Erikson's Life Cycle

Stage	Psychological Challenge	Description	Psychological Strength
Infant (birth to 12–18 months)	Basic trust vs. mistrust	Develops a sense of whether the world can be trusted	Hope
Toddler (12–28 months to 3 years)	Autonomy vs. shame and doubt	Develops a sense of self as independent or as shameful and Doubtful	Will
Pre-schooler (3-6 years)	Initiative vs. guilt	Develops ability to try new things and learns how to handle failure	Purpose
School-age (6 years to puberty)	Industry vs. inferiority	Learns basic skills within his or her culture, and learns to combat feelings of inferiority	Competence
Adolescent (puberty to young adult)	Identity vs. identity confusion	Determines own sense of self	Fidelity
Young Adult	Intimacy vs. isolation	Makes commitment to another, isolation and/or self-absorption occur if unsuccessful	Love
Middle Age Adult	Generativity vs. Stagnation	Seeks to guide the next gen-	Care

		eration or risks feeling incomplete	
Old Age Adult	Integrity vs. despair	Seeks a sense of personal accomplishments with life and accepts death or falls into despair	Wisdom

It is important to know the stages of the life cycle to understand how the self unfolds; this helps us to be prepared for what to expect at each stage to get through them successfully. However, the stage of the life cycle that has the most significance for relationships is childhood. Indeed, it is our first experiences with love that plays a significant role in who we attract, who we choose, how we love, and whether and how we continue our journeys.

Chapter 3 Exercises

Identifying Unfinished Tasks

The purpose of these exercises is to identify the level to which you completed the development task, and the level of psychological strength you think you gained at each stage in the life cycle. These exercises are also designed to help you identify how levels of task development and psychological strengths have affected your life, and how they might continue to affect you as you proceed through the life cycle.

EXERCISE 3.1. *The Life Cycle*

1. Put a circle and square (if you have a partner) around the number that corresponds to the level to which you successfully completed the developmental task and your psychological strength.

Stage	Developmental Task/ Psychological Strength	Low				High
Infancy (birth to 18 months)	Trust/ Hope	1	2	3	4	5
Toddler (12-3 years)	Autonomy/ Will	1	2	3	4	5
Pre-Schooler (3-6 years)	Initiative/ Purpose	1	2	3	4	5
School-age (6 years to puberty)	Industry/ Competence	1	2	3	4	5
Adolescence (puberty to	Identity/ Fidelity (Com-	1	2	3	4	5

young adult)	mitment)					
Young Adult	Intimacy/ Love	1	2	3	4	5
Middle Age	Generativity/ Care	1	2	3	4	5
		1	2	3	4	5
Old Age	Integrity/ Wisdom	1	2	3	4	5
		1	2	3	4	5

EXERCISE 3.2. *Narrative*

1. Describe how the level of task completion and psychological strength at each stage in the life cycle affects your life, and how they may continue to affect your life as you continue to go through the life cycle. In addition, describe how your development affects your interaction styles in relationships.

_____
_____
_____
_____
_____
_____
_____
_____
_____
_____
_____
_____
_____
_____
_____
_____
_____

40 Soul Partners

Additional Notes

4

Love and the Wounded Child

Love is the binding force of the universe. It is the force that binds the male and female to ensure the survival of the human race, the mother and child to ensure the survival of the child, and kinfolk to ensure the survival of the family, clan, tribe, and nation. It is also the force that connects humans to the Divine. It is our experiences with love that are significant to our success in attracting and keeping love.

Although love is the force that connects everything, it manifests on two levels. The first level is that which corresponds to the lower, physical, emotional, and mental aspects of the self. The second level is the higher aspects of the self that corresponds to Universe Love. There are also two factors that shape our approach to love. One is our social conditioning about love and the other is our early experiences with our caregivers.

The society in which we are socialized has underlying cultural ideas about love. The most pervasive idea about love in the U.S. is romantic love. Romantic love is thought to have emerged out of the 12th century with courtly love between a knight who, through the cultural idea of chivalry, dedicated himself to the care of a woman of high status that he could not have. Prior to that idea, marriages in Europe and throughout the world were typically arranged by family members motivated by political and economic interests. Although romantic love is thought to have emerged in Europe, it has been found to exist throughout the world and has a wide variety of definitions with the most common being physical and emotional attraction. Regardless of the role of society in shaping our approach to love, it potentially has all the dimensions of physical, emotional, mental, and spiritual. Love is also energetic, and it is eternal.

The second factor that affects how we approach love is our early experiences with our primary caregivers. If these experiences were healthy and we able to complete the tasks of each stage of the life cycle successfully, then we may only be affected by negative love experiences once we left our families. However, most of us are negatively affected in some way or other by our early family experiences irrespective of how well-intentioned our caregivers may have been or how much they strove to provide for all our needs. We are not referring to the more traumatic experiences of neglect and abuse, but those day-to-day experiences in our families that left scars on us psychically and energetically. When we go into the world, we take all of who we are, including our wounds from childhood, with us. These wounding experiences have affected us energetically which affects the level at which we are vibrating. Subsequently, the people we attract may have had similar wounding experiences and may be vibrating at similar or lower levels.

THE SOUL'S GUARDIANS & GUIDES

When a soul journeys to Earth, it comes with a double and cosmic and Earth guardians. The double (referred to as intuition, guardian angel, etc.) is that aspect of the self that is connected to the cosmic realm. Cosmic guardians may be family members (who have passed) or others in previous incarnations who help the soul on its journey. They may also include beings of other interdimensional realms that we may not be able to easily feel, see, or cognize with the limited faculties of our five senses.

Earth guardians and guides include our parents, grandparents, siblings, extended family members, etc., and others we meet throughout our lives including our partner. Our experiences with our parents are our first introduction to the world. Whatever issues our parents were working out while they were raising us affected how we developed. Factors that may have affected how our parents raised us includes the type of family or community support they received, their social conditioning, and where they were in their evolvement. In examining the effects of your parent's/caregivers in shaping who you are, you would reflect on the circumstances surrounding your conception, your parent's state when you were conceived, and how their interaction patterns affected you when you were in your mother's womb and during childhood.

Parental Love

The two primary types of love shown by parents are instrumental and expressive love. Instrumental loves provide for our basic physical survival needs of food, clothing, warmth, shelter, and safety. Expressive love provides us with our psychic needs to feel safe, secure, and loved. Both types of love help us to complete the tasks at each stage of the life cycle in childhood and build our sense of trust, will, competency, identity, and, ultimately, our sense of self. When these needs are met, the self can continue positive growth and development. When these needs are not adequately met or are met in excess (being spoilt by parents), it can cause an imbalance in how the self continues to evolve.

The factors that may affect how caregivers provide care include the communities around them and their physical, mental, and emotional capacities and interaction styles. Questions to ask are: Did your parents have the support they needed to provide you with your most basic physical and psychic survival needs? What was the state of the community surrounding them? Was it clean and safe? What was the quality of the institutional support in providing the necessities of food, clothing, housing, education, healthcare, etc.? Did they have the emotional support they needed from other family and community members? Not having the necessities or family and institutional support could have detracted from your parents' abilities to show both instrumental and expressive love.

A factor affecting whether and how parents show expressive love is their capacities to love, which may have to do with their makeup, and whether and how they were shown expressive love by their parents when they were children. If their parents did not show expressive love, they may have not known how to show it themselves. When parental love is deficient, it can have a negative effect on the child. In addition, a parent's way of showing love, although may work for one child, may not work for another one.

The Wounded Child

As indicated above, although our parents may have done the best they could, many of us have been wounded in some way or another. Some of these wounds may have occurred at different phases in our early development. It is important to understand some of the dynamics of our early experiences and how they may play out in our interaction patterns and love styles as adults.

Birth of the Physical Self: Pre-birth
The Neonate

When a soul journeys to Earth, it is born into the human family with an ancestral line. The factors that make up the human family, a family's genetics, and hundreds of years of the ancestral line's behaviors and interaction patterns, may be passed onto the child. The parents' genetic make-ups, their diets, what is going on in their lives, and how they interact with each other affect the development of the fetus. Whatever the mother is experiencing while carrying the fetus in the womb, also affects how it develops. If the mother and father are in conflict and she feels rejected, stressed, unloved, and unsupported, and/or use drugs and/or alcohol, the fetus will be exposed to environmental hazards, which will affect it biologically, psychically, and energetically. If the pregnancy is unwanted, the fetus may feel it energetically. Research has shown that experiences in the womb are linked to a host of physical and psychological problems throughout life, including, but not limited to: "heart disease, diabetes, cancer, hypertension, allergies, obesity, anxiety, depression, schizophrenia and autism" (Orlans & Levy, 2014, pp. 49-50). For example, if a mother experiences chronic anxiety, then high levels of the stress hormone, cortisol will enter the fetus's brain and body, programming its brain and nervous system to be on high alert for potential threats. "High levels of cortisol can result in anxiety, depression, and emotional dysregulation in childhood and throughout life" (Orlans & Levy, 2014, p. 50). Although much of what the mother experiences affect the fetus some of the damage from pre-birth can be mitigated with a healthy and nurturing post-natal environment.

Birth of the Emotional and Relational Self:
Attachment and Exploration
Infancy

As indicated, being connected is a fundamental need throughout the human life cycle. It is necessary for both our physical and emotional survival on Earth. Depending on the pre-natal environment, particularly if it was healthy, birth may mean that the infant is leaving a warm, secure, and safe environment, where all its needs were met. Thus, birth can be a traumatic experience, which is why it is often referred to as birth trauma. How the infant's needs are met in the first stage of life will lay the foundation for how it will become rooted in the earthly realm; that is, whether it will be able to securely attach to its caregivers. The first stage in life is also when the development of the emotional body becomes more prominent. It is this body that allows the child to respond to these early experiences and these responses lay the foundation for its emotional development and how it will relate in relationships with others throughout the rest of its life.

As indicated in the previous chapter, in the first stage of the life cycle, the infant is faced with the task of developing a sense of trust. How its primary caretakers respond to its needs will play a significant role in whether it is able to resolve what can be a potential crisis between trust and mistrust. When the infant's basic needs are adequately met, it lays the foundation for a healthy and secure attachment, which is significant for the successful completion of the first developmental task (i.e., to develop a basic sense of trust). Developing a good sense of trust means that the infant can trust that the world is a secure and safe place, making it feel good about the caregiver and itself. Being able to trust lays the foundation for healthy attachment and the development of the psychosocial strength of hope.

What happens if, during infancy, the infant's needs were not adequately met by its caregivers? How does this play out in how the infant feels about itself and its caregivers? How does it play out in how the infant continues to develop? More importantly, when the infant grows into an adult, how do these early experiences affect his or her interaction patterns in relationships? The attachment theory provides a basis for understanding how early childhood experiences shape adult attachment and love styles.

Attachment Theory

The attachment theory was first developed by John Bowlby (1969; 1997) and later used by Ainsworth et al. (1978; 2015) to study infants in an unfamiliar situation to see how they would react when separated from their caregivers. Using the findings from these studies, Holmes (1993) outlined the stages in the development of attachment. According to Holmes, the attachment system develops between birth to three years of age and has several stages. For the infant, from birth to approximately 6 months, there is little evidence of discriminating behavior toward any adult. Crying, clinging, grasping, and cuddling are directed toward any available adult. However, between six and seven months, the infant begins to discriminate between familiar and unfamiliar faces, voices, and interaction styles, and a clear-cut attachment begins to emerge. After three years, the attachment has been established. How caregivers responded during the formation of attachment helps to determine the type of attachment style that the infant has developed.

Two primary attachment styles that have been identified are secure and insecure. For adults, their attachment styles can be determined primarily by how they are able to talk about their early experiences when being interviewed using the Adult Attachment

Interview (AAI),[1] a questionnaire developed to explore adult attachment styles, as well as their responses to other self-report questionnaires designed to do the same thing. The attachment styles and how they develop are explained below.

Secure Attachment

Secure attachment occurs for those individuals with caregivers who were relatively responsive to their needs and provided the foundation necessary to form healthy, secure attachments. In the first stage of the life cycle, the need for food, warmth, and comfort was adequately met, giving them a sense that the world is a safe and secure place that can be trusted. During the second stage of the life cycle, the exploration stage when children begin to venture into and explore the world, they were given enough space, but not too much, to explore and test their ability to do things on their own. Such people, although they may not have received everything, they needed or desired from their primary caregivers during these stages, were given enough to develop a healthy attachment. Getting their needs met, in turn, helped them to feel firmly rooted in the earthly realm, provided the basis for healthy emotional development, and gave them a good sense of trust, which laid the foundation for healthy psychosocial development for the next stage of the life cycle and throughout the rest of their lives.

When being interviewed using the AAI, those individuals with a secure attachment style show that they value intimate relationships and acknowledge the effects that their relationships with their caregivers had on them. Whether these relationships were happy or troubled, the interviewees not only provide detailed memories of their childhoods but also demonstrate an ability to reflect on their experiences with an understanding of both their own behaviors and the behaviors of their caregivers. In addition, they are able to discuss these relationships in a coherent fashion. In adult relationships, they feel free to come and go without feeling insecure.

---

[1] The Adult Attachment Interview was created by Carol George, Nancy Kaplan, and Mary Main in 1984.

Insecure Attachment

Insecure attachment occurs for those individuals who did not get what they needed in the first stages of the life cycle. When their needs were not adequately met by caregivers, it posed a threat to their very existence, making them feel anxious. Such anxiousness lead to maladaptive coping styles with two primary reactions: a dramatic or exaggerated response where they maximized their behaviors to get what they needed or a withdrawal response where they minimized their behaviors. These response styles have been characterized as anxious-ambivalent and anxious-avoidant attachments.

Anxious-Ambivalent Attachment is a characteristic of those individuals whose caretakers were responsive to their needs, but inconsistent in providing them. Such caregivers may have been insensitive to their needs, but not altogether rejecting these needs. They may have been inept in physical contact with them as infants and showed little affection. It may also be characteristic of those individuals whose caretakers provided what they needed, but not in a timely fashion.

In general, when an infant needs something, it responds in the only way it knows how in the first stage: grasping, clinging, and crying. When the caregiver does not respond adequately, the infant responds dramatically or exaggeratedly, which may mean that it continues to grasp, cling, cry longer, or scream louder to elicit a response. In this case, the infant instinctively develops strategies to get what it needs. Due to the inconsistency of the caregiver, the infant has good and bad experiences with the caregiver, which causes it to develop an anxious-ambivalent attachment style. Thus, when it gets what it needs, it feels good. When it does not get what it needs, it feels bad. When the caretaker is inconsistent, the infant gets frustrated and angry because it must find ways to get the caregiver's attention. Such experiences result in ambivalence toward the caregiver: the infant is clingy, but when the caregiver responds, it pushes her away. Ultimately, the infant develops good/bad feelings about the caregiver and itself.

Clingy Adults—In adult relationships, individuals with an anxious-ambivalent attachment may become clingy adults whose needs are never met; as such they want to merge with their partner. They are often the type of individuals who cannot be pleased no matter what their partner does. When their partner needs space, they may get angry because it aggravates the wound of when their caregivers were unavailable. When their partners seek closeness, they may push them away because they are angry that they were not available when they needed them. Many of these adults cling desperately, on the one hand, because they fear abandonment, but push away, on the other hand, because they are ambivalent about how they feel.

In the AAI, these individuals may be preoccupied or entangled in the details of their lives and are unable to provide descriptions of their early childhood experiences. They may still be angry with their caregivers and have issues that they have not resolved with them. When describing their experiences, they may provide extremely long, incoherent stories.

Anxious-Avoidant Attachment is a characteristic of those individuals whose caregivers were consistently cold, rejecting, and slow to respond to their needs. In the first stage of life, some of these individuals may have had caregivers who were uncomfortable with close body contact, saw them as a burden, were not interested in them, and/or were depressed. Some of these caregivers may have never recovered from the wounds of their own childhoods. For these infants, because these experiences were painful, they withdrew from the primary caregiver, and, in more extreme cases, they withdraw into a shell.

Distancing Adults—As adults, these people are often extremely guarded, building a fortress around themselves and their emotions. They are independent doers and feel that they do not need others. Such individuals may hide in their work and other activities and may see others who desire time and attention as being too needy or dependent. While they feel this way, they also want to be able to be more needy and dependent. However, due to their fear of opening the wound of rejection that they experienced in childhood, they are afraid to show this side of themselves. They are often emotionally unavailable and are quick to withdraw from relationships when they are presented with challenges or conflict occurs.

When discussing their experiences in the AAI, such individuals might be dismissive; that is, they may have little to say about their childhood experiences and provide relatively short descriptions. Their ability to recount specific incidents is limited and they may minimize the effects of important relationships in their lives. For example, they might say, "I had a miserable childhood, but it has not affected me." Their attachment style as an adult may be distant and closed because they fear being rejected.

The type of attachment anxious-ambivalent vs. anxious-avoidant that a toddler develops continues in the exploration stage of the life cycle. During the exploration stage, the task of separating from the caregiver becomes more prominent as the toddler ventures out to explore the world. Although he/she is striving for autonomy, he/she wants to remain securely attached to the caregiver. One can see the need to remain attached when the toddler ventures out, but keeps looking back or leaves the room, and returns quickly to make sure the caregiver is still there. The toddler wants to venture out but return to a secure base, something that lasts throughout life. It is also important to test what he/she can do on his/her own during the exploration stage to develop willpower.

What happens if during the exploration stage there is too much restraint or too much freedom in this newfound need to explore the world? If there is too much restraint, then the toddler begins to doubt himself and feels shame. If there is too much restraint, it may mean that the caretaker is too clingy, which may stem from deficits in her own childhood. In such instances, the toddler needs to keep the caregiver physically close to feel secure but may distance himself/herself emotionally by developing an ambivalent style or an avoidant style. If the caregiver gives the child too much freedom, sending them off too soon, or encourages them to "be independent" and play by themselves because she feels trapped by the child's dependence, is disinterested in the child, or wants to pursue her own interests, the child may develop an ambivalent style. Too much freedom can make exploration a frightening experience, causing the child to be clingy. When the caregiver is emotionally cold, physically unavailable, and rejecting, then the child learns early not to depend on anyone and may withdraw into his/her own world, developing an avoidant style. Overall, too much freedom or too much restraint may undermine healthy development in the second stage of the life cycle.

Disorganized Attachment—Individuals with a disorganized attachment style might be classified in either of the above categories. They may have had caregivers who were inconsistent; that is sometimes the caregiver may have been overly attentive while other times they may not have been attentive enough, especially at times when it was most needed. Some individuals may have also been neglected, maltreated, or traumatized. As adults, they may suffer from unresolved mourning and may be clingy at times, avoidant at other times, and have difficulty with attachment in general.

These attachment styles are summarized in Table 4.1. Problems in adult relationships might occur if two people come together who have different attachment styles. For example, as shown in *Figure 4.1* an individual with an anxious-avoidant attachment style who is distant may meet someone with an anxious-ambivalent attachment style and is clingy. Likewise, as illustrated in *Figure 4.2*, an individual who has a secure attachment style might meet someone who has a disorganized attachment style. Such differences in styles may lead to misunderstandings and consequently conflicted interaction styles.

Table 4.1 Attachment & Relationship Styles

Attachment Style	Early Experiences with Caregivers	Intimate Relationships
Secure	Consistently warm and Available	Feels free to come and go as they please
Anxious-Ambivalent	Inconsistently warm and available	Clingy
Anxious-Avoidant	Unavailable and rejecting	Distant

Disorganized	Maltreated, abused, and/or neglected	Distant and clingy

Figure 4.1
Conflicting Attachment Styles I

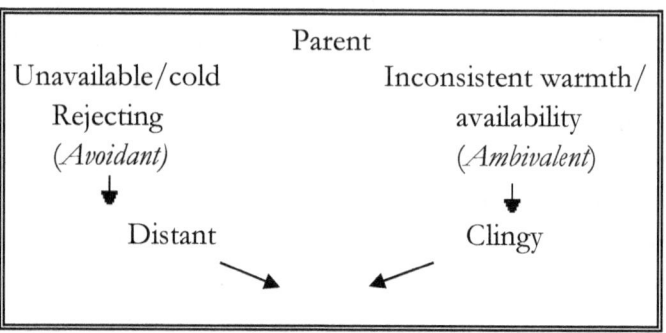

Figure 4.2
Conflicting Attachment Styles II

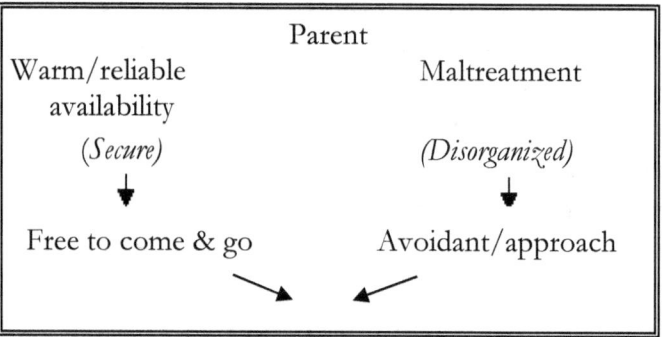

The Absent Parent

Since our souls are brought into the world by the joining of two people, it is natural to desire the presence and support of both our parents. If a parent is absent, and if there is no adequate family and community support to make up for the missing parent, then one parent will be left to provide all of the child's physical, emotional, mental, and spiritual needs. Even if that parent makes every attempt to do so, it is virtually impossible to do so without some consequences to either the child or the parent. Both genders are also needed for same and opposite-sex modeling as it is necessary for socialization not only for future relationships but life in general. Even if adequate family and community support exist, one can still be affected by an absent parent and may feel rejected and abandoned because, psychically and energetically, the question that might haunt them for the rest of their life is: why did that parent leave?

Entitlement

According to Audrey Chapman in *Getting Good Loving* (2005), when our needs were not met as children, we may enter the world feeling entitled to get from our partners what we did not get from our parents or caregivers. Some individuals may expect their partners to provide them with all their needs or make up for what their parents or society did not give them. In other words, what we expect from our partners may be directly related to the type of care we received or did not receive from our parents.

As outlined in Table 4.2, one who was raised with custodial care—that is, where the parents only provided instrumental love (provision of material needs)—may have felt unloved. This type of care may be characteristic of single-parent homes, where the parent lacks the time and energy to show expressive love. It may also be characteristic of parents who did not know how to show expressive love because they did not receive it themselves. Some individuals may have been reared by parents who were socialized to believe that showing too much affection might weaken children, making them ill-prepared to deal with the realities of society. Consequently, children whose parents used this type of rearing style may have felt unloved and emotionally insecure. Therefore, when they enter into relationships, because they have not been shown expressive love, they do not know how to show it. They, therefore, avoid getting too close or allowing anyone to get too close to them.

Those individuals reared in families where their parents did not acknowledge them for their special skills and talents, may have felt that they were not special. In adult relationships, they may not feel sure of themselves, and subsequently, may have an unstable sense of self.

Those individuals who experienced conditional love may have had parents who only showed love if certain conditions were met (i.e., received good grades, did well in sports, or performed chores). They may need constant demonstrations of love to feel sure of themselves. Individuals who were neglected (i.e., not shown instrumental or expressive love) may suffer from feeling unloved and unaccepted and may be preoccupied with looking for the love they never received in childhood. Overall, individuals experiencing entitlement may respond in adult relationships the same way they did when their needs were not met when they were children; with hurt, sadness, and disappointment.

Table 4.2 Entitlement

Type of Love	Definition	Interaction Style
Custodial	Instrumental/non-expressive love; provided the basic necessities of food, clothes, shelter, etc.	Perpetual mistrust and a rigid defense system to keep from getting too close
Lack of acknowledgment	Not given adequate attention; special talents and skills unnoticed; not made to feel special	May have difficulty sharing themselves because of shallow and unstable sense of Self
Conditional love	Based on performance; rewarded with love if certain conditions were met; did well in school, sports, etc.	May feel unsure of partner's affection and commitment and need constant demonstrations of love
Neglect	Did not receive emotional or instrumental support	May spend a lifetime looking for nurturance and attention not received during Childhood

Parent and Child Partners

Entitlement may show up in other ways. One way is that some individuals are looking for mommies and daddies or a parent-partner (someone who acts more like a parent) and expect to be the child-partner (to be parented). In such instances, if a parent-partner meets a child-partner, at first, they may seem compatible. The parent-partner, especially if he or she was an older child with a lot of responsibility, and a great deal of control in the family might like the sense of power and control that such a role requires. The child-partner may also have had a great deal of responsibility during childhood and is looking to be relieved or he or she may have never been taught to be responsible and, therefore, need a parent- partner. The problem arises, however, when one grows tired of the role and the other is not ready to relinquish theirs.

A notion also exists that love is unconditional. Probably the only unconditional love is that between a parent and a child. The reality is that most individuals are with their partners based on certain conditions being met (e.g., sharing mutually in economics, sex, companionship, and household and childcare responsibilities). Partners are also expected to show respect, be honest, faithful, committed and many other things to create a mutually satisfying and fulfilling relationship. Thus, for adults, the notion that love is unconditional may be just that, a notion. If either of the partners falls short on too many of the conditions, the relationship will likely dissolve. Needless to say, it is important to move from entitlement to a relationship in which the partners meet each other as equals and where there is mutual sharing. Giving up entitlement is indeed necessary for a healthy relationship.

Birth of the Mental and Individual Self: Purpose and Competency
Childhood

The next developmental task is initiative, which gives birth to purpose and industry, which, in turn, makes one feel competent. Here, the child tries out new things and wants to be accepted as a competent member of the social world. Being competent is the beginning of the development of the mental body and the individual self. As indicated previously, during childhood, the soul, still has not anchored entirely into the physical world; however, because of the limitations of the child's mental capacity, he/she does not yet recognize the limitations of the physical body and the world he/she inhabits. At this stage, the child tries to become different things and takes on new forms. Unlike adults who have repressed aspects of themselves to fit into the social world, the soul still knows the possibilities and still has contact with beings in other dimensions which the child can still see.

How caregivers and others respond to the child's quest for purpose, competency and acceptance will have a great effect on its emerging self. When trying new things, personalities, and forms, if children are made to feel bad about certain aspects of themselves, are not made to feel competent in the tasks they perform, or are not made to feel good about their accomplishments, whether at home, at school, or in other social settings, this could have detrimental effects on the development of their self-concept, self-esteem, self-efficacy and, overall sense of self.

The repression of aspects of the self particularly shows in ideas about gender. In most cultures, there are ideas about what it means to be a man and what it means to be a woman. Up until about the age of three, children do not know that they cannot change their sex. However, just as in other aspects of their lives, once they learn what it is to be a girl or boy, they seek to become competent members of their gender. For example, if a boy wants to engage in socially prescribed "female" activities and his parents make him feel bad about it, then he will begin to repress these aspects of himself. The same can be said for girls in similar situations. In general, to become competent members of society, we must begin dismembering aspects of ourselves. Extreme forms of self-repression can result in psychopathology, e.g., anxiety, depression, phobias, personality disorders, etc.

In adult relationships, those individuals who were made to repress aspects of themselves or were not given attention may have lost their initiative and have no sense of purpose. Others who were not accepted may be overdriven by purpose, subsequently making them emotionally unavailable to their partners and children. Being made to feel incompetent as a child may show as oversensitivity about being competent and accepted in adulthood.

Birth of the Social Self: Identity and Love (Intimacy)
Adolescence

Adolescence is the most critical stage in the life cycle; it is when the individual becomes solidified in the physical world and differentiation begins to intensify because the adolescent begins the process of individuating or detaching from the family of origin. At this stage, the teen is becoming a more social being outside of the family in search of identity and intimacy. Although the search for identity, or who am I, and intimacy, in the form of friendships, starts earlier in the life cycle, identity becomes prominent during adolescence and intimacy during young adulthood.

During adolescence, the search for what to commit one's life to rises to significance. It is during this time that the teen begins to explore possible identities. How he/she identifies is based on the social environment and social constructions within that environment. For example, in most societies, people identify with what makes them unique as a group, tribe or nation. In some societies, particularly traditional African societies, adolescents go through initiation rites to ensure that they are clear about who they belong to as a people. As part of these rituals, they are taught that since all of life is filled with divine essence, which is eternal, so too are they. To identify with the group is vital to one's survival and survival of the tribe or nation in the earthly realm. However, to identify with that part of the self that is eternal is critical for the evolvement of the soul.

In the U.S., because it is a multicultural society, different ethnic groups have different ways in which they identify that distinguishes who they are and there are multiple identities one can assume. These identities revolve primarily around statuses and roles, which may include race, class, gender, level of education, sexual orientation, work (and position), family, and roles within families (e.g., mother, father, sister, brother, and child). One of the primary ways in which people identify is by what they do. What we commit our lives to is a critical part of who we are and the developmental task that is most significant during adolescence.

As individuation becomes more prominent and the quest for identity is awakened, this is the time when the adolescent begins to question (and challenge) everything from their parents, teachers, minister, and they may question themselves, including their gender, sexuality, and their own existence. They may even question the existence of God. How parents respond to this critical period is important to how the teen continues to develop; this is connected to the parents' socioeconomic statuses as well as where they are in their evolvement. If the parents become more restricting, continue to use the same parenting styles, cannot respond to questions adequately, make them feel bad about exploring themselves, and/or force them to suppress aspects of themselves, then this will only compound previous repressive and wounding experiences. Conversely, if the parents do not set clear boundaries, give them too much freedom and/or overindulge their emotional and physical desires, not only at this stage but in the earlier stages as well, then it could lead to unhealthy development, which will contribute to problems in the next stage of the life cycle (i.e., the quest for love).

Young Adulthood

Adolescence is the period in which the quest for love is awakened, but it becomes more prominent in young adulthood. As the adolescent grows into adulthood, individuation from the family of origin continues as the quest for love finds expression in relationships with friends, partners, children, and work. As the young adult seeks love, his/her experiences in childhood provide opportunities to replay interactions from early childhood experiences. If he/she has unresolved issues from childhood, then they will play out in his/her interaction patterns in relationships with friends, associates, employers, children, and, most significantly, intimate partners. If the young adult is not able to love securely, freely, and unselfishly, then he/she will be unable to share himself wholly and completely. Over-guarding his/her heart or sense of self to avoid aggravating already existing wounds can create blocks to love in higher forms of expression and can hinder their evolvement.

Imago Theory

Imago Theory was first developed by Harville Hendrix. According to him, when we come into the world, we are whole and experience oneness with everything (Luquet, 1996). Many problems stem from a rupture of this essential connection from unconscious parenting. The effect is the separation of self-parts and alienation from others. Imago theory proposes that love functions as a selection process whereby we unconsciously seek out and form relationships with those who are like our caregivers and whose wounds are complementary to our own. In other words, we seek partners unconsciously, because we are seeking to heal and grow. We anticipate that they will facilitate the healing of emotional wounds and ultimately recovery of our wholeness. However, because we do not *consciously* recognize that we have chosen our partners because we want them to help us grow, we recreate childhood scenarios, leading to the recreation of the wounding experiences. The goal of Imago is for partners to *re-image* the other as a wounded child. Rather than recreating wounding experiences, through mirroring, validating, and showing empathy to each other, partners would serve as mutual therapists to help each other heal. Helping each other heal emotional wounds can lead to the resumption of developmental growth, spiritual evolvement, and ultimately the restoration of the oneness that was lost in childhood.

Recognizing the wounds of our childhoods is significant to understanding our love styles and interaction patterns. More important is to recognize how these wounds affect our health and well-being: physically, emotionally, psychically, and energetically, and, ultimately, who we attract, and how we interact with them.

Chapter 4 Exercises

Identifying Childhood Wounds

These exercises are designed for you to explore how early experiences with parents/caregivers have affected your attachment styles, whether you are experiencing entitlement, and the effect they are having on your relationship.

EXERCISE 4. 1. *Attachment*

1. Think about your early experiences with your parent/caregivers as far back as you can remember (or at least from 5-12). Based on what you can remember, answer the following by putting a circle (and square for your partner) around the response that corresponds to your experiences with your parents/caregivers according to the following scale.

Not True at All	Somewhat True	True
1	2	3

	Mother/ Caregiver 1	Father Caregiver 2
a. Felt loved as a child	1 2 3	1 2 3
b. Felt could depend on parents/caretakers	1 2 3	1 2 3
c. Felt parents/caretakers were attentive and responsive to my needs as much as they could be	1 2 3	1 2 3
d. Did not feel loved as a child by parents/caregivers	1 2 3	1 2 3
e. Felt rejected as a child by parents/caregivers	1 2 3	1 2 3
f. Feel that parents/caregivers couldn't care less about whether was dead or alive	1 2 3	1 2 3

g. Feel parents/caregivers were verbally and/or physically abusive	1 2 3	1 2 3
h. Feel parents/caregivers were horrible as parents	1 2 3	1 2 3
i. Feel parents/caregivers were loving sometimes and other times they were not	1 2 3	1 2 3
j. Feel parents/caregivers were attentive and responsive to needs at times and other times they were not	1 2 3	1 2 3
k. Feel parents/caregivers were accepting at times and rejecting at other times	1 2 3	1 2 3
l. Overall, feel that parents/caregivers had good and bad traits and did the best they could	1 2 3	1 2 3
m. Still struggling with trying to get past the horrible experiences with parents/caregivers during childhood	1 2 3	1 2 3
n. Do not think it is necessary to even think about or discuss childhood or the role parents/caregivers played in my/his/her life	1 2 3	1 2 3
o. Do not know what to think about childhood	1 2 3	1 2 3

If you answered True or Somewhat True to questions in the following manner, you might have received this type of care from your parents/caregivers.

Question	Parental Attachment Style
a, b, c, l	Consistent warmth/availability
i, j, k	Inconsistent warmth/availability
d, e, f, n, o	Unavailable/rejecting
g, h, m,	A mixture of those above or maltreatment, neglect, or abuse

2. Check the box that best describes how you responded to the statements above.

You	Your Partner
☐ Consistent warmth/availability ☐ Inconsistent warmth/availability ☐ Unavailable rejecting ☐ A mixture of those above or maltreatment, neglect, or abuse	☐ Consistent warmth/availability ☐ Inconsistent warmth/availability ☐ Unavailable rejecting ☐ A mixture of those above or maltreatment, neglect, or abuse

3. Continue to explore your attachment styles by putting a circle (and a square if you have a partner) around the number that corresponds to how you interact according to the following scale.

Not True at All	Somewhat True	True
1	2	3

Attachment Styles	You	Your Partner
a. Need to know where partner is always	1 2 3	1 2 3
b. Even though we spend a lot of time together, feel anxious when partner leaves	1 2 3	1 2 3
c. Must be in contact with partner all day	1 2 3	1 2 3
d. Get anxious when cannot find partner	1 2 3	1 2 3
e. Feel uncomfortable when partner wants to be close	1 2 3	1 2 3
f. Do not need someone around too often;	1 2 3	1 2 3

makes feel crowded		
g. Need a lot of space to feel comfortable with partner	1 2 3	1 2 3
h. Sometimes need partner to be around all the time and other times do not want him/her around at all	1 2 3	1 2 3
i. Feel partners should have freedom and independence to pursue own lives	1 2 3	1 2 3

If you answered Somewhat True or True to questions in the following manner you might have the following attachment style:

Statements	Attachment Style
I	Secure
a, b, h	Anxious-ambivalent
e, f, g	Anxious-avoidant
c, d	Disorganized

4. Check the box that corresponds to the statements above, for the attachment style that best describes you/your partner:

You	Your Partner
☐ Secure ☐ Anxious-ambivalent ☐ Anxious-avoidant ☐ Disorganized	☐ Secure ☐ Anxious-ambivalent ☐ Anxious-avoidant ☐ Disorganized

5. Describe relationship with parents/caregivers by giving examples and how you feel about it.

_____
_____
_____
_____
_____

EXERCISE 4.2. *Entitlement*

1. The following exercise explores the type of rearing you received from your parent/caregivers. Answer the questions by putting a circle (and square if you have a partner) around <u>True or False</u> for the response that corresponds to your parents/caregivers. Then proceed to the subsequent questions to see how your parents/caregivers' style of parenting may affect how you interact, and the expectations you have of each other.

Parents/Caregivers	Mother Caregiver 1	Father Caregiver 2
a. Did not have a lot of material things but gave lots of love	T F	T F
b. Did not know how to show expressive love maybe because it was never shown to them	T F	T F
c. Worked so hard trying to provide the necessities they did not have time for me/him/her	T F	T F
d. Really did not care about me/him/her	T F	T F
e. Were too involved in their own lives to be concerned about me/him/her	T F	T F
f. Did not provide the basic necessities nor did they provide love and affection	T F	T F
g. Essentially left me/him/her and siblings to fend for ourselves	T F	T F
h. Only showed love if I/he/she did what was told to do	T F	T F
i. Ignored me/him/her if did not do what was expected of me/him/her	T F	T F
j. Would not show love if did not please them	T F	T F
k. Rarely acknowledged accomplishments	T F	T F

l. Focused on the achievements of siblings and did not take notice of me/him/her	T F	T F
m. Made me/him/her feel as I/he/she was not there	T F	T F
n. Provided needs and showed expressive love	T F	T F
o. Did the best they could to provide both instrumental and expressive love	T F	T F

2. If you answered True or Somewhat True to questions in the following manner, your parents/caregivers might have provided this type of care:

Statement	Parenting Style
b–c	Custodial
d–g	Neglect
h–j	Conditional love
k–m	Lack of acknowledgment
a, n-o	Healthy balanced

3. Which parenting style best characterizes your parents/caregivers?

You	Your Partner
☐ Custodial ☐ Neglect ☐ Conditional ☐ Disorganized ☐ Lack of acknowledgment ☐ Healthy/balanced	☐ Custodial ☐ Neglect ☐ Conditional ☐ Disorganized ☐ Lack of acknowledgment ☐ Healthy/balanced

4. How do you/your partner feel about the type of care your parents/caregivers provided?

_____
_____
_____

5. Now explore how early parental experiences are affecting your expectations by putting a circle (and square if you have a partner) around the number that corresponds to how it applies to you according to the following scale.

| Not True at All | Somewhat True | True |
| 1 | 2 | 3 |

Your Styles	You	Your Partner
a. Need a lot of attention from partner to feel secure	1 2 3	1 2 3
b. No matter how much partner is there still feel(s) insecure	1 2 3	1 2 3
c. Need partner to constantly do things to feel secure	1 2 3	1 2 3
d. Need to constantly be complimented by partner to feel good about self	1 2 3	1 2 3
e. Hard to share self completely	1 2 3	1 2 3
f. Have difficulty trusting anyone including partner	1 2 3	1 2 3
g. Have difficulty letting guard down no matter how trustworthy partner is	1 2 3	1 2 3
h. Seems no one, not even partner, can give what need	1 2 3	1 2 3
i. No matter how much partner shows love, do not feel satisfied	1 2 3	1 2 3
j. Feel it is partner's responsibility to provide financially	1 2 3	1 2 3
k. Feel its partner's responsibility to take care of all needs	1 2 3	1 2 3
l. Feel should be able to get from partner what parents/caregivers did not give	1 2 3	1 2 3
m. Feel should be able to get everything need from partner	1 2 3	1 2 3

n. Expect partner to make happy	1 2 3	1 2 3

Your ways of interacting with each other, and the expectations you have, may have to do with the type of love you received from your parents/caregivers. You may also be experiencing entitlement. If you answered True or Somewhat True to the questions in the following manner, this may indicate that this is the type of love you received from your parents/caregivers.

Statement	Parental Style/Entitlement Issue
a–b	Lack of acknowledgment/unstable sense of self
c–d	Conditional/need constant demonstrations of love
e–f	Custodial/rigid defense system/perpetual mistrust/want to keep anyone from getting close
g–i	Neglect/looking for nurturing did not get in childhood
j–n	General entitlement/expect partner to make up for what your parents caregivers did not or could not do

6. Check the box that corresponds to the entitlement issue that best describes you.

You	Your Partner
☐ Unstable sense of self ☐ Need constant demonstrations of love ☐ Rigid defense system and/or mistrusting ☐ Looking for nurturing did not get from parents ☐ General entitlement ☐ None of the above	☐ Unstable sense of self ☐ Need constant demonstrations of love ☐ Rigid defense system and/or mistrusting ☐ Looking for nurturing did not get from parents ☐ General entitlement ☐ None of the above

> **EXERCISE 4.3.** *Absent Parent*

1. If one or both of your parents were not involved in your lives, describe the situation and how you feel about it.

> **EXERCISE 4.4.** *Attachment & Entitlement Narrative*

1. Discuss how your attachment styles, entitlement issues, and/or an absent parent affects you, how you interact, and how it affects your relationship.

Additional Notes

5

The Seven Chakras

If one were to leave a physical wound untreated, it may eventually fester, attracting all types of parasites, which could be detrimental, not only to the wound but the whole body. It is the same when unseen energetic wounds are left untreated. When there are scars, tears, or open wounds in the physical, emotional, or mental bodies, they can create energetic holes that leak out vital force, thereby detracting life force from the other bodies. Conversely, when blocks exist in any of the bodies it can lead to blocks in the energy body.

Untreated wounds can attract energetic parasites, which leave the energy field depleted, reducing your vibratory level, and subsequently attracts those individuals whose vibratory level is also low. When two people are trying to form a relationship with wounded bodies and depleted vitality, their incapacitated states make it difficult to form and sustain a healthy relationship. This is why healing the energy body is just as important as healing the physical, emotional, and mental bodies. Healing the energy body can begin with understanding the functions of the seven chakras, how they correspond with the various aspects of the self, and how they correspond with the stages in the life cycle.

THE SEVEN CHAKRAS

As indicated in Chapter 1 there are seven chakras. The etheric or energy body is the body that draws in the vital force from the universe and distributes it to the seven chakras. The seven chakras then distribute the vital force throughout the body through the 72,000 nadis and 12 meridians (pathways) throughout the body. For each chakra, there are several spokes (like on a wheel) through which the vital force flows in and out. Since these spokes look like the lotus flower, they are referred to as petals. Each chakra also has a vibration or spiritual correspondences that help to enliven it and increase the flow of vital force through it. The spiritual correspondences include, but are not limited to, elements, colors, sounds, etc.

For each aspect of the self, there is a corresponding chakra. Each of the seven chakras corresponds to a different stage of the life cycle and the four bodies. The four bodies can be healed by increasing the vital force to the chakra connected to them. Increasing the vital force increases the vibration level and, subsequently, consciousness. A raised vibration level can help one attract the right person for this life, and a raised consciousness gives one more insight, clarity, and discernment in all matters in life, including knowing when the person appears and sustaining a relationship with him or her. The chakras, including how they connect to the aspects of the self and the different stages in the life cycle, are outlined in this chapter. Since healing the chakras can facilitate healing and/or awakening of aspects of the self, this chapter outlines the vibration correspondences for each chakra. How they can be used to balance and heal the chakras is described in Chapter 6.

The Root Chakra *(Muladhara)*

Since all of existence is energy in different forms, our physical body is also energy and is the densest aspect of the self. It is the vehicle that allows us to reside in the earthly realm. The Muladhara or root chakra is the energetic correspondence to our physical reality and the social world that we inhabit. As the name 'root' suggests, it roots us in both our physical and social worlds. It is concerned with our foundation (i.e., the laws that hold our physical body together so that we can exist in the physical realm), and roots us to a social group in order to ensure that we have the support necessary for survival on Earth. The root chakra is located at the base of the body between the anus and genitals, near the coccygeal nerve plexus. Its physical correspondences are the adrenal glands and the body parts that support our physical foundation (feet, legs, bones, and spine).

The root chakra corresponds to the first stage in life, which is the stage that should provide us with a secure foundation so that we are firmly rooted. Since it corresponds energetically with our basic physical survival needs of food, clothing, shelter, warmth, and sleep, if these needs are adequately met in the early stages of life, then it will provide the foundation for healthy development and functioning. If they are not met, then it can result not only in physical health problems but also a shaky sense of security, potentially throughout the rest of our lives.

Any threat to our survival puts stress on the adrenal gland, which produces the hormone, cortisol, and increases the blood flow to the parts of the body (e.g. feet, legs, etc.) to prepare them for the fight, flight, or freeze response. When blood flows to these parts of the body, other parts of the body may be left in a state of deprivation because too much blood is being used to compensate for the response. If there were threats to our survival during childhood, this may mean that we began leaking vital force that should have been nurturing other parts of the body early in our lives. Over time, leaks to vital force could have consequences for how we continued to develop.

The experiences of one's childhood, as well as those that one has throughout one's life, reveal themselves in physical health problems that may stem from excessive worry about survival. Whether it is warranted or not, one may never feel secure and worry over their job, money, material possessions, etc. Such worry may lead to highly charged emotional reactions to real or perceived threats to anything that threatens one's sense of physical survival. Over time, excessive worry can lead to a drain on the vital force, creating not only an imbalance but lifelong ailments of the bones, legs (joints), and nerves as well as depression, anxiety, and, potentially, a host of other, more severe, physiological, and psychological problems. Healing the physical body can begin the process of healing all the bodies. This process can begin with a healthy diet and exercise, and therapy to address excessive worry, and balancing the vital force to the root chakra.

The vibration correspondences of the root chakra are the element Earth, the color red, and the sounds Lam and the C-note. It has four petals and its sacred symbol is the square: the symbol of foundation and all directions.

- Name/Meaning—Muladhara/support and basis of physical life
- Purpose/Function—to provide a foundation, ground us to the Earth and the physical body
- Location—at the base of the body between the anus and genitals; perineum in men; cervix in women
- Physical Correspondences:
  - Gland—Adrenals
  - Body Parts—Feet, legs, bones, and spine
  - Nerve Plexus—Coccygeal Plexus
- Mental/Emotional Correspondences—concerned with the foundation and basic survival needs of food, water, shelter, sex, sleep, and safety as well as the social connections that ensure that these needs are met.
- Spiritual/Vibration Correspondences:
  - Color—Red
  - Element—Earth
  - Sound/Musical Note—Lam/C-note
  - Symbol—Square, which is the symbol of the four directions: north, south, east, and west
  - Petals—Four

The Sacral Chakra (*Svadhisthana*)

The Svadhisthana or sacral chakra means 'dwelling place' or 'home' and is the energetic correspondence of our emotional body. It is located in the lower abdomen area near the sacrum. Its physical correspondences include the gonads (i.e., the ovaries in women and testes in men), womb, prostate, bladder, kidneys and muscles, and the sacral nerve plexus.

The sacral chakra corresponds to our desires and fuels our expansion capacity to procreate, create, produce, and fulfill our life purpose. Our desires underlie our emotional responses to wants and needs and begin developing in the first stage of life with our first relationships with our caregivers. If our physical and psychic survival needs were met in the first stage of development, then it laid the foundation for healthy emotional responses. If they were not met or were inconsistently met and we had to maximize our emotional responses, e.g. cry, scream, throw temper tantrums, etc. to get what we needed, then it may have created a drain on our vital force early in our development. If our caregivers were cold and rejecting and we withdrew or shut down emotionally, then it may have created blocks to the vital force, thereby depriving the emotional body of what is needed for healthy emotional development.

The experiences of our childhood and throughout our lives reveal themselves in our relationships through emotional overreactions to real or perceived threats to loved ones, by clinging or withdrawing, neither of which is healthy for continued development. If one continues over-reactive emotional responses throughout one's life, then it will drain one's vital force, which may show in physical manifestations in our reproductive capacity, bladder, kidneys, etc. Conversely, if one is emotionally cut-off or unavailable, it may block vital force and make intimacy difficult. Healing the emotional body can begin with balancing the vital force to the sacral chakra, thereby increasing one's procreative, creative, and productive capacities and the fulfillment of one's life purpose.

The vibration correspondences of the sacral chakra are the element water, the color orange, and the sounds Vam and the D-note. Its sacred symbol is a downward pointing triangle and it has six petals.

- Name/Meaning—Svadhisthana/dwelling place or home of the self
- Purpose/Function—Creativity, reproduction, expansion, and fulfillment of purpose
- Location—Sacrum/lower abdomen
- Physical Correspondence:
  - Gland—Gonads (ovaries and testes)
  - Body Parts—Bladder, prostate, womb, kidneys
  - Nerve Plexus—Sacral Plexus
- Mental/Emotional Correspondence—productivity, creativity, sexual interests, fertility, sensuality
- Spiritual/Vibration Correspondences:
  - Element—Water
  - Color—Orange
  - Sound/Musical Note—Vam/D-note
  - Symbol—Inverted-downward pointing triangle
  - Petals-Six

The Solar Plexus Chakra *(Manipura)*

The third chakra is the solar plexus. Its name 'Manipura' means gem or city of gems and it corresponds to our will and power to bring into manifestation our desires. The solar plexus is located between the navel and base of the sternum; its function is to provide the heat necessary for digestion, and assimilation. Its physical correspondence includes the pancreas, digestive organs, including the stomach, small intestine, liver, gallbladder and spleen, and the celiac nerve plexus.

The solar plexus corresponds to our sense of personal power, self-esteem, self-efficacy, and fuels our sense of empowerment. Our sense of empowerment begins developing in the second stage of life when the child begins individuating from the primary caregivers; it becomes more prominent in the third and fourth stages of the life cycle during the periods of initiative and industry when our mental capacity is developing and continues during adolescence, and throughout life. Our early experiences in our families and the social world (e.g., daycare, school, and church) can have a profound effect on our sense of personal power. It affects our self-esteem and sense of agency. If we were not encouraged and made to feel good about ourselves and our abilities to achieve, then it may be revealed throughout our lives through behaviors and habits that are used to assuage low self-esteem and feelings of inferiority, inadequacy, and incompetency. When we engage in bad habits like overeating, drug and alcohol use, etc. they can lead to a drain of our life-force because it is being utilized to help organs that are overworking to process too much and/or bad food and/or to mitigate tension in these areas of the body due to overreactions when childhood wounds are aggravated in response to what appears to be an attack on one's personhood. Such experiences can lead to a weakened vitality, which can weaken our will and subsequently our power to carry out our life purpose and in extreme cases, even weaken our desire to live. Conversely, if one was spoilt as a child, and allowed to do anything they wanted without regard for others, it may have led to one having an exaggerated sense of self and too much willpower. Too much willpower can lead to being overbearing, forceful, and can even lead to violence. Healing how we feel and think about ourselves can begin by balancing the vital force to the solar plexus chakra.

The vibration correspondences of the solar plexus are the color yellow, the element fire, and the sounds Ram and the E-note. Its symbol is an inverted triangle and it has 10 petals.

- Name/Meaning—Manipura/city of gems
- Purpose/Function—Power and enthusiasm
- Location—Between the naval and base of the sternum
- Physical Correspondences:
  - Gland—Pancreas
    Body Parts—Digestive organs, including stomach, small intestine, liver, gallbladder, spleen
  - Nerve Plexus—Celiac plexus

- Mental/Emotional—Concerned with thoughts
- Spiritual/Vibration Correspondences:
  - Element—Fire
  - Color—Yellow
  - Sound/Musical Note—Ram/E-note
  - Symbol—Inverted triangle
  - Petals—10

The Heart Chakra *(Anahata)*

The Anahata or heart chakra is the gateway to the higher self, which connects the heartbeat of the self to the heartbeat of the universe, opening the door to higher expressions of love. It is located at the center of the thoracic cavity behind the heart. Its physical correspondences are the thymus, heart, lungs, arms, hands, and the cardiac and respiratory nerve plexuses.

The heart chakra corresponds to how we love and share ourselves. Awakening of the higher self begins during adolescence and comes to ascendancy in the young adult stage of the life cycle. During this stage, we begin the journey from the lower world to the upper world by attuning to Universe Love. Since love is the binding force of the universe, when we awaken to Universe Love we begin to awaken to or our connection to others and our capacity to love, share and show empathy and compassion. How our early caregivers showed love plays a major role in how we love. If our experiences were positive and we have a good, healthy capacity for love, then we will be able to love openly, honestly, and freely. If our love experiences were not so good, and we are bound by love wounds, then we will have a decreased capacity for love and experience blocks to intimacy. Shutting down to guard our heart potentially blocks the flow of the vital force to the heart chakra, making it difficult to tap into Universe Love and love in higher forms of expression. Conversely, loving too much because we did not feel loved enough can lead to an overabundance of vital force flowing to the heart chakra.

Too much or too little vital force to or from the heart chakra can lead to physical and psychological ailments of the heart and other areas. This makes it difficult to share ourselves in balanced and healthy ways and can result in our being over or under empathic, understanding, and compassionate.

To awaken the higher self means healing the love wounds with parents and other family members, past lovers, and friends. Healing love wounds can open the door to health and well-being, the higher self, and allow us to tap into Universe Love. Opening the door to Universe Love can begin with balancing the vital force to the heart chakra.

The vibration correspondences of the heart chakra are the element air, the color green, and the sounds Yam and the F-note. The symbol of the heart chakra is two inverted triangles (the symbol of the Merkaba body—the body that helps the soul to travel to higher planes while in the physical body) and it has twelve petals.

- Name/Meaning—Anahata/unstuck, unhurt, etc.
- Purpose/Function—Higher love, compassion, transformation
- Location—Center of the thoracic cavity behind the heart
- Physical Correspondences:
  - Gland—Thymus
  - Body Parts—Heart, lungs, arms, and hands
  - Nerve Plexus—Cardiac and respiratory
- Mental/Emotional—Love and compassion
- Spiritual/Vibration Correspondences:
  - Element—Air
  - Color—Green
  - Sound/Musical Note—Yam/F-note
  - Symbol—Two inverted triangles/six-pointed star
  - Petals—12

The Throat Chakra *(Vishuddha)*

The Vishuddha, which means pure or throat chakra is the energetic correspondence of the communicative and expressive self and our capacity to hear. It is located near the throat and its physical correspondences are the thyroid, throat, ears, mouth and vocal cords, and the laryngeal and cervical nerve plexuses.

All of existence is sound in form. At higher levels of consciousness, the throat chakra gives us the capacity to hear the call to live by the Universe Law of MAAT—Truthfulness, harmony, balance, rightness, and justice: laws that shape our moral values and principles. Although the moral values and principles of our family of origin and society help to shape our own, it is during young adulthood that we become more aware of what is right and just and attuned to the universal law of "you reap what you sow." Thus, regardless of what we learned from our parents and society, we begin the journey of shaping our own moral values and principles, developing the courage to stand by them and the will to live by them.

Although the throat chakra can open us to higher levels of communication, many of us communicate based on emotional reactivity in response to experiences in the lower world of physical, emotional, and mental functioning. The way that we communicate may be based on modeling from our family of origin and/or filtered through our early experiences in our childhood as well as through those experiences throughout the courses of our lives. If these experiences were less than optimal, then we may have learned to communicate in ways to guard ourselves, making it difficult to express what we think or how we feel. We may shut down emotionally and/or disengage, cutting off communication or communicate in ways that are overly aggressive and/or attacking. When we shut down or overreact, we may block vital force, or expend too much of it through the throat chakra. In addition, when we internalize and externalize negative energy through negative communication, we can become toxic to ourselves and others. Becoming toxic can result in blocks to consciousness that calls us to live by Divine Laws and further block our ability to access higher levels of consciousness. Awakening the conscious self can begin with balancing the vital force to the throat chakra.

The vibration correspondences of the throat chakra are the element ether, the color blue, and the sounds Ham and G-note. Its symbol is an inverted triangle inside of a circle. It has 16 petals.
- Name/Meaning—Vishuddha/Purification
- Purpose/Function—Consciousness of universal laws, communication, and self-expression
- Location—Throat
- Physical Correspondences:
  - Gland—Thyroid
  - Body Parts—Throat, ears, mouth, and vocal cords
  - Nerve Plexus—Pharyngeal plexus and cervical plexus
- Mental/Emotional—Conscientiousness, moral values, and principles
- Spiritual/Vibration Correspondences:
  - Element—Ether
  - Color—Blue
  - Sound/Musical Note—Ham/G-note
  - Symbol—Inverted downward triangle inside a circle
  - Petals—16

The Third Eye Chakra *(Ajna)*

The Ajna, which means command or the third eye, is the chakra that connects the self to the upper world of light. Awakening to the world of light gives one vision, insight, and clarity, which increases wisdom and understanding and allows us to align with unlimited Universe Will and tap into unlimited Universe Power. The third eye is located on the forehead, slightly above and between the eyebrows. The physical correspondences of the third eye chakra are the pituitary gland, left and right cerebral hemisphere of the mind, and the medulla plexus.

Coming to wisdom and understanding can begin in the young adult stage of the life cycle, but, typically, rises to ascendency during middle life for some and old age for others. However, by the time many evolve to this stage in the life cycle, they are bogged down with the weight of their life experiences, making it difficult for them to see the "light." Due to wounding experiences by loved ones, as well as loss, trauma, stress, bad dietary habits, and wrong lifestyle choices, such individuals may now be weighed down by physical, mental, and emotional ailments and may see the world through the physical health problems and lenses of hurt, anger, fear, sadness, and grief. Too much vital force may have dissipated because of these life experiences and their life force is now being further weakened because it is being blocked by bad physical health and negative thoughts and feelings that are lodged in these respective bodies, making it difficult for vital force (and light) to flow through. Blocked vital force is evidence by seeing things only from one's own perspective, ignorance, cynicism, paranoia, and a lack of trust and faith. It also manifests in psychological disorders such as anxiety, depression, and personality disorders such as narcissism. In addition, more severe disorders may result from attracting dark energetic forces and parasites that attach themselves to those individuals suffering from these types of ailments. The effects may be even more severe if the soul is weighed down by the karmic debt of one's life choices.

Becoming enlightened means doing the work necessary to increase the light flowing through one's body, which can begin with balancing the vital force throughout the body and to the third eye in particular. Energy work can help open the third eye, giving one more insight and clarity so that one can see how one can use the gifts of one's life experiences, whether good or bad, as growth in one's soul's evolvement. Opening the third eye increases one's ability to see and gives one insight as well as the peace and knowing that comes with it. Awakening to the "light" may also give one the ability to see in other interdimensional realms, raise one's consciousness, increases one's wisdom and understanding, and subsequently facilitate awakening one their unlimited potential and spiritual power to bring things into manifestation.

The vibration correspondences of the third eye are the element light, the colors indigo and purple, and the sounds Aum/Om and

A-note. Its symbol is an inverted downward triangle inside a circle, and it has two petals.
- Name/Meaning-Ajna/Command
- Purpose/Function—Inner vision, insight, wisdom, and spiritual power
- Location—Slightly above and between the eyebrows
- Physical Correspondence:
    - Gland—Pituitary
    - Body Parts—Left and right cerebral hemispheres of brain
    - Nerve Plexus—Medulla plexus (Autonomic nervous system)
- Mental/Emotional—Peace and knowing
- Spiritual/Vibration Correspondences:
    - Element—Light
    - Colors-Indigo/Purple
    - Sound/Musical Note—Aum /Om/A note
    Symbol—Inverted downward triangle inside a circle
    Petals—Two

The Crown Chakra *(Sahasrara)*

Sahasrara or the crown chakra, which means no dwelling place, is the chakra of transcendence and liberation. The crown chakra is located at the top of the head and its physical correspondences are the pineal gland (referred to as the seat of the soul), the upper skull, and the central nervous system. Awakening to the eternal self enables the soul to unify with all of reality and ultimately, the Soul of the universe. The soul then becomes liberated from the social conditioning of this life, the karmic debt that it has created in previous lives and this life, and unites with the Universe Soul, while in its physical body on Earth. Uniting with the Universe Soul leads to peace, bliss, or heaven while on Earth, and once one loses the physical body, eternal life in the cosmic realm.

The vibration correspondences of the crown chakra are pure spirit, and the colors violet, white, and gold. It has no seed sound, but

has the musical note, B. Its symbol is a circle and it has a thousand petals.
- Name/Meaning—Sahasrara/No dwelling place
- Purpose/Function—Transcendence, liberation
- Location—Top of the head
- Physical Correspondences:
  - Gland—Pineal
  - Body Parts—Upper skull, cerebral skull
  - Nerve Plexus—Central nervous system
- Mental/Emotional—Peace, oneness, unity
- Spiritual/Vibration Correspondences:
  - Element—Pure spirit
  - Colors—Violet, white, gold
  - Sound/Musical Note—None or silence/B note
  - Symbol—Circle
  - Petals—1,000

Whatever one is experiencing that is a deterrent to one's health and well-being may indicate that work may need to be done in that respective area and/or on that chakra. Most of us are aware of therapies to heal the physical, mental, and emotional bodies, but few people are aware of therapies to heal the energy body and even fewer are aware that healing the energy body may be necessary to overall health. Ways to heal the energy body include a number of energy or vibration modalities, all of which can help increase the vital force flowing through the chakras, facilitating their healing, and increasing their vibration level. Being healthy and vibrating at a higher level, can ultimately help one to attract the right partner and sustain a relationship with him or her.

Chapter 5 Exercises

Identifying Energetic Wounds

The purpose of these exercises is to help you identify unresolved issues that may potentially be contributing to health problems in the area corresponding to the chakra. Healing modalities to work with the chakras are described in chapter 6, and steps to heal are outlined in chapter 7.

EXERCISE 5.1. *Root Chakra*

1. Use the chart below to circle the number that corresponds to health/issues you/your partner experience under each domain.

Physical/Social Aspect of Self	Correspondence	Low 1 2 3 4 5 High	
Survival/Social	**Psycho-Emotional**	You	Your Partner
	Insecure about Survival	1 2 3 4 5	1 2 3 4 5
	Worry about Survival	1 2 3 4 5	1 2 3 4 5
	Fearful	1 2 3 4 5	1 2 3 4 5
	Anxious	1 2 3 4 5	1 2 3 4 5
	Physical		
	Adrenal Gland	1 2 3 4 5	1 2 3 4 5
	Feet/Legs	1 2 3 4 5	1 2 3 4 5
	Bones	1 2 3 4 5	1 2 3 4 5
	Spine	1 2 3 4 5	1 2 3 4 5

2. Describe what is going on in any of the areas above.

_____
_____
_____
_____
_____

EXERCISE 5.2. *Sacral Chakra*

1. Use the chart below to circle the number that corresponds to your/your partner under each domain.

Emotional Aspect of Self	Correspondence	Low 1 2 3 4 5 High	
		You	Your Partner
Security/ Balance	Psycho-Emotional		
	Insecure	1 2 3 4 5	1 2 3 4 5
	Anxious	1 2 3 4 5	1 2 3 4 5
	Clingy	1 2 3 4 5	1 2 3 4 5
	Distant	1 2 3 4 5	1 2 3 4 5
Productivity	Interest	1 2 3 4 5	1 2 3 4 5
	Work	1 2 3 4 5	1 2 3 4 5
	Life purpose	1 2 3 4 5	1 2 3 4 5
	Creativity	1 2 3 4 5	1 2 3 4 5
Sexuality	Interest	1 2 3 4 5	1 2 3 4 5
	Fertility	1 2 3 4 5	1 2 3 4 5
	Sensuality	1 2 3 4 5	1 2 3 4 5
	Physical		
	Gonads	1 2 3 4 5	1 2 3 4 5
	Bladder	1 2 3 4 5	1 2 3 4 5
	Prostate	1 2 3 4 5	1 2 3 4 5
	Womb	1 2 3 4 5	1 2 3 4 5
	Kidneys	1 2 3 4 5	1 2 3 4 5

2. Describe what is going on in any of the areas above.
_____
_____
_____
_____
_____

EXERCISE 5.3. *Solar Plexus Chakra*

1. Use the chart below to circle the number that corresponds to your/your partner under each domain.

Mental Aspect of Self	Correspondence	Low 1 2 3	High 4 5
		You	Your Partner
Thoughts About Self & the World	**Psycho-Emotional**		
	Self-concept	1 2 3 4 5	1 2 3 4 5
	Self-esteem	1 2 3 4 5	1 2 3 4 5
	Self-efficacy	1 2 3 4 5	1 2 3 4 5
	Sense of empowerment	1 2 3 4 5	1 2 3 4 5
	Outlook on life	1 2 3 4 5	1 2 3 4 5
	Willpower	1 2 3 4 5	1 2 3 4 5
	Physical		
	Pancreas	1 2 3 4 5	1 2 3 4 5
	Digestive organs (stomach, small intestines, liver, Gallbladder, Spleen	1 2 3 4 5	1 2 3 4 5

2. Describe what is going on in any of the areas above.

_____
_____
_____
_____
_____

EXERCISE 5.4. *Heart Chakra*

1. Use the chart below to circle the number that corresponds to your/your partner under each domain.

Compassionate Aspect of Self	Correspondence	Low 1 2 3 4 5 High	
	Psycho-Emotional	You	Your Partner
	Guarded	1 2 3 4 5	1 2 3 4 5
	Over close	1 2 3 4 5	1 2 3 4 5
	Ability to be intimate (close)	1 2 3 4 5	1 2 3 4 5
	Ability to Share	1 2 3 4 5	1 2 3 4 5
	Ability to show compassion	1 2 3 4 5	1 2 3 4 5
	Ability to show empathy	1 2 3 4 5	1 2 3 4 5
	Physical		
	Thymus gland	1 2 3 4 5	1 2 3 4 5
	Heart	1 2 3 4 5	1 2 3 4 5
	Arms	1 2 3 4 5	1 2 3 4 5
	Hands	1 2 3 4 5	1 2 3 4 5

2. Describe what is going on in any of the areas above.

_____
_____
_____
_____
_____

> **EXERCISE 5.5.** *Throat Chakra*

1. Use the chart below to circle the number that corresponds to your/your partner under each domain.

Conscious Aspect of Self	Correspondence	Low 1 2 3 4 5 High	
		You	Your Partner
Moral Values and Principles	Psycho-Emotional		
	Conscious of a force greater than self	1 2 3 4 5	1 2 3 4 5
	Sense of what is right and wrong	1 2 3 4 5	1 2 3 4 5
	Sense of what is just	1 2 3 4 5	1 2 3 4 5
	Lives by moral values and principles	1 2 3 4 5	1 2 3 4 5
	Understands the consequences of one's actions	1 2 3 4 5	1 2 3 4 5
	Interest in doing the right thing	1 2 3 4 5	1 2 3 4 5

Expressive	Negative communication (profanity, gossip)	1 2 3 4 5	1 2 3 4 5
	Difficulty communicating thoughts and Feelings	1 2 3 4 5	1 2 3 4 5
	Difficulty with effective communication in conflict	1 2 3 4 5	1 2 3 4 5
	Physical		
	Thyroid gland	1 2 3 4 5	1 2 3 4 5
	Throat	1 2 3 4 5	1 2 3 4 5
	Ears	1 2 3 4 5	1 2 3 4 5
	Mouth	1 2 3 4 5	1 2 3 4 5
	Vocal cords	1 2 3 4 5	1 2 3 4 5

2. Describe what is going on in any of the areas above.

_____
_____
_____
_____
_____

EXERCISE 5.6. *Third Eye Chakra*

1. Use the chart below to circle the number that corresponds to your/your partner under each domain.

Enlightened Aspect of Self	Correspondence	Low High 1 2 3 4 5	
	Psycho-Emotional	You	Your Partner
	Stuck in social conditioning	1 2 3 4 5	1 2 3 4 5
	Negative outlook	1 2 3 4 5	1 2 3 4 5
	Open/flexible	1 2 3 4 5	1 2 3 4 5
	Seeks knowledge	1 2 3 4 5	1 2 3 4 5
	Seeks truth	1 2 3 4 5	1 2 3 4 5
	Seeks wisdom	1 2 3 4 5	1 2 3 4 5
	Seeks understanding	1 2 3 4 5	1 2 3 4 5
	Physical		
	Left and right hemisphere of the brain	1 2 3 4 5	1 2 3 4 5
	Autonomic nervous system	1 2 3 4 5	1 2 3 4 5

2. Describe what is going on in any of the areas above.

_____
_____
_____
_____

EXERCISE 5.7. *Crown Chakra*

1. Use the chart below to circle the number that corresponds to your/your partner under each domain.

Eternal Aspect of Self	Correspondences	Low　　　　　　High 1　　2　　3　　4　　5	
	Psycho-Emotional	You	Your Partner
	Attachment to social conditioning	1 2 3 4 5	1 2 3 4 5
	Attachment to worldly things	1 2 3 4 5	1 2 3 4 5
	Seeks unity with self and Others	1 2 3 4 5	1 2 3 4 5
	Seeks peace	1 2 3 4 5	1 2 3 4 5
	Seeks unity with God	1 2 3 4 5	1 2 3 4 5
	Seeks God	1 2 3 4 5	1 2 3 4 5
	Physical		
	Upper skull & cerebral skull	1 2 3 4 5	1 2 3 4 5
	Central nervous system	1 2 3 4 5	1 2 3 4 5

2. Describe what is going on in any of the areas above.

_____
_____
_____
_____
_____

EXERCISE 5.8. *Narrative*

1. Summarize the areas that are affecting your lives and what you need to do work on.

___

Additional Notes

6

Healing the Energy Body

One path to good health is to maintain one's vibration frequency at an optimal level. All of existence vibrates at its own frequency. Frequency means the number of waves or oscillations per second, measured in Hertz. A healthy body usually has a frequency of between 62 and 78 MegaHertz (MHz). Disease begins to occur when the body has a frequency of about 58 MHz. Vibration work means surrounding oneself with frequencies high enough to ward off disease and raising one's vibration to a healthy level. Raising one's vibration helps to raise one's consciousness. Raising one's consciousness helps to connect to Universe Consciousness. Below is a chart of how frequencies are measured:

1 Hertz = 1 Hz = 1 oscillation per second
1 Kilo Hertz =1 KHz = 1,000 oscillations per second
1 MegaHertz=MHz = 1,000,000 oscillations per second
1 GigaHertz = 1 GHz = 1,000,000,000 oscillations per second

SOUND

According to the oldest spiritual tradition in the world, among the Egyptians, the universe was created through sound. This idea is also found in other spiritual traditions. Even in the Christian tradition, the world was created through God speaking: "Let there be light..." and then everything was created. In science, the universe was created by sound—a big bang. In *Cymatics*, which means matter pertaining to waves, Hans Jenny suggests that all matter is formed and shaped by sound. Whether moving or still, all matter is sound vibration in unique patterns in visible form (Dale, 2009, p. 142).[1] Scientists have even found that "cells interact and form patterns first through sound and second through light" (Dale, p. 124). It has also been found that the primary function of DNA is not to synthesize proteins as was originally thought, but to perform bio-acoustic and bioelectrical signaling (Dale, p. 143). Additionally, it has been found that "chromosomes work like holographic biocomputers using the DNA's electromagnetic radiation to generate and interpret spiraling waves of sound and light that run up and down the DNA ladder" (Dale, 2009, p. 143).

Sound can be used to enliven the chakras. As indicated in the previous chapter, each chakra has a seed sound, which is the subtle sound at the center of the seed made by its vibration. The seed sound has also been referred to as a vibration or energy pattern in the region of the body where the chakra can be found. Seed sounds are words or mantras that, if chanted, vibrate in a way as to enliven the corresponding chakra. There are numerous mantras and words of power that, if chanted, tap into the spiritual power of that vibrational sound. The most significant mantra is Aum (also Om) because it is considered to contain the entirety of the universe.[2] In addition, each note and sound in the musical scale corresponds to one of the chakras. Therefore, playing music containing a specific note helps to activate the energy of that chakra. The seed sound and musical note for each chakra are outlined in Table 6.1 below.

Table 6.1 Chakras and Sounds

Chakra	Seed Sound	Musical Note	Musical Scale
Root	LAM	C	Do
Sacral	VAM	D	Re

---

[1] Powerful video that attests to shapes arriving out of sound can be found at www.cymatics.org.
[2] In Eastern spirituality (i.e., Hinduism, Buddhism, Jainism, and Sikhism).

Solar Plexus	RAM	E	Mi
Heart	YAM	F	Fa
Throat	HAM	G	So
Third Eye	AUM	A	La
Crown		B	

Color

Color is a measure of the frequency at which a light wave is moving. It is essentially light moving at a frequency that our eyes can detect. The lowest frequency that our eyes can detect is red, while the highest frequency is violet. How we see color is based on the color it is reflecting from. When the sun emits light, it emits all colors. When it hits an object with a specific color, the object reflects that color more, while all the other colors are absorbed. White reflects all colors and black absorbs all colors.

The chakras can be enlivened by the color that corresponds to the frequency of its light waves or the color of the vital force that works through it. To utilize color to enliven a particular chakra, one might surround oneself with that particular color by painting a room, or placing gems, crystals, candles, or color lights in a room and/or taking color baths. Outlined below is an explanation of the colors and the chakras to which they correspond.

- ■ *Red* has the longest wavelength and lowest frequency of visible light. It corresponds with the root chakra. It is a hot and stimulating color that energizes. Physically, it is associated with the bloodstream and therefore, covers the entire body. Red is closely associated with the heart and exposure to red quickens the heart rate and increases blood circulation, which means that it can help the body to heal. However, because it energizes, if one is ill, it can energize the illness as well. Red is also associated with sexuality and the arousal of sexual energy. Emotionally, red is associated with love. However, it is also associated with aggression and anger. When white is added to red, it transforms into pink, which is a softer color of love and is associated with femininity.

- ***Orange*** corresponds with the sacral chakra, sexuality, and reproduction. It is also warm but does not have the vibrant heat of red. Physically, it is linked to the sexual organs. Emotionally, it is a vibrant color that heightens emotional energies, inspiring happiness, joy, sensuality, and creativity.
- ***Yellow*** corresponds to the solar plexus and, like the sun, powers us with vitality that stimulates the nerves and mind. Emotionally, it helps with mental activity, clarity, alertness, concentration, and focus. Yellow also brings about cheerfulness, empowerment, self-esteem, and self-confidence.
- ***Green*** corresponds with the heart chakra and is a cool color. Being that it is the primary color in nature, it provides nourishment for the body and a balance for the emotions and mind. Generally, green is associated with money, prosperity, new beginnings, and growth. Since it is associated with the heart chakra, it corresponds to love, sharing, truth, harmony, and balance.
- ***Blue*** corresponds to the throat chakra. It is a cool color, which is associated with inner peace and calmness. At higher levels, it corresponds to sounds at higher frequency levels, giving us the ability to be clairaudient; to have "clear hearing" in other interdimensional realms. Opening the gateway to communication at higher frequency sounds increases wisdom and understanding.
- ***Indigo*** is a mixture of blue and violet and corresponds to the third eye. It facilitates opening doors to "clear seeing," or clairvoyancy, which is the ability to see at higher frequencies, giving one access to interdimensional realms and higher levels of consciousness.
- ***Violet*** is a mixture of red and blue and has the shortest wavelength and highest frequency of all the colors that can be seen. It corresponds to the crown chakra. Violet facilitates illumination, transcendence, and unity of the masculine and feminine, further facilitating merging and unity with the Universe Soul.
- ***White*** corresponds to the crown chakra and contains all light in the color spectrum. It is a reflection of all of creation; an

expression of the universe in all its manifested colors. White facilitates illumination, transcendence, unity, and merging with the Universe Soul, leading to a state of bliss.
- ■ *Black* is the absence of or complete absorption of light. It is the source of creation where all things; all of existence, comes from.
- ■ *Silver* is a combination of black and white and was called the "crystallized moon" by the ancient Egyptians. It is associated with femininity and intuition. It facilitates cleansing, purification, and clairvoyance.
- ■ *Gold* was called the "crystallized sun" by the ancient Egyptians, essentially meaning solidified vital force. It is a mixture of yellow and orange and contains the properties of both colors. Physically, gold gives vitality to the body, particularly to the skeletal structure and nervous system. Since it is believed to be the crystallized sun or vital force, it is also used for illumination and transcendence.

SACRED GEOMETRY

As indicated above, physical shapes are sound vibrating. Geometric shapes result from sound vibrations that repeat themselves throughout the universe. Due to the vibration of the sound through which the shapes come into existence, they have special significance for how they affect the energy body and, subsequently, the physical, emotional, mental, and spiritual bodies. Filling one's environment with various shapes can help with energy work. Some of the shapes and what they represent are outlined below.

- ■ **Circle**—Wholeness, completeness, infinity, and perfect balance
- ■ **Square**—Foundation
- ■ **Triangle**—Illumination/spiritual attainment
- ■ **Two triangles** (with one inverted)—Astral/spiritual travel[3]

---

[3] Merkaba—the light body that allows the soul to travel.

THE ELEMENTS

All of reality is comprised of one or more of the five elements: fire, water, earth, air, and ether (the medium of the subtle bodies).[4] Since we are made of the elements, they can be used as healing and strengthening, and conscious raising tools.

Earth

Tuning into the Earth, its mineral and plant life, and all that it gives us can help assist in the healing process and raise our vibration levels. The Earth is powerful and has generative, regenerative, and grounding qualities. Touching the Earth, the original place of our birth, allows us to know and feel its power. Our ancestors were in touch with its powers and all that it provided due to their direct relationship with it through planting and harvesting. The gifts it gave spoke to their hands and hearts, which, ultimately, spoke to their souls. When we open our eyes and see, we find that practically all physical phenomenal (i.e., everything, whether in a natural or in a transformed state) comes from the Earth—wood, metals, herbs, vegetable life, etc. In fact, 66 elements found in the Earth's crust can be found in the exact same proportions within the blood's hemoglobin.

Trees are deeply rooted in the Earth and those trees that have been around for a long time have seen and experienced a lot. They are the Earth's guardians and can speak to our souls when we turn our ears to their vibrations.

Gems and crystals have numerous healing qualities; they have guardians, entities, or beings who are involved in their creation, evolvement, and protection. They have extraordinary color, shapes, and vibration and are used not only for healing but for spiritual attunement. Gems and crystals have memory and can be programmed with energies to help guard and protect all of the bodies.

---

[4] Ether is finer energy that cannot be seen and is thought to be the medium of the subtle energy bodies discussed in Chapter 1. Since the other four elements are used to help to heal and raise the consciousness of all the bodies, including the subtle energy bodies, ether is not discussed here.

By laying various shapes, sizes, and colors on the body and/or surrounding oneself with them, and by putting them in various places throughout the home, crystals can help clean, heal, and awaken the chakras.

Herbs, flowers, and bushes of all sorts provide colors, shapes, and scents, all of which provide healing for the body, mind, and spirit. They also have guardians, entities, or beings (often referred to as nature spirits) who are involved in their creation, evolvement, and protection. There are numerous works on herbs that provide information on their healing properties. Flower and herbal scents are the essences of essential oils that are used to awaken the senses and facilitate healing and consciousness.

Essential oils from flowers and herbs have their own vibrational frequencies. They are called essential because they are the components of the plants that are essential for their survival; parts that fight parasites. When concentrated, essential oils can create an environment in which disease cannot survive. The essential oils that have the highest frequencies range from 52 MHz to 320 MHz

Essential oils can be used in several ways via aromatherapy. The three primary methods include: topical, applying them directly to the body through a message; inhaling them through steam (including putting them in bath water); and/or ingesting them. A combination of these methods can also be used. See the vibration level properties of some of the more commonly used essential oils below alongside some of the foods we consume:

- Processed canned foods—0 MHz (below 1,000,000,000 hertz)
- Fresh produce—up to 15 MHz
- Dry herbs – 12 MHz to 22 MHz
- Fresh herbs – 20 MHz to 27 MHz
- Essential oils—52 MHz to 320 MHz
  - Rose - 320 MHz
  - Frankincense - 147 MHz
  - Lavender - 118 MHz
  - Myrrh - 108 MHz

- Sandalwood - 96 MHz
- Peppermint - 78 MHz

Air

According to the Akan people of Ghana, since air contains the vital force that provides the breath of life, God is everywhere; omniscient and omnipresent. Air is also vital for change. When the wind blows, things move, therefore, air represents movement and change. Deep breathing or prana is the key to vitality and consciousness.[5] Deep breathing during meditation not only helps to circulate more vital force throughout the body but by focusing on breathing, it helps to calm the internal chatter that blocks your ability to tap into other interdimensional realms and ultimately Universe Consciousness. Incense scented with natural essential oils: myrrh, frankincense, opium, aloe vera, etc., are objects that can be used to represent air and help enhance healing and awakening work.

Water

Water is soothing and has a cleansing effect on all the bodies. It can be programmed with sound to help heal the bodies as well. In *the Messages in Water,* Masaru Emoto (2001) found that when words like love, gratitude, and other kind words were spoken, water formed beautifully shaped solid crystals. Likewise, when he prayed over the water and played beautiful music, beautifully shaped solid crystals were formed. When he exposed water to violence and ugly words, the crystals were fragmented. Since our bodies are 70% water, what we think and say can affect our bodies significantly. Before drinking water, praying over it, exposing it to peaceful and calming music, and sending it messages of love, gratitude, and other life-affirming messages can help heal the bodies. The same can be done while showering and before bathing in water. Ask the water to wash away

---

[5] See Reiki Masters Training Manual by Kaia (2014) in the list of references for a practical guide on how different types of breathing techniques help to increase vital force to the glands which help to heal the bodies.

weaknesses, to strengthen you, and to heal your mind, body, and spirit.

Fire

Fire gives light and heat and has a transforming effect. It burns away the old, allowing for the new. Fire transfers energy to new forms, releasing what was old. Since it rises and is transforming, it connects us to spirit. Candles and incense can be used for clearing and cleansing and can help with healing. When using a candle, you can make a prayer over it before lighting it. In the prayer, you can ask for what you want. When the candle is lit, the prayer then goes to the universe.

MEDITATION

Meditation is truly the path to health, vitality, and enlightenment. Meditation focuses on quieting the mind of the internal and external chatter that distracts the self from aligning with Universal Consciousness and can give one the wisdom and understanding to stay on the path of one's soul's journey. Whatever work that needs to be done can be achieved through mediation. Through meditation, one can transcend the phenomena of this world (e.g., negative thoughts, beliefs, patterns, and behaviors) and connect with other worlds and vibrations with which the soul shares space. One is also able to project (i.e., bring into manifestation phenomena, such as new thoughts, beliefs, patterns, and behaviors) and accomplish the things that bring one success, prosperity, peace, and joy. More importantly, mediation helps to heal and rejuvenate all aspects of the self. When going into meditation, surrounding oneself with the elements and vibration modalities in the form of colors, scents, and sounds as well as and deep breathing are the keys to increasing the vital force circulating through the energy body, thereby increasing its vibration; this ultimately leads to awakening to higher levels of consciousness.

Attunements

Vital force, referred to as Reiki in Japanese, Qi or Chi in Chinese, and Prana in Hinduism, can be increased via an attunement. An attunement is a procedure during which a person passes on an energy structure to another person's energy body. They may have attuned by the source (an energetic force/intelligence) and received the energy directly from that source, or they may have received it from someone else who is already attuned to the energy. Receiving an attunement can increase the life force channeling through the energy body and, therefore, through the physical, emotional, mental, and spiritual bodies. Attunements not only facilitate healing and awakening but also speed up these processes. What once took people years to achieve through meditation and mantras can be achieved more quickly through an attunement. Receiving an attunement increases the light quotient within the body at the cellular level changing how the body and its senses process everything that it consumes and everything around it.

Sekhem is an energy structure from ancient Egypt.[6] If one looks at the early translations[7] from their sacred temples and tombs, one can see that Sekhem was used as a word of power to access God's spiritual power. It not only provides healing for the physical, emotional, mental, and spiritual bodies, but it is also a love and light energy. Sekhem was rediscovered by Patrick Ziegler in 1980 when he visited Egypt and spent a night in the Great Pyramid. He bought it back to the U.S. and passed the energy on to others. Individuals who have been attuned to its power can attune others to it.

The most known energy structures or attunements are referred to as Reiki (life force energy). Although accessing the energy structure of the universal life force is an ancient practice, Reiki was rediscovered in the mid-1800s by Mikao Usui after he went into mediation and fasted on Mount Kumara for 21 days.

---

[6] The various spellings of this energy are seichem, seichim, sekhem, and skhm.
[7] See the numerous works by E.A. Wallis Budge.

Reiki is a healing modality from the universe that serves to heal the physical, emotional, mental, and spiritual bodies. It is a healing energy that is transmitted through the hands of the person who has been attuned to it. Since its rediscovery, Reiki has been transformed by individuals who are attuned to the energy transmitted to them by other individuals who are attuned to it.

By utilizing Reiki and attuning to other energy structures (i.e. crystals, flowers, etc.); some individuals have attuned to additional types of Reiki that serve various healing and conscious raising functions. These various types of Reiki can be used to help heal one or all the bodies. They can also be used for certain types of diseases of the different bodies as well as for clearing, cleansing, and protecting, and to increase one's ability to do psychic and energy work. One may seek out and/or receive an attunement from someone who has been attuned to the energy, most likely a Reiki practitioner. Receiving an attunement, particularly higher levels of Usui Reiki (healing Reiki) gives one the ability to not only heal oneself but to heal others. A few attunements have been prepared for you. Follow the instructions below to receive them.[8]

Instructions
To receive each attunement below, do the following:
1. Sit down in a comfortable position or lie down;
2. Place your hands on your knees and open them;
3. Close your eyes;
4. Recite the words out loud or say them mentally for the particular attunement;

---

[8] See Reiki Masters Training Manual by Kaia (2014) in the list of references for a more extensive discussion on Reiki and practical application. You should not activate any of these attunements if you are experiencing medical issues or are taking medications. Please note that by accepting any of these attunements, we nor our publisher, or any affiliates of ours are responsible for any injuries or problems of any kind mental, physical, emotional, or spiritual acquired from accepting these attunements. By accepting any attunement, energy, or healing modality, you agree that you accept complete responsibly for the undertaking and that nothing provided you is a replacement for proper and complete medical care.

5. Sit for 12-15minutes for the energy to run. If you can, sit for another 10-25 minutes to give the energy a chance to become absorbed into your energy system more rapidly;
6. At the end of the session, say the word, "abide." to stop the energy flow. You can also say the word "ground" to ground you back to earth;
7. You should activate one attunement a day, 3-7 days apart to avoid taking in more energy than your body can handle in a period of time.

ATTUNEMENTS[9]

1. **Protection Attunement**—This attunement is designed to put protection around you. It should be done before any other attunement is called down and should be activated before doing energy work.

  i. ***DNA Psychic Protection***—Use before doing energy work.
  Say the following:
  > *I now call forth the awakening and grounding of the DNA psychic protection attunement prepared for by Ra Heter; in, through, and around my entire energy field matrix and four body systems.*

2. **Clearing and Cleansing Attunement**—These attunements can be used to clear your energy field & chakras of negative energy. They can be used daily and in the combination described below.

  ii. ***White Flame***—Can be used daily.
  Say the following:
  > *I now call forth the awakening and grounding of the White Flame attunement prepared for by Ra Heter; in, through, and around my entire energy field matrix and four body systems.*

  iii. ***Seven Chakra Flush***— Can be used weekly.
  Say the following:

---

[9] Although some of these energies can be used daily, it is highly recommended that you take precautions and use them weekly to see how they feel and how your body adjusts to them.

> *I now call forth the awakening and grounding of the Seven Chakra Flush attunement prepared for by Ra Heter; in, through, and around my entire energy field matrix and four body systems.*

iv. **Meridian Flush**—Can be used weekly.
   Say the following:
   > *I now call forth the awakening and grounding of the Meridian Flush attunement prepared for by Ra Heter; in, through, and around my entire energy field matrix and four body systems.*

When using these attunements in combination (once a week) say each of the following and allow 1-3 minutes for each to run before saying the next one:

   —*White Flame*
   —*Seven Chakra Flush* (to cleanse all the chakras, or can say seven chakra flush for each chakra for more intense cleansing work)
   —*Meridian Flush*
   —*Grounding Cord* (to help ground you back to Earth)

3. **Healing Attunement**—can be used for healing the four bodies. Usui Reiki is the universal life force energy that is used to heal.

v. ***Usui Reiki***—Can be used as needed.
   Say the following:
   > *I now call forth the awakening and grounding of the Usui Reiki Levels I, II, and III attunements prepared for by Ra Heter; in, through, and around my entire energy field matrix and four body systems.*

4. **Spiritual Power/Love & Light** –increases feelings of love and increases light, awakening, and consciousness.

vi. ***Sekhem***—Can be used as needed.
   Say the following:
   > *I now call forth the awakening and grounding of the Sekhem attunement prepared for by Ra Heter; in, through, and around my entire energy field matrix and four body systems.*

5. **Clearing, Healing & Transmuting**— clearing of negativity blocked energies and transmutes DNA mutations.

vii. *Violet Rose Flame*—Can be used daily.

<u>Say the following:</u>
> *I now call forth the awakening and grounding of the Violet Rose Flame attunement prepared for by Ra Heter; in, through, and around my entire energy field matrix and four body systems.*

<u>Daily Invocation</u>
I am a being of the Violet Rose Fire. I am the purity God desires.

Attunement Use

The attunements may be used daily, weekly, or as needed. To use the attunements after you have activated them, just sit in a comfortable position or lie down with your hands open. Say the name of the attunement, (i.e. DNA psychic protection, white flame, etc.) Then sit for 3-5 minutes or longer if you use them during meditation. When you are finished say "abide," to stop the energy flow. You can also say "ground' to ground you to earth. If you use the attunements regularly, you should make sure that you stay hydrated (drink lots of water). Below is a prayer that you might use daily for cleansing and before meditation.

<u>A Daily Invocation</u>

Higher Self, I now ask my body to remove all negative feelings, my speech to remove all residual expressions, and my mind to remove all residual thoughts, energies, entities, and beings connected to me that are not truly my own. I want to be healthy, please remove any and all things that are not in my highest joyful good to carry. Please do that now.

Doing Energy Work

To engage in energy work there are a few things you may want to consider doing first.

Seeking out an energy teacher—It is important to seek out and work with an energy practitioner/teacher. It is important to work with someone who has the experience to not only guide you but to make sure you are protected.

Creating a space—If you do not already have one, creating a space where you can do energy healing work is important. It should be clear of clutter and surrounded with objects that make you feel happy, healthy, and whole. This also means cleaning the environment of objects with high levels of electromagnetic frequencies (EMF) as much as you can or doing the work in a space with less of it.[10]

Building a shrine—A shrine can be built as a point of focus for prayer, meditation, and connecting with ancestors and other cosmic guardians and guides. Since tapping into other realms can be potentially dangerous, benevolent ancestors are our guardians. When using the shrine you should first give reverence to and pray to God for guidance and protection. Since ancestors who have lost the physical body can see in both worlds; the earthly and cosmic realms, you may then proceed by asking benevolent ancestors and other

---

[10] Electromagnetic frequencies (EMF) waves come from a variety of sources, in extremely low frequency (ELF up to 300 Hz), immediate frequency (IF—300 Hz -10 MHz), and high frequencies or radio frequency (RF—10 MHz- 300 GHz). They can affect the body depending on the level to which they are blocked by metal shields, building materials, trees, walls, or distance from the source. ELF sources include electrical power supply and appliances using electricity; computer screens, and security systems are the sources of IF fields and TVs, microwave ovens, and cell phones, etc. produce RF fields. Since the body is energy and is comprised of tiny electrical currents for it to carry out normal bodily functions from brain and heart activity to digestion, EMF can induce currents in the body and subsequently affect it and the energy field around it. Although research is not conclusive on the effects of EMF on health, some attribute a host of symptoms to EMF Hypersensitivity (EHS) including headaches, fatigue, sleep disturbances, skin problems including burning and rashes, anxiety, depression, and suicide. It is also thought to contribute to a host of diseases including attention hyperactive deficit disorder (AHDD), fibromyalgia, and cancer ("What are electromagnetic fields," n.d.).

cosmic guides and guardians to help and guide you. A shrine and items you might include the items outlined below.

1. A small table or space on a table
2. White cloth—to cover the table or space
3. Pictures of the ancestors who have passed
4. An object of each of the four elements, e.g., a candle for fire, a glass of water, crystals, gems, flowers, etc. for earth, and incense for air.
5. Any other objects that make you feel happy, healthy, and whole. For those who are interested in deeper spiritual work with "light" energies and/or are interested in becoming practitioners, you should seek out a teacher to guide you.

Putting protection around yourself—Before engaging in energy work, particularly if you are attempting to connect with energies in other interdimensional reams, it is absolutely necessary that you make it clear that you are interested only in energies of light and to put protection around you. Again, working with an energy/spiritual teacher is necessary.

The modalities outlined in this chapter are just a few of the numerous energy or vibration modalities that can be used to heal the energy body and increase vitality. Indeed, healing the energy body and increasing the vital force to our physical, emotional, mental, and spiritual bodies gives us more vitality and increases our vibration, which increases insight and clarity. However, more work must be completed to attract your soul's partner, and if you have already done so, continuing the journey toward spiritual evolvement together. These vibration modalities can be used as you ascend the steps to healing the three lower aspects of the self and awakening the four higher aspects of the self. The steps to health and awakening are outlined in the next chapter.

Chapter 6 Exercises

Healing the Energy Body

The purpose of these exercises is to guide you through a plan of action for healing the energy body. Using the list below, fill in the table for the vibrational modality you will incorporate into your lives (if you have a partner). If you have already incorporated a modality, just write "current" and indicate the frequency you practice it. In the spaces that follow, write in detail how you will practice energy healing.

EXERCISE 6.1. *Energy Healing Modalities*

1. List the vibrational modalities you will use in the table that follows.
i. Make environmental changes—type, e.g., change colors, get rid of, or useless high levels of electromagnetic frequency (EMF) items, e.g., not sleep with a cell phone next to you, eliminate the use of microwave oven, etc.
ii. Create a space—for healing and consciousness work.
iii. Build a shrine—for prayer focus, connection with ancestors, etc.
iv. Classes/activities—you will attend, e.g., energy healing, yoga, healing retreats, initiation, etc.
v. Other spiritual/religious practices—you will engage in, e.g., attend church, masjid, monastery, etc.
vi. Colors—you need for types of healing and consciousness work and how you will incorporate them in your healing practices, e.g., color lights, color baths, color objects, etc.
vii. Gems/crystals—you will use and how you will use them.
viii. Sounds—types, e.g., reiki music, chakra-specific sounds (for the chakras that need the most work), mantras you will cite, etc.
ix. Breathing practices—type and frequency, e.g., daily, 3 times a day, during meditation, etc.

x. Meditation—what days of the week, how often, how long, etc.
xi. Attunements—types, e.g., clearing and cleansing, healing, love, etc.
xii. Other practices— you will use

Energy modality	Date you will begin/ frequency you will use
1._____	_____
2._____	_____
3._____	_____
4._____	_____
5._____	_____
6._____	_____
7._____	_____
8._____	_____
9._____	_____
10. _____	_____

> EXERCISE 6.2. *Energy Healing Narrative*

1. Write in detail your energy healing practices or those you will incorporate in your life.

___

Additional Notes

7

Seven Steps to Healing and Awakening

If you recall in ancient Egypt, the step pyramid represented the steps to a life of bliss. Initiates went through initiation to help increase mastery over aspects of themselves as they climbed the steps to unify with the Universe Soul. How can these steps be used to help you gain mastery and raise your level of vibration so that you attract your soul's partner and continue towards spiritual evolvement? The answer is the same way in which they were used for initiates. However, healing goes hand-in-hand with mastery. Therefore, the path to healing and awakening includes the following seven steps:

1. Healing the Physical Body
2. Healing the Emotional Body
3. Healing the Mental Body
4. Awakening to Universe Love
5. Awakening to Universe Consciousness
6. Awakening to Universe Light
7. Unifying with the Universe Soul

Before going through the steps to healing and awakening, the first and most crucial step is self-recovery. There is the self, based on the person, *persona*, or mask of the soul. This self is based on your conditioning and experiences from the social world in which you were cultivated. Then, there is the self-based on the eternal aspect of the self. Self-recovery means recognizing your eternal self and making that the foundation of your identity. You can then begin the process of healing and awakening.

STEP 1: Healing the Physical World
Physical Body

The physical body is the vehicle through which the soul exists in the earthly realm, allowing it to experience the physical world. It is the densest part of your being and has the lowest level of vibration. It is also the vehicle that houses all the physical functions that allow your soul to experience other interdimensional realities. There are two levels: your physical body, and how you survive and thrive in the social world. The goal of healing and mastery of the physical body is to eliminate all habits and behaviors that are counter to its health and well-being.

Our physical body has to do with our health which includes our genetics (i.e., what we inherited from our ancestors and families) and how we take care of ourselves. The primary factor affecting our physical health is our lifestyle, which includes dietary and other habits. Our dietary habits are those that we carry from our families of origin and level of knowledge about healthy dieting. When you have an unhealthy diet, you may be feeding other biological and energetic parasites that use your body to feed on because of its unhealthy state. You are not only what you eat, but you also attract what you eat. What we eat shows in the energetic field around us (i.e., our aura) and can affect who we attract. People with unhealthy dietary habits and a dense aura tend to attract each other. Because of their unhealthy habits, they then have to expend their life forces dealing with the emotional, mental, and physical consequences of these habits. The health of the physical body can begin with managing the health problems that we have inherited from our families and ancestors and developing dietary and lifestyle habits crucial to physical health. It is also important that we eliminate stress and other habits that detract from our physical health.

Self-Examination
1. What physical health problems did you inherit from your family of origin and ancestors and how are you managing them?
2. What does your diet consist of and what are your eating habits?
3. What other lifestyle habits are you engaging in including those that cause stress and diminish your health and well-being?

Tasks
1. Diet—Become educated about and practice healthy dieting, which includes eliminating processed and denatured (overcooked) foods that do not offer the body any nutritional value and makes it sick. You should also learn about the different types of fasting/detoxing and cleansing diets, and when it is important to practice them. For example, one reason to detox and cleanse is that the internal organs of the body, like everything else, need rest (fasting provides the organs with rest) and cleansing. Different types of fasts include water, liquid (e.g., lemon and maple syrup), juice, dry (no food or water), fruit (partial elimination of certain types of food) intermittent (one meal per day or after a certain time of day). Also, detoxing and cleansing is probably best done during the winter and summer solstices and equinoxes, when the seasons and weather are changing to avoid getting ill. Many people get sick around these times because it is nature's way of helping us to detox and cleanse. Since we are made of the elements of earth, water, and air, our bodies must be fed from the matter we are made of including vegetables, fruits, whole grains, seeds, nuts, and water.
2. Exercise—It is important to develop an exercise regimen. An exercise regimen will help to increase oxygen (air) throughout the body, which helps to increase the vital force flowing through it. Exercises that are more specifically focused on increasing vital force throughout the body include yoga, tai chi, and qigong, etc. Since each organ has its own sound, qigong is focused specifically on sounds and movements to heal the organs.
3. Eliminate—other lifestyle habits and behaviors including stress, that might cause damage to your body in both the present and future.

To help reduce stress, incorporate meditation and the vibration modalities discussed in Chapter 6, into your life.

Social World

The primary driving force of the physical body is the survival instinct. It is concerned with the necessities of water, air, food, shelter, and sleep. The social world in which we exist is important to ensure that we are able to meet our basic survival needs. How we respond to the survival instinct goes back to our early experiences with our caregivers and our socialization within the broader society as we continue through the life cycle.

A value underlying socialization in the U.S. is materialism. Materialism is the doctrine that material possessions constitute the highest good in life; the belief is that if one has a high socio-economic status they are living the "good life." If during our early years, our basic survival needs were not adequately met, and we accept materialism as a guide for our lives, then we may focus primarily on our material reality. Being focused in this way may reveal itself in an over-focus on livelihood and money as well as an obsession over material possessions. Subsequently, we may be led to make social connections based primarily on physical and material needs and desires, which causes us to open our lives to others based primarily on their material and/or social capital. When we evaluate people based primarily on their material/social capital, we are evaluating them at the lowest aspect of themselves. When we allow people into our lives based primarily on their material/social capital, we are operating at the lowest aspect of ourselves.

Attempting to build a relationship with someone who has not solved the problem of meeting their basic survival needs (or, at least have a plan for how they will do so) can potentially negatively affect one's health and well-being. Therefore, these matters should be considered. However, they should not be the primary consideration for a potential partner. When a relationship revolves primarily around survival and/or materialism it is operating at its lowest level.

Seven Steps to Healing and Awakening 119

Self-Examination
1. What issues are you carrying from childhood around survival, and how are they affecting your life (e.g., excessive worry, stress, and/or obsession over livelihood, money, etc.)?
2. Are your approaching life and relationships in a survival mode (e.g., barely existing day-to-day without a plan for improving your life); looking for someone to take care of you?
3. Are you evaluating potential partners primarily on their material/social capital (e.g., physical attractiveness, career, money, social status, etc.)?
4. Are you operating in a survival mode or focused primarily on materialism and/or your social status?

Tasks
1. If you are struggling with anxiety around survival, put a plan in place, and if necessary, a secondary one and then stop worrying about it. Once you have a sound plan and put it to action, know that with good choices and right living, the universe will provide what you need.

2. Living in a survival mode, where you are living day to day, just barely making it, makes it difficult to see clearly and make good decisions, because all your focus is on surviving. Because existing in survival mode is so difficult some people are looking for someone to take care of them. Put a plan in place for your life so that you do not choose the wrong person because you need them to survive.

3. When evaluating partners primarily based on their material/social capital, you may miss the opportunity for a relationship with your soul's partner because on the surface he/or she may not present with societal ideas e.g. physical attractiveness, career, money, etc. When evaluating whether someone has potential, focus on whether they have a plan for their life, their personal attributes, and their life purpose. Then think about how you can merge your social and material capital in ways to expand and carry out your life purposes together.

4. Regardless of where we are in the socio-economic strata, many of us feel pressure to achieve societal ideas about what constitutes the good life. Really think about what constitutes a good life for you. Be honest about what you really need and evaluate what is driving what you think you want. If your relationship is in survival mode, put a plan in action to get out of the survival mode.

STEP 2: Healing the Emotional Body

Our desires activate our senses and our emotional responses. They are the primary force driving our procreative, creative, and expansive capacity. There are two factors to consider when it comes to our emotions. The first is that many people struggle with emotional pain. When an expectation is not met, they may respond with highly charged emotional reactions or they may shut down emotionally. Both may be responses to guard against repeat wounding experiences. These emotional responses may be similar to how they responded when they were children and can hinder their creative and expansive capacity.

The other factor is emotional responses to physical and/or sexual attraction. Although both physical and sexual attraction is important, in materialistic societies, many people make choices about a potential partner based primarily on emotional responses to physical and sexual attraction. The goal of healing the emotional body is to eliminate all emotional responses and choices that are counter to its health. In addition, is being conscious of making choices about a potential partner based primarily on emotional responses to physical and sexual attraction.

Self-Examination
1. What emotional pain are you still struggling with?
2. How do you respond emotionally when your expectations are not met?
3. Do you make choices about potential partners based on emotional responses to physical and/or sexual attraction?

Tasks

1. Heal the pain. One of the most significant factors that some people struggle with is how to heal emotional pain. If one were careless about healing a physical wound, then it might become infected and infect the whole body. The same applies to emotional wounds. If one puts a bandage on an emotional wound without really dealing with it, then it can infect all aspects of the self and, eventually, all of whom one comes into contact with. We are hesitant about really dealing with emotional pain because of societal norms of being seen as weak or because it makes us feel vulnerable. It is important to heal emotional pain. It can be done using the steps that follow.

 i. Face the pain. This can be done by admitting that whatever it is/was and/or who did it caused you pain.

 ii. Examine the emotional wounds and feelings attached to the pain.

 iii. Work through the feelings attached to the pain via one or more of the following methods:

—Crying is probably the easiest and most accessible way to deal with pain. Since water is a cleanser, tears are the soul's cleanser. Unfortunately, many people are afraid to face their vulnerability and will not cry. This may especially be true for men.

—Talk therapy is useful because talking and emoting to a third party helps to release the feelings attached to the pain.

—Telling those who caused you pain that they hurt you also helps to release feelings attached to pain. Writing a letter can be a way to release the feelings attached to pain and then discarding it if you decide it is not worth confronting the person and want to deal with it yourself.

—Wallow if you need to for a while until you have cried and/or talked it out.

—Forgive who hurt you and then release them. When you release them, you release yourself. Most people do not hurt others intentionally. They do so just by being who they are or because they have been hurt or wounded in some way themselves. Having empathy, understanding, and compassion regarding what may have occurred in their lives to make them hurt others helps you to release them.

—Decide to move on and get back to the business of living.

2. Devise strategies for healthy, emotional responses by managing your expectations. Much of how we respond to things has to do with our expectations. If we do not get what we feel we need or want, or if someone else does not meet our expectations, then some of us respond the same way we did when we were children. If your emotional responses are over-reactive or emotionally disengaging do the following:

i. Go back as far as you can and try to remember how you responded when you were a child to unmet needs and wants. Examine how these emotional responses have carried over into your adult life.

ii. Come to terms with the emotional responses of your childhood and see where you got stuck. Taking into consideration and having empathy and understanding for the limited social, economic, and personal capacities of our caregivers and others can help us get unstuck.

iii. Meditate and use your imaginative ability to manifest your wishes and desires. See yourself responding to matters more healthily. To do this, some strategies include, but are not limited to:

—When a situation presents itself, take a moment to practice deep breathing and/or affirmations/prayers to help you calm down if you overreact or to keep you from shutting down if your response is to emotionally distance yourself.

—Spend time working through your thoughts and feelings on matters, including examining your expectations and whether they are realistic. You will want to look at whether you are asking people to be who you want them to be versus who they really are.

—Reframe how you think about the person or situation if possible. Make a decision and be at peace with it.

—Cut the energetic ties to the person or thing. Use your hand in a circular chopping manner, while simultaneously saying "cut the strings" three times, and then move on.

3. If you make decisions about potential partners based on emotional responses to physical and/or sexual attraction, be aware that this is what you are doing and make a commitment to change this behavior. See Chapters 8 and 9 for guidelines on dating and choosing a partner.

STEP 3: Healing the Mental Body

The mental body consists of both the left brain (thoughts and language) and the right brain (creative and imaginative ability). How we think is based on our conditioning in the social world and our experiences in this world. Social conditioning consists of the ideas, values, and beliefs of the cultural group into which we are born. The ideas, values, and beliefs are perpetuated through the society's various institutions (e.g., family, schools, church, and various forms of media) as group thought. The health of the ideas, values, and beliefs underlying your thought world is as healthy as the group thought that you are cultivated into. Group thought that promotes materialism, individualism, survival of the fittest (unhealthy competition), sexism, racism, (sex and race inequality), etc. are not a healthy foundation upon which to build a society or a relationship.

Our thought world is also shaped by our experiences. Experiences of the physical and emotional bodies are filtered through the mental body, and it memorizes those experiences. Unpleasant experiences may get lodged into one's memory as negative thought patterns that can begin early and continue throughout life. Things that were done or said to us shape how we feel and what we think about ourselves. They affect our self-esteem, self-efficacy, and sense of personal power and agency, and ultimately our vitality and will to live life to the fullest. If they were negative or hurtful, we may harbor negative thoughts about ourselves and/or those individuals who hurt us by playing these statements and experiences over and over in our minds, which feeds our wounds, making them larger, and, subsequently, making them toxic to the mind, body, and spirit. Since all physical reality begins with thought, negative thoughts can manifest in physical reality and can create a life of their own, causing disease. The goal of healing and mastering the mental body is to eliminate all thoughts that are bad for your health and replace them with positive thoughts.

Self-Examination
1. What ideas, values, and beliefs of society are you holding on to?
2. What thoughts are you harboring around past injuries and how are they manifesting in your life?
3. How have your experiences affected your self-esteem, sense of personal power, and your will to live life to its fullest?

Tasks
1. Examine the group thoughts that you are holding on to, and discard those ideas, values, and beliefs that are no longer supporting how you are evolving (See Chapter 9—mental compatibility).
2. Reframe how you think about injuries to the physical and emotional bodies. For example, rather than taking something someone said or did personally, try to understand it from the perspective of the person who caused your injury. If it were intentional, try to have empathy for what may have happened to them that would make them want to cause you harm.
3. Life experiences can diminish our self-esteem, sense of personal power, weaken us, and ultimately deplete our will to live to our fullest capacities. Follow the guidelines in Step 2, Tasks 1-3 above to help bring about health and well-being in your thought world.

STEP 4: Awakening to Universe Love

Universe Love is the bridge to the three upper worlds of the higher self. Awakening to Universe Love awakens us to the unifying force of the universe that expands past our personal experiences with love and opens us to the currents of God's love. Our capacity to cross the bridge to Universe Love has to do with our experiences with love. If we feel we cannot trust, have to shut down, or over-guard our hearts, then we jeopardize our capacity to open to Universe Love and ultimately, the love we are seeking.

A limited capacity to love also inhibits our ability to show empathy, compassion, and understanding, and share ourselves in balanced and healthy ways. In addition, since love is the doorway to the higher self, a limited capacity to love can block our ability to live through our higher selves and access to higher levels of consciousness.

Self-Examination
1. How have early experiences with love affected your ability to love and share yourself openly, honestly, and freely, to show empathy understanding, and compassion for others and to live through your higher self?

Tasks
1. Remove yourself from the center of love experiences that have wounded you. As indicated above, rather than harboring negative thoughts and feelings about someone who has hurt you, have empathy and compassion for what happened to them.
2. Follow the guidelines in Step 2, Tasks 1-3 above, and engage in energy healing practices outlined in Chapter 6 to help you heal love wounds.

STEP 5: Awakening to Universe Consciousness

Crossing the bridge of personal experiences with love to Universe Love, awakens us to Universe Consciousness, giving us the ability to access sounds of the upper worlds. An awakened consciousness awakens us to the laws of the universe, MAAT—which among many things means rightness, justice, truth, harmony, and balance. Attuning to the laws of MAAT awakens us to the understanding of our free will choice to live by them and helps to shape our moral values and principles. These moral values and principles in turn make us more conscientious of what is right and just, the consequences of our actions and attune us to the part of the self that judges the self. Living based on the laws of MAAT, helps us to live through our higher selves and opens the doors to higher levels of consciousness.

Unfortunately, for many, the sounds of the wound of our life experiences block access to Universe Consciousness. Also, overindulgence in the "noise" from the world around us, e.g., radio, television, internet, etc., also blocks access to Universe Consciousness. This is why it is important to meditate so that one can block all the internal chatter and external noise. In addition, how we use our communicative faculties can block us. When we communicate in ways that are not good, we can block the gifts that come from access to God's wisdom, understanding, and power.

Self-Examination
1. What inner chatter are you replaying over and over in your mind, potentially blocking you from higher levels of consciousness?
2. What are your moral values and principles? What choices are you making with your free will? What choices are detracting from your health and well-being and the health and well-being of those around you? How are your choices and actions affecting you and others?
3. How are you using your communication faculties? Are you using them based on the emotions and thoughts driven by the lower self?

Tasks
1. Engage in energy healing and awakening practices to increase your ability to access Universe Consciousness (e.g., your inner voice that has access to other interdimensional realms).
2. Examine your moral values and principles, and if necessary, revise them. Having values and principles based on MAAT will shift how you connect to all of reality.
2. Be cognizant of how you use your voice (e.g., profanity, gossip, etc.) See chapter 10 for how to communicate in healthy ways.

STEP 6: Awakening to Universe Light
Awakening to Universe Light opens the doors to wisdom and understanding gives us access to higher levels of consciousness. Wisdom and understanding give us the ability to see with more clarity and opens the doors to our unlimited potential and spiritual power. Many are unable to see the light because they see the world through

the lenses of their social conditioning and the experiences of their lives.

Self-Examination
1. Are you stuck, rigid, inflexible, and only able to see the world through the lenses of your limited social conditioning?
2. What experiences throughout your life cause you to see the world through the lenses of hurt, anger, fear, sadness, grief, ignorance, cynicism, paranoia, and lack of trust and faith, blocking your ability to see the light?

Tasks
1. Engaging in awakening and enlightening practices outlined in chapter 6 helps to increase your light quotient (light energy flowing through your body). This gives you the ability to see with more clarity.
2. Become more devoted to your spiritual or religious practice. If you do not already have one, consider seeking out a spiritual teacher for guidance.

STEP 7: Unifying with the Universe Soul
Unification brings about oneness, peace, and a bliss state. Awakening to the eternal self means that you shed yourself of social conditioning and detach from the world of form. The universe opens to you and you can now access the place where God sits.

With continuous and intense spiritual work, you may be able to able to attain unification in this lifetime. Unfortunately, most people will not attain such a goal. However, with conscious awakening practices, you may be still able to experience glimpses of the bliss state and awakening to higher levels of consciousness. A higher level of consciousness increases the frequency at which you are vibrating, enabling you to attract the right person for this life. Once you attract each other, the goal is to help each other fulfill your purposes for this life, continue spiritual evolvement together, and become the best expression of yourselves so that you become vessels through which the Universe Soul can express itself on Earth.

In summary, the quest for mastery over the lower aspects of the self takes a lot of work. It begins with health and well-being. Achieving health and well-being is one thing, staying there is another thing. The same applies to the quest to awaken the higher aspects of the self. It not only requires work, but a tremendous amount of time spent participating in awakening practices. Depending on where you are in your evolvement, unity with the Universe Soul can happen in this lifetime or may take many more lifetimes. No matter where you are, what is important is that you are on the right path. Your soul's partner is the one to help you continue on this journey. When you begin the journey of awakening the higher self, you will begin to vibrate at a higher frequency. This gives you the ability to hear your soul's partner with your soul's ear and see him or her with your soul's eye when he or she appears. If you have already found each other, putting into practice the health and awakening practices outlined in this and previous chapters will help you to continue your spiritual evolvement together.

Chapter 7 Exercises

Healing and Awakening

The purpose of these exercises is for you (and your partner if you have one) to lay out a plan of action for health and awakening, utilizing the steps outlined in this chapter. In each section, you will start with a self-examination, and then describe your healing and/or awakening plans.

STEP 1. *Healing the Physical World*

Physical Body
1. <u>Self-Examination</u>: Describe the following as they apply to you:
i. Physical health problems inherited from your family of origin
ii. Diet and eating habits
iii. Other lifestyle habits (e.g., stress, substance abuse, etc.) that detracts from physical health

_____
_____
_____
_____
_____

i. <u>Tasks</u>: Describe what changes you will make if necessary: _

ii. Diet changes—classes on healthy dieting, eliminating processed and overcooked foods, adding more healthy foods, fasting, etc.
iii. Exercise agenda—exercise regimen you will incorporate if you do not already have one, e.g., aerobics, tai chi, qigong, yoga, etc.
iv. Other lifestyle habits you will change

_____
_____
_____

Social World

2. <u>Self-Examination</u>: Describe the following as they apply to you/your relationship:
i. Issues you are carrying from childhood around survival
ii. Your approach to life/relationships (e.g., in survival mode, barely making it day-to-day without a plan, looking for someone to take care of you, etc.)
iii. How you evaluate potential partners or each other (e.g., based on their material capital, e.g., physical attractiveness, socio-economic status, etc.)
iv. Your relationship status and focus (e.g., survival mode, materialism, social status, etc.)

_____

3. <u>Tasks</u>: Describe changes you will make if necessary:
i. A plan for your life so that you stop worrying about survival and/or so you can get out of the survival mode
ii. An expanded list of attributes you will use to evaluate potential partners and each other *(see Chapter 9 on compatibility)*
iii. A shift in relationship focus (e.g., from survival mode, materialism to self-development, spirituality, etc.)

_____

> **STEP 2.** *Healing the Emotional Body*

1. <u>Self-Examination</u>: Describe the following as they apply to you:
i. Emotional pain you are still struggling with

ii. How you respond when expectations are not met
_____
_____
_____
_____

2. <u>Tasks</u>: Heal emotional wounds by describing your experience and what you will do to work through the pain if necessary:
i. Healing the pain
a. What was done, by whom?
_____

b. What is the wound and the feelings attached to it (e.g., how did it make you feel)?
_____

c. Methods you will use to work through your feelings (e.g., crying, talk therapy, confronting the person, writing a letter, and discarding it, etc.).
_____

d. What other feelings emerged as you wallowed (continued to work through the pain by crying, talking, etc.)?
_____

e. How will you forgive the individual (e.g., saying to yourself, "I forgive you for. . . " telling him or her, writing a letter, etc.)?
_____
_____

f. What else you will do so you can move on?
_____
_____

ii. Strategies for healthy emotional responses to unmet expectations:
a. As far back as you can remember, recall how you responded to unmet needs and wants when you were a child and how the emotional responses carried over into your adult life.

_____

b. How will you come to terms with emotional responses (e.g., having consideration, empathy, and understanding of limitations of supportive figures)?

_____

c. What strategies will you incorporate in your life for healthier emotional responses (e.g., meditation, breathe, work through thoughts and feelings before responding, reframe how you think about a person or situation, cut the energetic strings, etc.)?

_____
_____
_____

> **STEP 3. *Healing the Mental Body***

1. Self-Examination: Describe the following as they apply to you/your relationship:
i. Societal ideas, values, and beliefs that you are holding on to
ii. Thoughts you are harboring around physical, emotional, and mental injuries
ii. How life experiences have affected your will to live to your fullest capacity

_____
_____
_____
_____
_____

1. Tasks: Describe changes you will make if necessary:
i. Societal ideas, values, and beliefs that are no longer working for you that you will discard:

ii. Strategies for healing from thoughts you are harboring and ruminating on around physical, emotional, and mental injuries (e.g., reframing, energy healing practices—meditation, attunements, etc.).
iii. Strategies from steps 1-3 above that you will use to help promote healing and increase your will to live to your fullest capacity
iv. Healing practices you will use to help you regain your strength and vitality

_____
_____
_____
_____
_____
_____

> **STEP 4.** *Awakening to Universe Love*

1. <u>Self-Examination</u>: Describe the following as they apply to you/your relationship:
i. How early experiences with love has affected your ability to share yourself openly, honestly, and freely, and to show empathy and compassion

_____
_____
_____
_____
_____
_____

2. <u>Tasks</u>: Describe changes you will make if necessary:
i. Strategies you will use to heal from love wounds so that you can love, share yourself freely, and increase your ability to feel empathy, and show understanding and compassion

_____
_____
_____

STEP 5. *Awakening to Universe Consciousness*

1. <u>Self-Examination</u>: Describe the following as they apply to you/your relationship:
i. Wounds and other life experiences that are blocking your ability to hear your inner voice
ii. Moral values and principles that may need to be revised
iii. Choices you are making that are detracting from your health and the well-being of those around you
iv. Negative ways in which you use your communication faculties that may be blocking the gifts of God's wisdom and understanding

___

2. <u>Tasks</u>: Describe changes you will make if necessary:
i. Energy healing and awakening practices you will engage in to increase your ability to access Universe Consciousness (your inner voice) (e.g., meditation, mantras, music, etc.)
ii. Revisions you will make to your moral values and principles so that they are in alignment with Universe laws (e.g., MAAT—rightness, justice, truth, harmony, balance, etc.)
iii. Ways in which you will change how you use your communication faculties (e.g., eliminate profanity, gossip, promote healing and awakening through teaching, music, art., etc.)

___

> **STEP 6.** *Awakening to Universe Light*

1. <u>Self-Examination</u>: Describe the following as they apply to you/your relationship:
   i. Idea, beliefs, values that are you rigid and inflexible about, and other social conditioning you may need to let go of
   ii. Experiences throughout your life that cause you to see the world through the lenses of hurt, anger, fear, sadness, grief, ignorance, cynicism, paranoia, and lack of trust and faith, blocking your ability to see the light

   _____
   _____
   _____
   _____
   _____
   _____

2. <u>Tasks</u>: Describe changes you will make if necessary:
   i. Seek truth by seeking out the wisdom of the ages
   ii. Engage in awakening practices to increase your light quotient so that you can see with more clarity
   iii. Seek out a spiritual or energy teacher for guidance

   _____
   _____
   _____
   _____
   _____
   _____

> **STEP 7.** *Unifying with the Universe Soul*

1. <u>Self-Examination</u>: Describe the following as they apply to you/your relationship:
   i. The kind of attachments you have that you may need to let go of.
   ii. Issues with oneness, unity, and peace with yourself, in relationships with others, and with God

2. <u>Tasks</u>: Describe changes you will make if necessary:
i. Awakening practices to help facilitate detachment from the world
ii. Awakening practices to help facilitate oneness, peace, and unity

---

STEP 8. *Healing and Awakening Narrative*

1. Describe and discuss areas not covered that are significant to you and/or you need to work on and practices you will put into place.

Additional Notes

8
~~~~~~~~~~~~~~~

Seven Principles of Conscious Dating

Many people long to find their soul's partner, but do not recognize the time, energy, and effort it may take to do so. Nor do they have skills or strategies for dating in a way that leads to mating. We are referring to dating that leads to mating as conscious dating. The following are the seven principles of conscious dating.

1. Know Yourself
2. Put a Plan into Action
3. Be Conscious
4. Value Yourself
5. Value who You Date
6. Take Your Time
7. Have Fun

PRINCIPLE 1: Know Yourself
The ancient African proverb, "know thyself," is probably the most important principle for conscious dating. To know yourself, you might ask yourself the following questions: Who am I really? What issues am I still struggling with? What wounds am I still recovering from? How are they playing out in my life? What is my plan for working through these issues and wounds and how do they affect

how I interact in relationships? Other questions you might ask yourself include: What is important to me? What are my moral values and principles? What are my strengths and weaknesses? What are my gifts? What is my life purpose? Dig down deep and face who you really are. Knowing yourself helps you be clear about what you are bringing to a relationship and what you need to work on so that you have clarity about who is the right person for you. More importantly, knowing yourself helps you to be clear about who is the right person to help you fulfill your purpose for this life and continue to evolve spiritually.

PRINCIPLE 2: Put a Plan into Action

The second principle of dating is to develop a plan and put it into action. A plan entails first making meeting your soul's partner a priority and then putting into practice the principles outlined in this chapter. Most people put their time, money, and energy into things that are important to them. Prioritizing meeting your soul's partner means making this just as important as anything else in your life. This translates investing your time, money, and energy into meeting them, which means taking time out of your life to meet people and date.

Meeting people and dating can start by letting people know you are available. You may already be acquainted with your soul's partner, but they do not know you are available. He or she may already be among your friends, associates, or co-workers. When your family, friends associates, co-workers know you are available they may begin to think about people they know and send them your way.

You can also meet people through the places you attend regularly like your job, church, or community organizations you are affiliated with. In addition, you can meet people through online dating and match-making companies. Different types of online dating sites cater to specific orientations like religion, ethnic group, age, etc. Some matchmaking companies do extensive background interviews to obtain information that helps to match you with the right person. They also provide a variety of other services, including how to dress, dating advice, etc. Finally, your plan would include following the rest of the principles outlined in this chapter.

PRINCIPLE 3: Be Conscious

Being conscious simply means being aware of which self is in the driver's seat, and which brain is dominating your dating patterns and choices.

The Triune Brain

Although continuous research reveals how complex the human brain is, and a lot more research is being done to understand its complexity, Paul MacLean's triune brain theory may be useful for increasing awareness of which brain may be dominating when making certain choices in our lives, particularly around dating and mating. According to the triune brain theory, three areas of the brain includes the Reptilian Complex (R-complex), Paleomammalian Complex (Limbic Core), and the Neomammalian Complex (Neo-cortex). They are outlined briefly below.

The Reptilian (R-Complex) or Physical Survival/ Animal Brain— is–the core of the brain at the base of the forebrain and is made primarily of the upper brain stem. It is the part of the brain that humans share with reptiles and birds and is connected with behaviors associated with physical survival. The survival brain is based on instinctive behaviors of feeding, fighting, fleeing and includes aggression, dominance, territoriality, and ritual displays—behaviors necessary for safety and survival.

The Paleoamammalian Complex (Limbic-Cortex) or Emotional Brain—is the part of the brain that is responsible for memory and the emotion and behavior involved in the acquisition of food for feeding, reproductive behavior, procreation, maternal love, and parenting. The emotional brain is responsible for behaviors that are essential for the survival of the species.

The Neomammalian (Neocortex) or Reasoning/Intellectual Brain— is the source of language, use of symbols, reason, and logic, as well as planning and processing of culture and traditions. The intellectual brain is responsible for behavior associated with the survival of the tribe or the social group.

The Fourth Brain

A fourth part of the brain area that has been identified is the prefrontal lobe or spiritual brain. It is the part of the brain that is associated with consciousness. When dating it is important to be conscious of which brain is dominating your behaviors. The brain that is being used while dating will affect your behavior and ultimately who you select as a partner. If you are using the survival and/or emotional brains, then you are operating by the animal instinct and/or emotions which are based on satisfying needs at the physical survival and emotional levels. At the intellectual brain level are the cultural ideas and beliefs of what constitutes a good mate. When you engage in conscious dating, the spiritual brain is dominant and guiding your behaviors and choices.

PRINCIPLE 4: Value Yourself

Valuing yourself means that you recognize that you are a descendant of the Divine. You should therefore be respected and treated that way. Valuing yourself also means that you take care of yourself. How you take care of yourself is reflected in your physical appearance and your aura energetically and how you present yourself to the world. It shows in the physical shape you are in, the clothes you wear, and how you carry yourself. If it appears that you do not care about yourself, then it makes it difficult for others to care about you. If your aura shows that you are bogged down with a lot of emotional baggage and that you engage in unhealthy habits and behaviors, you may repel who it is that your soul needs the most.

Personality Repellents

Some personality characteristics that show low self-value and may be unappealing, turn people off, or even set one up to be exploited or abused include low self-esteem/confidence, being too needy, desperate, egotistical, etc.

Low Self Esteem/Confidence—Self-esteem has to do with the beliefs we hold about ourselves, and self-confidence has to do with trust in our abilities, qualities, and judgment. Low self-esteem and self-confidence may stem from experiences in our families and/or socialization from society. How members of our families and circle of friends in our churches and communities treat us can play a significant role in shaping our self-esteem and confidence. If we have been treated badly by others, it may make us feel bad about ourselves. Ideas perpetuated in society can also undermine our self-esteem, and confidence. In materialistic-driven societies shaped by race, class, and gender, hierarchies, women are supposed to be physically attractive and men are supposed to be wealthy and powerful. Wherever one believes one is on the beauty and wealth hierarchies can have some effect on how they feel about themselves. Having high self-esteem and being confident is important, as neither men nor women are attracted to people who are low on these qualities.

Being too Needy—There is the idea that men feel a sense of themselves and get in touch with their feelings when they feel needed. However, this depends on how they are needed. If a man is needed in ways that he does not feel he can adequately fulfill, such a need can be a repellant. Since many men do not know how to deal with their own emotions, an emotionally needy woman can be a turn-off because they may feel they cannot fulfill this need. They also want to have their own life and do not want to feel that they have to be responsible for yours. Although men get in touch with their feelings when they feel needed, it is the opposite for women. Most women enjoy giving and sharing themselves. However, just as men, they want to be able to do these things freely. When a woman feels too needed, she may lose touch with her own feelings and ultimately herself. Being too needy can kill the potential for a relationship.

Being Desperate—When someone acts desperate, it can be a turn-off because the person feels like they are being pulled into a relationship, without giving them the opportunity to explore whether they want to be in it. If a man or woman feels too much pull too fast, then they may begin to pull back and eventually shut down. Also, when someone is desperate it shows energetically. When either a man or woman appears to be desperate, they can set themselves up to be exploited, and if they are too forceful or smothering, it can shut down the other person's natural responses and potentially scare them off.

Being a Sour Puss—People with a sour puss personality, may just sit around (some watching television) and seem uninterested, unattentive, and non-engaging and not have much to say. When they do say something, occasionally, it may be short and negative. They may also lack a sense of humor.

Being Overly Dramatic—Drama queens and kings are the common way of referring to women and men who overdramatize events in their lives. Although having a lively personality can be attractive to some people, there is good drama and bad drama. Too much drama can be a turnoff, especially if it is bad drama. One factor that can lead to drama is when people engage in physical and/or emotional intimacy too early in the dating process. Because expectations increase when we engage in intimacy too early in the process, it can agitate recent emotional wounds and open old ones. To cut down on potential drama it is important to be cognizant of time in the dating process which is dealt with extensively in the next section of this chapter.

Being Bitter—Some people have had negative experiences throughout their lives, making them bitter. Underlying bitterness is anger stemming from hurt or disappointment one may be still struggling to recover from. Contributing to the anger may be experiences from repeating dating patterns that are not working. If you are still recovering from old wounds it may be better to put off dating until you have healed enough to permit you to date in a healthy way.

Being Emotionally Unavailable or too Available—Some people are emotionally unavailable, while others are emotionally too available. Some people are emotionally unavailable because they have been hurt in the past and want to avoid being hurt again. Others, on the other hand, are too emotionally available too early in the dating process. There may be several reasons for this including that they have not recovered from a past relationship, are seeking someone to help them heal childhood wounds, or are motivated by the emotional brain, etc. Whatever the case may be, whether one is emotionally unavailable, or too available it may be because they have not learned how to balance the emotional aspects of themselves.

Being Egotistical—It is good to have high self-esteem and to have confidence in oneself, but some people have an exaggerated sense of themselves, which can be just as much as a turn-off as someone with low self-confidence. Being egotistical may mean that the person is self-centered and more focused on themselves, which is a turn-off for someone who is dating him/her.

These are not all; there may be other personality characteristics that need work. No one is perfect and we all have aspects of ourselves that we need to work on. If you find that you have some areas that you need to work on, then do so. This is necessary to attract your soul's partner. While it is important to show that you value yourself, it is also important to show that you value the person you are dating.

PRINCIPLE 5: Value Who You Date

What is it that we all want? We all want to feel that we matter, that we are valued and that we are special. Therefore, it is important to make the person you are dating feel valued and special. This can be done in several ways.

Be Present—The most significant way to make the other person feel valued is to be present. This means that when they are in your presence, you are paying attention and letting other things go for the moment, including your cell phone. You are the *looking glass*— which means that people are generally looking for a reflection of themselves, or what they might want to be. They get clues about who they are by the way you respond to them. How do you be present? By listening and showing interest in who they are.

Listening—Many of us are good talkers, but we are not good listeners. Hone your listening skills. You could probably learn as much about a person as you will over the course of dating them by listening intently in the first 15 minutes of the first conversation. If you are a talker, talk less and give the other person a chance to talk and share themselves. It shows them that you are not just self-interested but are interested in who they are.

Showing Interest—What are the signs that someone is interested? They affirm you by paying attention to what you are saying, they look you in the eyes, smile at you, etc.

Do not Judge—If you do so, stop judging people based on negative experiences in previous relationships. Each person should be judged on their own merit. If you use the strategies outlined throughout this chapter and take your time, then there is no need to worry about being hurt or disappointed.

Be Courteous, Kind, and Show Appreciation—No one has to give you anything including their time. Anything someone does for you is a gift. You should always show appreciation when someone does something nice for you. Acknowledging a gift can be done with a simple smile and thank you.

PRINCIPLE 6: Take Your Time

One of the single most important principles you can incorporate in your dating practice is to take your time. Far too many people meet someone and rush the process. This may particularly be the case when we feel extremely attracted to someone. If someone has that much potential, then it is even more important to slow things down so that you do not rush the process and blow something that has potential. Rushing the process may mean we are delving into lower levels of physical and emotional intimacy before connecting on higher levels of mental and spiritual intimacy.

Intimacy

What is intimacy? Intimacy has to do with sharing oneself in a way that allows one to experience connectedness with another person. There are several types of intimacy that we engage in as we get to know each other. These include physical, emotional, mental, and spiritual.

- *Physical intimacy* is the sharing of one's body with another and is driven primarily by physical attraction.
- *Emotional intimacy* is the sharing of feelings and emotions.
- *Mental intimacy* is the sharing of thoughts and ideas about various aspects of the world, for example, political, social, and so forth. This is typically undergirded by worldview, values, and beliefs, which are further influenced by social conditioning and level of education; both formal and informal.
- *Spiritual intimacy* is sharing oneself at a deeper level, which may depend on the level to which there is connectedness on the other three types of intimacy. It also includes sharing religious/spiritual beliefs.

The problem is that some people engage in physical intimacy too early in the dating process without connecting emotionally, mentally, or spiritually. This prevents the natural unfolding of getting to know a person, which may, in turn, lead to the death of the relationship before it has had the chance to be born, mature, and transform into something higher.

It is important to decide at what stage in the dating process to enter into various levels of intimacy. This allows one to get to know the person so that one can find out the reason they are in one's life, which reveals itself in the events that take place in the experiences with him or her. The following might be a general guide for the levels of intimacy that might be shared in the stages of dating. Let us review the concept of time again.

Time

To prevent confusion that results from pre-mature intimacy, it is important to know some things about time, including how it works in the dating process. If you recall, all phenomena go through a time process. Planets undergo cosmic time, earthly beings undergo vital time, nature undergoes natural time, and social systems go through a time process that consists of four stages. As shown in *Figure 8.1*, the first stage is the beginning of things; the seed, the idea. It is considered the period of conception. The second stage is birth, the formation stage. The third stage is maturity. And the fourth stage is the transformation or death stage.

Figure 8.1
Four Stage Time Process

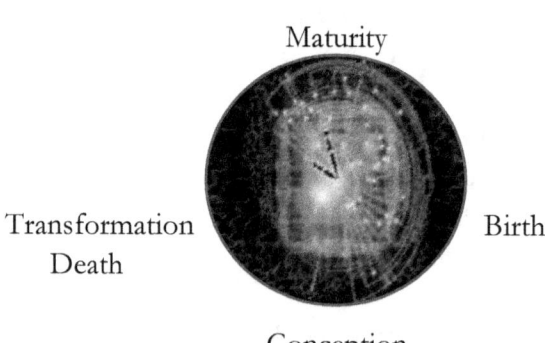

Maturity

Transformation
Death

Birth

Conception

Four Stages of Dating
Dating goes through this same time process. Getting to know a person unfolds in stages as well. How the time process translates into the stages of dating and what to focus on at each stage are outlined below.

Conception (Attraction)
Conception in the time process translates into attraction in dating. What is attraction? Attraction is a quality, feature, action, or power that evokes interest, liking, appeal, etc. It means that there was something about the person that prompted you to pay attention. There was something about her that prompted you to ask her out. There was something about him that prompted you to accept his invitation. If the person has potential, the most significant task in the conception stage is to sustain the attraction. Although sustaining attraction is important throughout all the stages of getting to know a person, and even in marriage, it is extremely critical in the first stage of dating because it is easy to move on from a person one has not invested any time, emotions, or anything else in. The close to 50 percent divorce rate is an indicator that people do not understand the importance of sustaining attraction throughout the relationship and even in marriage. Unfortunately, many people do not have the skills to keep the attraction going long enough to sustain it to the next level of commitment, let alone to marriage. The conception stage begins with the thought "I am interested in this person." If you already know the person, the thought is "I would like to get to know this person for the possibility of something more." It is at this stage that you might consider going out on a date. Some considerations and strategies at the conception stage are outlined below.

Considerations

Purpose of dating—Although many people date with hopes of meeting someone to share their lives with, others date for other reasons like to have fun, occupy their time, sex, etc. The first step then is to be clear on why you are dating yourself and to listen carefully to those you are dating so that you are clear about why they are dating.

Who will pay—People have different ideas about who should pay for dating. Some people believe that whoever initiates the date should pay for it, while others believe that the man should pay. A strategy might be to discuss it. The risk, however, is that this may lead to a discussion that delves into worldview and values around gender roles too early in the dating process. To avoid having such a discussion before the first date, you could opt to do something that does not cost money, for example, a visit to a bookstore, park, or museum. Another strategy could be to just go on the first date and let it work itself out and both parties show a willingness to contribute, and do this until you are comfortable with discussing it.

Where you will meet—This depends on the purpose of the date. If you want to find out more about the person to see if he or she has potential then you might opt to meet where you can talk, for example, a park or a place to have coffee or tea.

Dating Strategies

Date in public spaces—When just meeting someone, you may not want to invite them to your house or go to their house for the first few dates. Because of tight economic times, and the diverse forms of entertainment that technology brings with the Internet and Big Screen TVs many people are opting for the convenience of dating at home. Although it may be economically feasible, doing so makes you vulnerable to physical intimacy too early in the dating process. This may particularly be the case if alcohol is part of your entertainment. You may want to avoid alcohol altogether while dating because it causes people to let their defenses down. Two people who are attracted to each other together alone make it too easy for them to what is most natural, become physically intimate, especially if the attraction is strong. No matter how attempting it may be, do not meet at a place where you will be alone. You should meet in a public place, not just for these reasons, but also for safety.

Be your best self—People often complain that the problem with dating is that people show their representative. Being your representative does not mean that you are being someone that you are not. It means that you are being the best of who you are. The idea is that when you present your best self, the person has the chance to get to know and grow to love that person. When they grow to love that side of your personality, they may be inclined to be more tolerant of you when you are not at your best, as long as that side of your personality is not so bad that it detracts dramatically from the best of who you are. The questions to ask yourself are: Who is my best self? How am I when I am this person? How often is this self present? If this side of yourself is not present most of the time, what is preventing her/him from being present? What can you do to bring her/him out more? How can you practice your best self so that it becomes habitual?

Manage your expectations—Since no one has committed at the conception stage, you should manage your expectations (and throughout the relationship and even marriage). What does that mean? It means you should have not expectations at this stage in the dating process. Not having expectations at the conception stage prevents you from responding negatively when things do not turn out as you would like them to. For example, because some women generally expect to receive a phone call after a date, they might get upset if their date does not call. How they feel may then be reflected in how they respond when their date eventually calls. Having premature expectations and responding negatively in the conception stage of dating may make it difficult for the process to continue to evolve, killing the possibility for the development of a relationship. Even after a few dates, you should not have expectations, because there has been no discussion of commitment. If you find that you do not have a mutual interest in continuing to explore the possibility of an intimate relationship, you might find that the person has potential for some other purpose in your life, for example, a business alliance, a confidant, mentor, or friend.

Do not chase—Let the person know you are interested without chasing or being overly aggressive. It is important to show that you are interested, but if you are overly aggressive to the point of seeming smothering or forceful, you might turn the person off.

Cleanup your house—If you decide to invite someone to your home, clean it up. How people keep their home tells a lot about them at least in some peoples' minds. If your house is unclean and/or disorganized, it may be an indication that there is something unclean and/or disorganized about you that has not come to the surface yet. Those who like a clean, orderly environment might see your housekeeping skills as a potential liability. The thinking is, "How much time will I have to spend cleaning up after this person?" It is difficult for someone to see you if they cannot get past seeing how disorganized, unclean, and chaotic your house is. Cleaning up your house also means cleaning up your physical, psycho-emotional, and spiritual houses.

Leave the baggage at home—Some of us have baggage, some have suitcases, and some of us have trunks. Leave the baggage at home. Nobody wants a liability. It is important to do the work discussed in previous chapters to heal from wounds of the body, mind, and spirit.

Pay attention to the small stuff—Some of the simplest things in life are a big deal to some people. Being present, paying attention, and listening can give you insight into what is really important to a person. Most of us would be surprised to learn how simple and inexpensive some of the things that people value are and how easy it is to make some people happy. This is particularly important for men to know. Some men think they have to spend a lot of money or do big things to make women feel happy. Something as simple as a gaze, a flower, a cookie, or candy can make a person feel really happy.

Be aware that money is not everything—Some people, especially men, think that having and spending money is all it takes to make a person happy. Only a woman who does not think much of herself will date a man for his money. Meeting a financially stable man is a plus. All people are attracted to people who have a sense of purpose and who can bring something to the table financially. However, many women have their own money and do not need a man for that, although it is important that he has his own so that he is not a drain on hers. However, women are also looking for other qualities like being a good conversationalist, having a good sense of humor, etc.

Keep it moving—This means to continue to date others. This is particularly important for women. Some women stop dating once they have met someone who has gotten their attention. And while they are waiting, men are having all the fun. Keeping it moving keeps you from being too focused on whether a person is interested in you, and from becoming disappointed if they are not.

Intimacy

In the first stage of dating, intimacy on all levels should be kept at a minimum. Below are strategies for intimacy at the conception/attraction stage of dating.

Physical—You might elect to not engage in physical intimacy on the first date or in the first stage of dating. When two people enter into physical intimacy, they are also entering into each other's energetic fields at a deeper level. Because there was an energetic exchange, without higher levels of intimacy, you feel may feel exposed and vulnerable.

Emotional—Premature physical intimacy may lead to emotional intimacy and you began making decisions based on emotions that are derived from physical intimacy, though the signs may be there that this is not the right person for you. It is important to not invest feelings into a person before getting to know them.

Mental—It may not be good to get into deep conversations on issues that delve into your worldviews and values as it may turn you off before getting to know the person. You may not share some views and values, but that might not be enough to prevent the development of a relationship. No two people are going to be completely compatible on their views and values. Topics to avoid include those that open the door to physical intimacy, focus on the past; particularly negative experiences, and topics that people have strong opinions about. Some topics not to discuss on the first few dates include but are not limited to sex, past relationships or ex-partners, politics, religion, and problems in your life.

Sex—Do not talk about sex on the first date and early in the dating process. Particularly for women, if a man brings up sex on the first date, he is testing to see if you are open to it. If you have some rules with regard to a time frame when it comes to physical intimacy, for example, some people have a three-month rule; keep it to yourself. If you start talking about that, then the person may see this as a challenge and begin to focus not on getting to know you, but on how to get you to break your rules.

Ex-partners—Two is company, three is a crowd. Do not talk about your ex-partners or previous relationships. The goal is to be present with the person you are with, making them feel special.

Politics & religion—These are areas that people typically have strong opinions about. When you have differences in opinions on these topics, and because they may cause us to become emotional, it may deter you from further exploration. As you continue to get to know each other, you may find that you have other things in common, and that you have more in common in these areas as well, and/or that you may be able to live with your differences.

Problems in your life—When you focus on problems in your life, you may be perceived as being too needy and a liability; and nobody wants to take on a liability. It can be a turn-off for someone to have to hear your problems before getting to know your good qualities. You might be perceived as a person with too much baggage rather than a person who has a lot to offer.

Spiritual—People can feel spiritually connected without even trying. However, it is important to distinguish between spiritual attraction and physical attraction. Physical attraction may make people feel that they are experiencing a spiritual attraction. It, therefore, can be blinding and lead to physical intimacy. You should not get into deep conversations about religion, because people have strong ideas about it. Our ideas about religion, however, may have nothing to do with spirituality, but they are thought by many to be the same thing. If you delve into conversations about religion too early in the dating process, you may find that your ideas about religion are radically different without knowing that although you do not share the same religious ideas and beliefs, you share the same spiritual values. This may deter you from further exploration.

The Task

Overall, at the conception stage, it is important to put your best foot forward. You should treat the date, whether it is on the telephone, Internet, or in person, like a job interview. You should show your best self. Although you may have some shortcomings (we all do), they may only be your perceptions and may not be perceived as shortcomings by the person getting to know you. Also, since you have good qualities and some that are not so good, it is important that the person sees your good ones, giving him or her the opportunity to see the best of who you are. After the person sees the best of you, characteristics that are not so good might not seem as bad, and the good ones may very well outweigh them.

Ending the Getting-to-Know Process

It is important to develop strategies for ending the getting-to-know process at least for a relationship. Everyone who comes into your life may be sent for a reason, for example, to bring a message, to teach a lesson, or to help you at a critical moment, which could be some time in the future. This is why it is important to honor and respect all who come onto your path (unless it is a force that could bring harm or destruction). If, after dating for a while, you find that you are no longer interested in exploring the person further, at least for a partner, you can let the person know. If, on the other hand, you find that the person has potential as a partner, you might continue to date him or her. If the feeling is mutual, you now enter the next stage which is the birth of a relationship.

Birth (Commitment)

Birth in the time process in dating translates into commitment in relationships. Commitment translates into "we are going to give it a try." What you are saying is that there is enough that makes this person worthy of your commitment and to see if he/she is worth exploring potentially for marriage. This is the stage at which a commitment is made by both parties to explore each other at deeper levels. A significant task at the birth stage is a commitment to how you will interact together.

The Touchstone—What might be considered is an open discussion about expectations and setting ground rules for how you will interact. Some things that might be discussed include the importance of being truthful and being able to self-disclose without being judged, what commitment means to each of you, including exclusivity and fidelity, your expectations with regard to physical intimacy, and how you are expected to interact socially with each other and with family members and friends. The touchstone can be a place to return to when misunderstandings arise.

The Task—At the commitment stage you can disclose more about yourselves. You should continue to put your best foot forward and be the best person you can be. At this stage, you can also show more of who you are, even when you are not at your best. Although you can reveal more about yourselves, it is important to avoid taking each other for granted. You should continue to do the things you did at the conception stage, so you can sustain the relationship to the next stage.

Meeting Family & Friends—You should meet each other's family members and friends. Getting to know and observing family members and friends and how you both interact with them, helps you learn more about each other.

Intimacy—At the commitment stage you still should consider what you can and cannot handle. It might be wise to consider using strategies suggested for the conception stage to avoid the temptation to move to physical intimacy without moving through mental, emotional, and spiritual intimacy.

For mental intimacy, you will now begin to explore your worldviews and values. For emotional intimacy, you will explore your feelings for each other. You might also disclose more personal things about yourselves—things that you would not share with just anyone. Although you may feel more comfortable sharing problems, it is still important to not "dump" all of your problems onto each other. A partner is someone to be supportive; they are not responsible for your problems or your healing. At the commitment stage, you want to be careful not to give off the impression that you are an emotional liability.

With regard to spiritual intimacy, the commitment stage is the stage to share ideas and beliefs about religion. You should be careful not to impose your beliefs on each other. The objective is to explore each other's beliefs, whether or not you are of the same faith, as you might find that you can have a relationship despite religious differences, as long as you both understand the necessity of spirituality for spiritual and relationship health.

Maturity (Engagement)

Maturity in relationships translates into engagement and is the stage that you decide to marry. The key tasks are not only to continue to explore and share as the relationship matures and unfolds, but to also engage in activities (counseling, self-help books, classes) to find out your levels of physical, emotional, mental, social, and spiritual compatibility. The areas of compatibility are discussed in more detail in Chapter 9. For those areas in which you find that you are incompatible, this is the time to explore whether you are willing to respect your differences and engage in practices that show your willingness to do so. If you find that it is too difficult to get along in areas in which you are incompatible, this may be the time to terminate the relationship. It is better to terminate the relationship at this stage than to get married and have to terminate it later.

Transformation (Marriage)

Transformation in time translates into marriage in relationships. If you do not seek to marry, then it can mean the death of the relationship—at least an intimate one. If you decide to marry, although the relationship continues to mature, it begins a new process that also goes through the four-stage time process with different challenges, many of which revolve around children and how to live together. The four-stage process begins with (1) conception—the idea that you are married; the physical reality, "we are married"; (2) birth—the marriage itself, and how you mature through mental, emotional, physical, and spiritual intimacy as a result of living together and after the birth of the first child or with already existing children; (3) maturity—making it past the challenges faced by areas of incompatibility and children, and what happens as you evolve as individuals with your own goals and destinies, and as you evolve together; (4) transformation—of the marriage to a point where the challenges level off and you know and accept each other's shortcomings and your differences, and move the relationship to a high- er level; or to the death of the marriage relationship through divorce or death of a partner. There is also a continuing cycle of highs and lows based on daily interactions and life events.

Intimacy—During engagement and when you marry, intimacy on all levels deepens. If you do not make the necessary adjustments and do the work that is necessary to sustain physical, emotional, mental, and spiritual intimacy, it may lead to the end of the relationship before you marry or an unhappy, unfulfilling marriage. The marriage may then transform into a dead marriage—where you stay together because of financial ties, children, or for other reasons. The other outcome may be the death of the marriage through divorce. If the work is done to sustain physical, emotional, mental, and spiritual intimacy, the marriage might transform to a higher level until the death of one of the spouses.

PRINCIPLE 7: Have Fun

Meeting your soul's partner is serious business, as the person you choose to share your life with is probably the single most important decision that you can make. However, do not be so serious that you take the joy out of it. Being easy and having fun increases your attractiveness and people are drawn to attractive people. People are drawn to those who like to have fun because it helps them to relax and have fun. So if you make finding your soul's partner a priority and are dating with some skills you will be successful. Be serious about finding your soul's partner, but also have fun doing so.

We have discussed the time process for dating and the levels of intimacy at each stage. During the maturity stage, or engagement, is when you should engage in activities through self-help books, classes, and/or counseling, to explore levels of compatibility. It is important to examine your levels of physical, social, emotional, mental, and spiritual compatibility which is explored in Chapter 9 that follows.

Chapter 8 Exercises

A Plan for Dating

The purpose of these exercises is for you to examine your dating patterns while simultaneously developing a plan for dating utilizing the seven principles for dating.

EXERCISE 8.1. *Knowing Yourself*

For the following describe:
i. Issues you are still struggling with and/or working on
ii. Your strengths and weaknesses
iii. Your gifts
iv. The most significant qualities you bring to a relationship
v. Your life purposes

_____
_____
_____
_____
_____

2. Given all the above, discuss the most significant qualities you need in a person to help you heal, fulfill your life purpose, and continue to evolve spiritually.

_____
_____
_____
_____
_____
_____

EXERCISE 8.2. *A Plan for Dating*

1. Describe your plan for meeting people.

_____
_____
_____
_____
_____

EXERCISE 8.3. *Being Conscious*

1. Check the box for which brain dominates your primary decisions and behaviors while dating.

☐ Physical—make decisions based on survival and/or physical attractiveness
☐ Emotional—make decisions based on emotions
☐ Intellectual—make decisions based on intellectual attractiveness and or material based societal ideas, e.g., social class, career, money, etc.
☐ Spiritual—allow spirit to guide decisions

2. Describe what you need to change and how you will do so when it comes to behaviors when dating.

_____
_____
_____
_____
_____

> **EXERCISE 8.4.** *Valuing Yourself*

1. Check the boxes for personality characteristics you present when dating if any apply to you.

☐ Low self-esteem ☐ Needy ☐ Desperate ☐ Egotistical ☐ Other_____ ☐ Other_____	☐ Dramatic ☐ Bitter ☐ Emotionally unavailable or too emotionally available ☐ Other_____ ☐ Other_____

2. Changes you will make in how you present when dating if necessary.

_____
_____
_____
_____
_____

> **EXERCISE 8.5.** *Valuing Who You Date*

1. Circle the number that corresponds with how much of the following you do when on a date.

Behavior	Not at all				A Lot
Talk	1	2	3	4	5
Listen	1	2	3	4	5
Show interest	1	2	3	4	5
Show appreciation	1	2	3	4	5
Guarded	1	2	3	4	5
Untrusting	1	2	3	4	5
Judgmental	1	2	3	4	5

2. Changes you will make in how you interact when you date if necessary.

_____
_____
_____
_____

EXERCISE 8.6. *Dating Strategies*

1. Check the box below that corresponds to the things you need to work on when dating

☐ Showing more self-care 　-losing weight 　-getting in shape 　-how to dress ☐ Where I meet for dates ☐ Entering into physical intimacy too early in the dating process ☐ Getting emotionally involved too quickly in the dating process	☐ Being more positive ☐ Presenting my best self more often ☐ Not talking about my problems ☐ Not bringing emotional baggage ☐ Paying attention to the small stuff ☐ Managing my expectations ☐ Chasing/being forceful

2. Describe your typical dating patterns.

_____
_____
_____
_____

3. Describe what you will do differently if necessary.

_____
_____
_____
_____

EXERCISE 8.7. *Having Fun*

1. Finding your soul's partner is a serious matter. However, some of us kill the joy of dating by being too intense. Circle the number that corresponds to your level of intensity when dating.

A little			Very	
1	2	3	4	5

2. What can you do to lighten up and make dating more fun?

_____
_____
_____
_____
_____

EXERCISE 8.8. *Dating Narrative*

1. Describe and discuss anything not covered that is significant in dating for you and the things you need to work on.

_____
_____
_____
_____
_____
_____
_____
_____
_____
_____
_____
_____

Additional Notes

9
~~~~~~~~~~~~~~~

Seven Compatibilities

Now that you have initiated the steps to attract love, and are dating, you will attract people. People come into our lives at different times for different reasons. They come into our lives for mutual awakening for the fulfillment of certain aspects of ourselves, to achieve goals, to provide protection at critical moments, and/or to learn lessons. What distinguishes your soul's partner from others is that he or she is the person who will be most significant in bringing the love, happiness, and joy, that comes with an intimate relationship, and helping you fulfill your mutual life purposes and continual spiritual evolvement together.

When you meet your soul's partner, or if you think you already have, it is important to explore various areas of compatibility. Exploring compatibility should be done even if you are already married. A reason that some married couples experience great difficulty is that they failed to examine their areas of compatibility before marrying. Examining areas of compatibility allows you to see the areas in which you complement each other and the areas in which you differ. Since there are inevitably going to be some incompatibilities, once you are aware of what they are, you can have discussions about how you are going to deal with them, which may mean agreeing to change some things and learning to accept other things. If the incompatibilities are not too great, and you decide to continue the relationship, it is important to consider whether you have the foresight to see the lessons you can learn from each other and the fortitude and willpower to help each other continue to grow and evolve despite your incompatibilities.

Compatibility may be categorized under the four bodies and seven aspects of the self: physical (including your social worlds), emotional, mental, and spiritual (which includes the compassionate, conscious, enlightened, and eternal aspects of yourselves).

Physical Compatibility

Your Physical Selves

Physical compatibility includes all matters in the physical realm, including your physical bodies and your social worlds. Your physical selves include physical attractiveness and health which are discussed in this section and sexuality which is discussed in Chapter 11. Physical attractiveness is how you feel about yourselves in terms of attractiveness, the degree of attractiveness you feel toward each other, and how important it is to you. Physical health concerns the health issues you inherited from your ancestral lines and families of origin and how you manage them, and your dietary and exercise habits. It is important to consider genetic-related health issues because they can potentially affect not only your physical health and that of the children you have together but can detract from the health of the relationship.

Our dietary and exercises habits have a lot to do with patterns carried over from childhood, emotional attachment to food, and ignorance about healthy dieting and exercise. In addition, consumption of and/or addiction to substances, such as sugar and salt, and drugs and alcohol, may indicate unhealed wounds to one or more of the bodies and/or leaks or blocks to the energy body. Your physical selves also include how you feel about and take care of yourselves in general including your hygiene and your physical appearance, for example e.g., how you dress, manage your hair, etc., and present yourselves to each other and the world.

Compatibilities to explore: How do you feel about yourselves and each other in terms of physical attractiveness and how does it affect your interaction patterns? What are the genetic-based health problems in your families of origin? What mechanisms are or will you put in place to manage these problems? What is your willingness and openness to learning about and changing unhealthy dietary and lifestyle habits that could potentially lead to health problems down the road? What is your willingness to incorporate new dietary and lifestyle habits for good health and well-being? How well do you take care of yourselves in general, i.e., your physical hygiene, your physical appearance, and how you present yourselves to each other and the world?

Your Social Worlds

Social compatibility has to do with the level to which you are compatible in a number of areas, some of which include your families of origin, friends, children, social class background, levels of education, occupations, credit history, and legal background, and your ideas about living arrangements, gender roles, money, how time will be spent, and goals.

Families of Origin—When two people join, two families also join. Therefore, it is important to consider whether you can integrate with each other's families and whether your families can mesh. Depending upon their culture, people have varying degrees of responsibility to their families of origin. Therefore, it is important to take into consideration how involved family members will be in your day-to-day lives, the roles they will play in your choices and decisions, and how much of your time and resources will be shared with them. It is important to pay attention to the habits and practices of family members as well. For example, if any of your family members have unhealthy dietary practices and/or use alcohol or drugs, and either of you and/or your children spend a lot of time with them, you may be influenced by them which can affect your health and the health of your relationship.

Social Class Backgrounds—Has to do with the educational level, occupation, and income of your families of origin, which influenced where they lived, their social groups, their attitudes, and dispositions, their values, and their overall lifestyles. Radical differences in social class backgrounds can present potential challenges in your relationship.

Gender Roles—The society we live in and our experiences in our families, shape our ideas about gender/roles. Traditional ideas about gender roles in the U.S. are that women are the nurturers and men are the providers and protectors. Even though many people believe they are non-traditional and adaptable when it comes to gender roles, they still internalize these ideas. What happens if one internalizes traditional gender role ideologies, but their circumstances make it impossible to carry them out? How will this affect the expectations they have of themselves, their partner, and their interaction styles?

Early experiences in our families also shape our ideas about members of the same and opposite sex. If one experienced an absent parent, neglect, or abuse from a caregiver, or hurt and/or disappointment from a friend or intimate other, feelings from these experiences can lead to negative opinions of members of that sex. What can also contribute to what we think and feel about members of the same or opposite sex are stereotypes generated by society.

Compatibilities to explore: What are your ideas about who should work outside the home, contribute to the household finances (and how much), pay the bills, cook, do household chores, do outside work, car maintenance, take care of the children, etc.? Based on your experiences in your families and with intimate others, and societal generated stereotypes, what unhealthy thoughts and feelings are you holding on to about the same or opposite sex? It is important to explore your ideas, thoughts, and feelings around gender because different ideas and negative thoughts and feelings can be a major source of conflict in relationships.

Children—Important considerations if you desire to have children include family health background, whether you can have children when you will have them, and how many you will have. You should consider your ideas around who will be primarily responsible for child-care (and all that comes with it), parenting, and discipline. The primary parenting styles are authoritarian (i.e., where parents discuss matters with their children), authoritative (i.e., where parents direct their children), and permissive (i.e., where parents allow their children a lot of freedom). Also consider your ideas around discipline, (e.g., physical punishment). In addition, consider your ideas regarding goals for your children, such as what type of schools they will attend and what types of activities they will be involved in. Parenting and discipline styles for children born outside the new relationship (i.e., stepchildren), including how the children's other biological parent and extended relatives will be incorporated into the family should also be considered.

Living Arrangements—Include your ideas about where you will live and how you will live. Some considerations include preferences for where in the world you will live, type of community in which you will live (e.g., urban, suburban, racially mixed), whether you will live together in the same house, house, and furnishing styles (e.g., contemporary vs. traditional) and your living environment (e.g., where you are on the continuum of orderliness, and cleanliness).

Education—Is a source of expansion and growth. People have different ideas and values about what education provides. Some people see it as a means for intellectual growth, while others see it as a means for upward mobility. Having similar educational backgrounds is not only a common value, but having similar knowledge levels, interests, and things to talk about helps to increase intimacy and relationship satisfaction.

Occupations—An unstable foundation will make for an unstable relationship. A stable foundation provides a secure base upon which to build a strong relationship. What people do for a living has different meanings for different people. For some people, work provides a means to provide for their families, while, for others, it is a source of fulfillment. For some, it provides both.
    Compatibilities to explore: What do you do for a living and do you have a plan in place to ensure that you can meet your basic survival needs? What does work mean to you? Is it a means to make

a living and provide for your family or is it a source of fulfillment? Important to note is that our work, or what we do for a living, may or may not have to do with our life purpose.

Finances—Our early childhood and life experience shape our ideas, goals, and values around money. People have different ideas about who should pay what when it comes to household expenses. They also have different ideas about how money should be spent, especially regarding debt, saving, and investing. They have different ideas about whether money should be kept in separate accounts or merged in the same account. In addition, people have different values around what money provides. For some people, money means security, for others, it means status, for others, it means power, while for others it means freedom or happiness.

If you have different ideas and values around money, you might consider a joint account for household bills and savings, and separate accounts for personal spending. Having your own money helps prevent you from being judgmental about what each other spends their money on. You should also create a budget.

Compatibilities to explore: What were your childhood experiences with money and how have they shaped your ideas and values? What does money mean to you? Is it a source of security, status, power, freedom, or happiness? How good are you with budgeting and managing money? What are your ideas regarding who should manage the money? What are your ideas about spending, especially as it relates to debt, saving, and investing? What are your short-and long-term financial goals, both individually and collectively?

Credit History & Legal Background—A person's credit history can tell you a lot about their spending patterns and habits as well as their values (i.e., whether they handle their responsibilities, pay their bills, follow through on financial obligations, etc.). It is important to know a potential partner's credit history so that you are aware of how much debt you are potentially getting into once you combine your lives. In addition, credit is an indicator of spending power, because it can determine how much house you can afford, access to credit for an automobile, business, etc.

Knowing a person's legal background is also important. If one has a criminal record, it can affect their ability to find employment, and a felony background can limit access to grants and loans for education and numerous types of jobs. Negative credit history and a potentially negative legal background, however, can be managed; it is just important to be aware so that you can be prepared for the work and time it may take to remedy the situation.

Time—It is important to consider how you will spend your time, including how much time will be spent pursuing individual interests and how much time will be spent engaging in activities together. How much time will be time spent with family members, friends, associates, and children; and quality time alone should also be considered.

Goals—We all have hopes, dreams, and aspirations. You should explore your hopes, dreams, and aspirations, those you share, and your short-and long-term goals for achieving them.

Compatibilities to explore: What are your personal and hopes, dreams, and aspirations (i.e., go back to school, open a business, write a book); what are those you share (e.g., purchase a home, travel), and what are your short-and long-term goals for achieving them? Are you open and willing to support each other's individual goals?

Friends—Can play a significant role in your lives and the choices you make. It is important to consider how significant a role they will continue to play in your lives and your relationship and whether you can mesh with each other's friends. Maintaining friendships is important because they can last a lifetime. Friends might even be there for you when things get tough or in the event that the relationship dissolves. Developing new friendships with other couples can also provide another social support system.

Emotional Compatibility

The personality consists of three components: emotional, mental, and behavioral. The emotional side is the feeling side of your personality and how you react to things. An aspect of your emotional make-up is temperament. Temperament is thought to be shaped by biology, which is shaped by genetics; the health of your parents at conception; what happened while in your mother's womb; e.g. state of health during gestation); the season into which we were born; the element most dominant in your personality, the celestial bodies and corresponding energetic fields acting on the Earth's field when you were born; and how your caregivers responded to your needs during infancy and childhood (as discussed in previous chapters).

An ancient model that has been used to understand temperament is the four temperaments. The four temperaments were believed to be shaped by the seasons which correspond to the four elements and their qualities: spring-air, warm and moist; summer-fire, hot and dry; fall-Earth, cold and dry; and winter-water, cold and moist. Since we are made of the elements, depending upon the dominance of one or more of the qualities associated with them, they play a role in shaping our temperaments.

Although the ancient model of temperaments originated in Egypt, it was further developed by a Greek physician, Polybus. Galen, another Greek physician, later identified nine temperamental types: one that was balanced (i.e., a good mix of the four qualities; warm, cool, dry, and moist), four that were less balanced (i.e., where one quality was dominant) and four that were even less balanced (i.e., where two qualities were dominant). The latter four include the following:

Sanguine (hot and wet)—These individuals are characterized as outgoing, optimistic, graceful, artistic, and possessing leadership qualities; however, they can be overcome by excess sensuality.

Choleric (hot and dry)—These individuals are characterized as bold and courageous leaders; however, they are impatient, easily angered, and irritated, and short-tempered.

Phlegmatic (cold and wet)—These individuals are good-natured, kind, compassionate, nurturing, and caring. They are calm, relaxed, and take life easy; however, they can do so to the point of being slow and sluggish.

Melancholic (cold and dry)—These individuals are reflective, conscientious, intellectual, and philosophical; however, they are prone to moodiness, depression, and pessimism.

The four temperaments have played a major role in how we think about temperament as this model is the basis for frameworks that were developed later to understand personality. Societies also have different systems to provide a way for understanding the role of cosmic energetic forces in shaping temperament and personality types.

The dominant celestial bodies and their energetic fields that acted on the Earth's energetic field and body when we were born are thought to play a role in shaping our personalities. These celestial bodies are the planet that is most dominant on the day of the week and the astrological constellation when we are born. Although it originated in Egypt, in the West, the Zodiac is used. The zodiac—which means "wheel of animals" contains 12 signs on a belt of stars that the sun passes through every 30 days over a year. For the Akan of Ghana, West Africa, the Ntoro, or the 12 agnatic groups one is born under is used. Similar to the zodiac, the Ntoro are essentially groups of people with the same essence due to celestial bodies. People born under one of the groups may be associated with certain elements, objects, and bodies of water or rivers, and are bound together by idiosyncratic characteristics. In addition, among the Akan as well as peoples all over the world, is the belief that each of the seven days is governed by different planets, energies, deities, and/or qualities of God, all of which have direct bearings on a person and, subsequently, his or her personality.

MENTAL COMPATIBILITY

The mental side of your personality has to do with how you cognize the world and your experiences in it. It also has biological and social bases and is shaped by the culture you are cultivated in. Culture is a people's general design for living and interpreting reality. It consists of two levels: *deep structure* and *surface structure* (Nobles, 1985). The *deep structure* level of culture has two levels *cultural factors* and *cultural aspects*. Cultural factors are based on the following:

- *Cosmology*—a people's ideas about the structure and origins of the universe;
- *Axiology*—a people's ideas about how universal relations are governed and defined;
- *Ontology*—a people's ideas about the nature of being.

Cultural factors underlie the *cultural aspects* which include:

- *Worldview*—a people's comprehensive ideas about order;
- *Ideologies*—a people's directions for solving social problems;
- *Ethos*—a people's character, tone, and style.

Both levels of *deep structure* level of culture underlie the *surface structure* level of culture, which are cultural manifestations, which include, but are not limited to, a people's ideas, values, beliefs, and behaviors in their overt daily expressions. Thus, our mental world is shaped by how we cognize the world, which is shaped by biology, and how we experience the world, which starts with our experiences in our families and continues via our cultivation in the broader society. Important to consider is your level of awareness of the historical, political, and economic ideologies driving the society in which you live as well as your place within that society. It means your level of awareness of the role of the various institutions (e.g., political, economic, religious, media, familial) in shaping your thought world. Being conscious of your level of awareness helps to understand your ideas, values, beliefs and, ultimately, what motivates your expectations and behaviors in a number of areas that will affect your day-to-day functioning and whether you can co-exist together.

Compatibilities to explore: How do you see the world and your place in it? Is the world a good or bad place? Are people inherently good or bad? What is your level of awareness about the historical, political, and economic ideologies shaping your lives? What ideologies are driving your expectations and behaviors? Are they in need of revision?

Our emotional and mental make-up influences our behaviors and shapes our essential personality, which is derived from the word 'persona,' which means a mask for the soul. Numerous frameworks have been developed to understand and explain personality types. One of the early frameworks was created by Carl Jung, who theorized that personality is shaped by conscious motivations (i.e., those we are aware of) and unconscious motivations (i.e., those we are unaware of). According to Jung, our conscious and unconscious motivations render two personality or attitude types: introvert and extrovert. These two personality types are distinguished by the direction of our interests and function types; how we think and feel (rational, judging functions) and sense and intuit (irrational, perceiving functions) the world around us.

Introverts are more inward-oriented and, as such, are more focused on the internal world of thoughts, ideas, concepts, and reflections, while extroverts are more outward-oriented and more focused on the external world of objects, things, people, and behaviors. These two attitude types have been used to develop typologies on personality types and are the basis for personality instruments such as the Myers-Briggs Type Indicator (MBTI), which identifies 16 personality types.

There are other theories on personality types. A commonly used one is Type A and Type B theory on personality types. Those with a Type A personality are described as impatient and achievement oriented, and those with a Type B personality are described as relaxed and easy-going. Personality traits have been used to understand differences in people. A commonly known model is the Five-Factor Model. Numerous studies have confirmed that five personality traits exist on a continuum of extraversion, agreeableness, conscientiousness, neuroticism, and openness to experience.

Neuro-Linguistic Programming (NLP), which has to do with the connection between neurological processes, language, and behavior learned through experiences, has been used to understand how people process the world around them. It has also been used as a tool for behavioral change. Although there are five ways in which we sense the world, proponents of NLP identify the three primary sensory modes of hearing, seeing, and feeling as being dominant in how people process information. Some individuals sense and process information primarily through what they hear (auditory), what they see (visual), or what they feel (kinesthetic). The idea is that we create subjective experiences through the five senses and language and if we understand the sense that dominates our personality, then it can be used to help make behavior changes.

Although both sides of the brain work interdependently, another model that has been theorized to show that how people process information is based on whether they are more left-brain dominant (i.e., thinking or analytical) or right-brain dominant (i.e., more intuitive or feeling). The energetic qualities of Yin and Yang have also been used to understand personality. Some individuals may be more dominated by Yang (i.e., outward-focused) or Yin (i.e., inward-focused). Personality attributes that people find desirable include being loving, warm, kind, caring, open, flexible, patient, and understanding as well as having a good sense of humor.

Compatibilities to explore: Are you more introverted or extroverted? Where are you on the continuum of the five personality traits? Are you Type A or Type B, auditory, visual, or kinesthetic, right-brain or left-brain dominant, and/or yin, or yang in your expression? What are your other general personality attributes and how do all your personality characteristics complement each other and how do they differ? How will you deal with your differences?

SPIRITUAL COMPATIBILITY

Spirituality helps to shape our moral values and principles and helps us heal. More importantly, it helps us evolve and awaken us to true selves. Spiritual practices are exercises that we engage in, to cleanse, heal, and feed the spirit. Spiritual compatibility has to do with your practices, and where you are in your spiritual evolvement. It includes your levels of compatibility with the four bodies of the higher self, including your compassionate selves, conscious selves, enlightened selves, and eternal selves.

Your Compassionate Selves

Your compassionate selves have to do with your capacities for empathy and understanding, and how you share yourselves with the world and each other. It is based on the level at which you have evolved past self-based love (i.e., love based on personal experiences) and have become open to the currents of Universe Love.

Compatibilities to explore: How do your past experiences with love affect your capacity to show empathy and understanding, and share yourselves in general, and with each other in particular?

Your Conscious Selves

Your conscious selves have to do with the level to which you have awakened to Universe Consciousness and the moral values and principles upon which you base your lives. It is the part of yourselves that attunes to the laws of the universe-MAAT and shapes your judgment and the strength of your character.

Compatibilities to explore: What are the moral values and principles guiding your lives? How do these values and principles shape your character? What work needs to be done to help you evolve to be your higher selves?

Your Enlightened Selves

Your enlightened selves have to do with where you are in your awakening to wisdom and understanding. There are generally three levels of spiritual practice and awakening. They are myth, ritual, and understanding. Some people understand religion at the mythical level, which means that they get stuck on religious doctrine, often taking what is meant to be symbolic as literal. Others engage in spiritual practices (e.g., pray, meditate) with little understanding as to why they are engaging in such practices. They are just doing what they are told or what they see others doing. Then, there are those individuals who go past the myth and ritual to a deeper understanding.

Compatibilities to explore: What are your spiritual practices? Where you are in your understanding of what it is that you practice? What is your level of openness to continue to deepen your understanding so that you continue to evolve in wisdom, understanding, the light?

Your Eternal Selves

Your eternal selves have to do with where you are with regard to understanding the aspect of yourselves that is eternal—your souls. Most people have difficulty awakening to this level of understanding because they are caught up in the illusion of the physical world. That is, they do not recognize, on a deeper level, the connectedness of all of existence through spirit (i.e., that all physical reality is spirit that has taken on form for a time) as well as the temporal reality of all form and experience in the earthly realm. Therefore, you may be at different or similar levels of awakening to this reality.

Compatibilities to explore: Where are you on your respective paths on this level of awakening? Where are you in regard to the commitment, dedication, and practice that will help you continue to evolve?

Finally, since sharing religious/spiritual practices helps increase spiritual connectedness and can help you evolve, factors to consider on a more practical level are whether you share the same religious/spiritual beliefs and practices and, if you do not, how you will reconcile these differences. Other factors to consider are how you will be involved in your practices, whether you will engage in them together, the frequency that you will practice, and, if you have different religious/spiritual practices, what your children will be raised under. Ultimately, it is your spiritual/religious practice that is necessary for spiritual evolvement.

In summary, it is important to take your time to get to know the people who come into your life. When, or if, you think you have met your soul's partner, it is important to explore physical, social, emotional, mental, and spiritual compatibility. Inevitably, you will not be completely compatible. It is how you navigate through your incompatibility that is important to sustaining a relationship, and if you decide to marry, marriage. If you think that you can help each other fulfill your life purposes and continue your journeys, then your work has just begun.

Chapter 9 Exercises

Compatibility Check

The purpose of these exercises is to explore your different areas of compatibility. They are designed to explore the areas in which you complement each other and how you will reconcile the areas in which you differ.

EXERCISE 9.1. *Physical Compatibility*

1. <u>Physical Attractiveness:</u> Discuss the following:
How do you feel about yourselves and each other in terms of physical attractiveness, how does it affect your self-esteem, and how does it affect your relationship?

_____
_____
_____
_____
_____

2. <u>Health Status</u>: Check the box that corresponds to health problems in your respective families.

☐ Diabetes	☐ High blood pressure	☐ Heart disease
☐ Cancer	☐ Sickle cell anemia	☐ Strokes
☐ Cirrhosis	☐ Multiple sclerosis	☐ Arthritis
☐ Alcoholism	☐ Drug addiction	☐ Alzheimer's
☐ Kidney failure	☐ Lupus	☐ HIV/AIDS
☐ Dementia	☐ Other_____	☐ Other_____

3. Discuss the following as they apply to you:
i. Heath issues in your families of origin, those you experience yourselves, and the effect they may have on your relationship and future children
ii. How you currently manage health issues and/or goals for doing so

_____
_____
_____
_____

4. <u>Diet & Exercise</u>: Check the box that corresponds to your diets.

You	Your Partner
☐ Vegan ☐ Vegetarian ☐ Poultry ☐ Fish ☐ Red meat ☐ Other _____	☐ Vegan ☐ Vegetarian ☐ Poultry ☐ Fish ☐ Red meat ☐ Other _____

5. Rank your diet and exercise regimens.

Not good			Excellent	
1	2	3	4	5

	You	Your Partner
Food type (whole, processed canned, frozen)	1 2 3 4 5	1 2 3 4 5
Food preparation (fried, overcooked, fresh, steamed, etc.)	1 2 3 4 5	1 2 3 4 5

| Exercise regimen | 1 2 3 4 5 | 1 2 3 4 5 |

6. Describe and discuss the following:
i. Your consciousness about diet and exercise
ii. Your goals for diet and exercise
iii. How you complement each other, how you differ, and how you will reconcile these differences

_____
_____
_____
_____
_____

EXERCISE 9.2. *Mental & Emotional Compatibility*

1. <u>Personalities/Ways of Being</u>: Check the box that corresponds to your personality/predominant way of being.

You	Your Partner
☐ Introverted (inward focused, quiet, reserved, etc.) ☐ Extroverted (outward focused, talkative, people oriented, etc.)	☐ Introverted (inward focused, quiet, reserved, etc.) ☐ Extroverted (outward focused, talkative, people oriented, etc.)
☐ Emotionally distant ☐ Emotionally close ☐ Emotional in general ☐ Unemotional in general	☐ Emotionally distant ☐ Emotionally close ☐ Emotional in general ☐ Unemotional in general
☐ Moody (up and down) ☐ Even-tempered ☐ Happy/cheerful ☐ Depressed	☐ Moody (up and down) ☐ Even-tempered ☐ Happy/cheerful ☐ Depressed
☐ Pessimistic ☐ Optimistic	☐ Pessimistic ☐ Optimistic

☐ Right brain (analytical) ☐ Left brain (intuitive, creative, etc.)	☐ Right brain (analytical) ☐ Left brain (intuitive, creative, etc.)
☐ Type A (high energy impatient) ☐ Type B (easy-going, patient)	☐ Type A (high energy, impatient) ☐ Type B (easy-going, patient)
☐ Auditory (hearing dominant) ☐ Visual (seeing dominant) ☐ Kinesthetic (feelings dominant)	☐ Auditory (hearing dominant) ☐ Visual (seeing dominant) ☐ Kinesthetic (feelings dominant)
☐ Disorganized ☐ Organized	☐ Disorganized ☐ Organized

2. Discuss how your personalities/ways of being complement each, how they are different, and how you/will reconcile these differences.

_____
_____
_____
_____
_____

3. <u>Personality Characteristics</u>: Using the chart below for suggestions, describe personality characteristics you like about each other (including those that are opposite to those in the chart), the challenges they present to your relationships, and how you/will deal with them. You may include other personality characteristics not listed on the chart.

Honest	Dependable	Reliable
Loyal	Committed	Faithful
Conscious	Conscientious	Sincere
Warm	Kind	Compassionate
Hardworking	Intelligent	Goal oriented
Intelligent	Open minded	Flexible

Caring	Affectionate	Interesting
Good sense of Humor	Funny	Communicative

_____
_____
_____
_____
_____

4. <u>Things You Value</u>: Using the chart below, write in the space that follows, the things that you value, or are important to you. You may add things that are not on the chart.

Being God-centered/ spirituality	Living a meaningful and fulfilling Life	Fulfilling a purpose	Having a strong sense of purpose
Living a healthy lifestyle	Pursue interests and hobbies	Autonomy/ independence, time to self	Emotionally satisfying work
Recognition/status	Helping others	Making a difference	Humanitarian Causes
Community/ activist causes	Relationship with family	Relationship with friends	High-paying/ status job
Political interest/ involvement	Learning/ knowledge/ education	Financial success	Safe & clean environment

You	Your Partner
a. _____	a. _____
b. _____	b. _____
c. _____	c. _____
d. _____	d. _____
e. _____	e. _____

5. Discuss your similarities and differences in terms of the things that are important to you and how you/will reconcile the differences.

_____
_____
_____
_____
_____

EXERCISE 9.3. *Social Compatibility*

Socio-economic Backgrounds

1. <u>Parents' Socio-Economic Background</u>: Describe and discuss the following:

i. Your parents' education, occupations, income, outlooks, etc.

ii. Neighborhoods you grew up in, the schools you attended, etc.

iii. Your responses in Chapter 2 exercise: *Shaping Factors*

iv. Similarities and differences in your backgrounds, how they affect your relationship, and how you/will reconcile the differences.

_____
_____
_____
_____
_____

2. <u>Current Education, Occupation & Income</u>: Describe and discuss your education, occupations, and income levels, how similarities and differences in these areas affect your relationship, and how you/ will reconcile the differences.

_____
_____
_____
_____
_____

Gender

1. Put a circle (and a square if you have a partner) around the number that corresponds to your ideas about who should be primarily responsible for what. If both of you think certain responsibilities should be shared, then put a triangle around number 3.

Tasks	You	Your Partner	Shared
a. Work outside the home	1	2	3
b. Finances (sort mail, pay bills, budgeting, balancing check book, phone calls, taxes, etc.)	1	2	3
c. Childcare	1	2	3
d. Daily household (cooking, dishes, sweeping, etc.)	1	2	3
e. Weekly household, (cleaning, laundry, carpet, bathrooms, mopping, etc.)	1	2	3
f. Outside maintenance	1	2	3
g. Appliance maintenance	1	2	3
h. Automobiles	1	2	3
i. Legal matters	1	2	3
j. Entertainment	1	2	3
k. Extended family	1	2	3

2. Discuss the ideas you hold about gender responsibilities and how you/will reconcile any differences.

_____
_____

_____
_____
_____

3. Based on your experiences (with caregivers, in past relationships, cultural ideas, stereotypes, etc.) discuss general ideas, thoughts, and beliefs you hold about men/women, and how they affect your relationship.
_____
_____
_____
_____

Family Friends & Children

1. <u>Family</u>: Check the box that corresponds to your ideas about family.

It is important that my partner ...	*It is important to my partner that I ...*
☐ Likes my family *(and my family likes him or her)* ☐ Accepts me spending time with my family ☐ Likes to spend time with me and my family *(discuss how much time is acceptable)* ☐ Accepts my family living with us if the need arises ☐ Wants to live near my family	☐ Like his/her family *(and his or her family likes me)* ☐ Accept him/her spending time with his/her family ☐ Like to spend time with him/her and his/her family *(discuss how much time is acceptable)* ☐ Accept his/her family living with us if the need arises ☐ Want to live near his/her family

2. <u>Friends</u>: Check the box that corresponds to your ideas about friends.

It is important that my partner ...	*It is important to my partner that I ...*
☐ Likes my friends *(and my friends like him/her)* ☐ Accepts me spending time with my friends ☐ Likes to spend time with me and my friends ☐ Likes to spend time with our friends ☐ Accepts my same-sex friends ☐ Accepts my opposite-sex friends	☐ Accept him/her spending time with his/her friends ☐ Like to spend time with his/her friends ☐ Like to spend time with our friends ☐ Accept his/her same-sex friends ☐ Accepts his/her opposite-sex friends

3. Describe and discuss your different ideas about family and friends and how you/will reconcile these differences.

_____
_____
_____
_____
_____

4. <u>Children</u>

i. Fill in the space with the number that corresponds to your current statuses and goals for children.

You	Your Partner

No of biological children you already have:
  With your partner_____
  With someone else_____
	No of biological children your partner already has:
	  With you_____
	  With someone else_____

No of children you would like to have with your partner_____	No of children your partner would like to have with you_____

No of children you already have/would like to foster/adopt_____	No of children your partner already have/would like to foster/adopt_____

ii. Put a circle (and a square if you have a partner) around the number that corresponds to your ideas about who should be primarily responsible for childcare. If both of you think certain responsibilities should be shared, then put a triangle around number 3.

Tasks	You	Your Partner	Shared
a. Daily care (bathing, feeding, dressing, shopping, haircare/cuts, health care)	1	2	3
b. Transporting (school, extra-curricular activities)	1	2	3
c. Education (homework, meeting teachers, etc.)	1	2	3
d. Nurturance (spending time with them, addressing emotional issues, etc.)	1	2	3
e. Discipline	1	2	3

iii. Check the box that corresponds to your ideas about how children should be parented.

I believe children should be parented by ...	*My Partner believes children should be parented by...*
☐ Primarily discussing things with parents ☐ Primarily by being told what to do by parents ☐ Discussing things primarily and being told what to do by parents somewhat	☐ Primarily discussing things with parents ☐ Primarily by being told what to do by parents ☐ Discussing things primarily and being told what to do by parents somewhat

☐ Being told what to do by parents primarily and discussing things somewhat ☐ Decide what they want to do Primarily	☐ Being told what to do by parents primarily and discussing things somewhat ☐ Decide what they want to do Primarily

iv. Check the box that corresponds to your ideas regarding whether children should be disciplined by spanking.

I believe children should ...	*My partner believes children should ...*
☐ Not be disciplined by spanking ☐ Be disciplined by spanking generally ☐ Be disciplined by spanking depending on the infraction and/or their age	☐ Not be disciplined by spanking ☐ Be disciplined by spanking generally ☐ Be disciplined by spanking depending on the infraction and/or their age

v. Check the box that corresponds to your goals for children. It is important to remember not to impose your unfulfilled dreams on your children. They have their purpose.

You	**Your Partner**
Education ☐ Public ☐ Private ☐ Charter ☐ Homeschooled ☐ Other_____	Education ☐ Public ☐ Private ☐ Charter ☐ Homeschooled ☐ Other_____
Activities ☐ Sports ☐ Arts ☐ Other_____	Activities ☐ Sports ☐ Arts ☐ Other_____

5. Describe and discuss the following:
i. How other biological parents and extended family members will be incorporated into your lives
ii. Areas in which you complement each other, areas in which you differ, and how you/will reconcile these differences

_____
_____
_____
_____
_____

Living Arrangements

1. Describe and discuss the following:
i. Where you prefer to live, e.g., International, U.S. (what city), suburbs, city, same race community, mixed community, etc.
ii House style (e.g., contemporary, traditional, single-story, two-story, etc.)
iii. Furniture style (traditional, contemporary, etc.)
iv. How your preferences and styles complement each other, how they differ, and how you will reconcile your differences

_____
_____
_____
_____
_____

Leisure Time

1. Describe and discuss your thoughts and feelings about the following:
i. The type of activities (interests you pursue and/or things you enjoy doing that does not include your partner) and the amount of time you will spend doing them
ii. The type of activities and amount of time you/will spend doing them together
iii. The type of activities and amount of time you/will spend doing them with family and friends

iv. The type of activities and time you will spend doing them with children
v. How your ideas about how time is/will be spent are similar, how they are different, and how you will reconcile your differences

_____
_____
_____
_____
_____

Goals
1 Describe and discuss the following:
i. Individual goals and your willingness to support each other's goals (and how you will do so)
ii. Goals you share
iii. How your goals complement each other, how they differ, and how you will reconcile the differences

_____
_____
_____
_____
_____

Money
1. Check the box that corresponds to how you think money should be kept.

You	Your Partner
☐ In separate accounts	☐ In separate accounts
☐ Joint accounts	☐ Joint accounts
☐ Each has his/her own account and we have a joint account for bills we share	☐ Each has his/her own account and we have a joint account for bills we share
☐ Other_____	☐ Other_____

2. Check the box that corresponds to how you think money should be handled and how you think bills should be paid.

I Think ...	*My Partner Thinks ...*
☐ I should handle all the money and pay all the bills	☐ I should handle all the money and pay all the bills
☐ My partner should handle all the money and pay all the bills	☐ He/she should handle all the money and pay all the bills
☐ I should pay the bills we owe collectively, and my own bills and my partner should pay his/her own bills	☐ I should pay the bills we owe collectively, and my own bills and he/she should pay his/her own bills
☐ My partner should pay all the bills we owe collectively, and his/her own bills and I should pay my own bills	☐ He/she should pay all the bills we owe collectively, and his/her own bills and I should pay my own bills
☐ We should pay all the bills Together	☐ We should pay all the bills Together
☐ Other_____	☐ Other_____

3. Rank in order of importance what money means to you by placing a number between 1 and 5 next to each value in the chart below, with "1" being the most valued, "2" being the next most valued, and so on.

You	**Your Partner**
___Status	___Status
___Security	___Security
___Enjoyment (doing and buying things you desire)	___Enjoyment (doing and buying things you desire)
___Control (over others)	___Control (over others)
___Independence	___Independence
☐ Other_____	☐ Other_____

4. Describe and discuss your values and practices around spending, debt, saving, and investing.

_____
_____
_____
_____
_____

5. Describe and discuss the following:
i. Short-term and long-term financial goals (e.g., developing a budget, getting out of debt, saving, investing, preparing will, etc.)
ii. How your ideas, values, and goals are complementary and different, and how you/will reconcile the differences

_____
_____
_____
_____
_____

Credit History & Legal Background

1. Check the box that corresponds to your credit histories and legal backgrounds.

You	Your Partner
Credit History ☐ Excellent ☐ Good ☐ Fair ☐ Needs improvement ☐ Needs much improvement	Credit History ☐ Excellent ☐ Good ☐ Fair ☐ Needs improvement ☐ Needs much improvement

Legal Background	Legal Background
☐ Felon	☐ Felon
☐ Misdemeanor	☐ Misdemeanor
☐ Probation	☐ Probation
☐ Parole	☐ Parole
☐ No legal issues	☐ No legal Issues
☐ Other_____	☐ Other_____

2. Discuss your thoughts and feelings about how your credit histories and legal backgrounds affect your relationship and your goals for improving them.

_____
_____
_____
_____
_____

EXERCISE 9.4. *Spiritual Compatibility*

1. <u>Moral Values and Principles</u>: Using the chart below list the moral values and principles you hold that you appreciate about each other. You may include values and principles, not on the list.

Honest	Dependable	Responsible
Committed	Fair	Just
Does the right thing	Has good character	Respectful
Loyal	Considerate	Compassionate
Kind	Empathic	Other_____

What you Appreciate About Your Partner	What Your Partner Appreciates About You
a. _____	a. _____
b. _____	b. _____
c. _____	c. _____
d. _____	d. _____
e. _____	e. _____

2. Check the boxes that correspond to your religious/spiritual practice.

You	Your Partner
☐ Christianity	☐ Christianity
☐ Islam	☐ Islam
☐ Traditional African	☐ Traditional African
☐ No specific practice	☐ No specific practice
☐ Eastern _	☐ Eastern____
☐ Spiritual/draw from several	☐ Spiritual/draw from several
☐ New Age	☐ New Age
☐ Agnostic or atheist	☐ Agnostic or atheist
☐ Other____	☐ Other____

3. Check the box that corresponds to your predominant type of religious practice.

Your Practice	Your Partner's Practice
☐ Attend religious service 　☐ Once a week 　☐ Twice a week 　☐ 3 or more times a week	☐ Attend religious service 　☐ Once a week 　☐ Twice a week 　☐ 3 or more times a week
☐ Pray	☐ Pray
☐ Meditate	☐ Meditate
☐ Get spiritual/psychic readings	☐ Get spiritual/psychic readings
☐ Attend classes	☐ Attend classes
☐ Other____	☐ Other____

4. Describe and discuss your religious or spiritual practices, how they complement each other, and if there are differences, how you will reconcile these differences.

_____
_____
_____
_____

5. Your missions/purposes and legacies: Discuss and describe the following:
i. The lessons you can learn from each other so that you grow as individuals and as a couple
ii. Your life missions and legacies you would like to leave
iii. The reasons you think you came to Earth this time
iv. Your purposes and how you can help each other fulfill them
v. Things you can do to help each other grow and evolve spiritually

_____
_____
_____
_____
_____
_____
_____
_____
_____

EXERCISE 9.5. *Compatibility Narrative*

1. Describe and discuss anything not covered in the previous sections and summarize major incompatibilities you will need to work on and those you will accept. In addition, describe and discuss how you generally feel about each other and your relationship.

_____
_____
_____
_____
_____
_____
_____
_____
_____
_____
_____
_____
_____
_____

200 Soul Partners

Additional Notes

10

Talking and Listening with Care

Thus, said Ra, the Lord of all, Lord of the Utmost Limits, after he had come into being. I am the one who came into being as Kheper... *He who comes into being and brings into being.* All beings came into being after I came into being. Many were the beings that came forth from the *commands* of my mouth. (Karenga, 1989, p. 5).

THE POWER OF WORDS

Translated from the sacred writings of ancient Egypt, these words speak not only to the creative power of the word but to how power powerful words are. The creator creates himself and then goes on to create the world. We find this same story in the Judeo-Christian faith. Genesis 2 reads: "And the earth was without form and void, and darkness was upon the face of the deep. And the spirit of God moved upon the face of the waters. *And God said:* "And through spoken word, God goes on to create the world and everything in it. In still another story of creation among the Fulani and Bambara of West Africa, we find that God, or Maa Ngala, also creates humans by the spoken word. Amadou Hampaté Bâ (1981), in an article entitled "The Living Tradition," explains how God creates Himself and then the world through the spoken word.

> *There was nothing except a Being.*
> *That Being was a living emptiness,*
> *brooding potentially over contingent existences.*
> *Infinite Time was the abode of that One Being.*
> *The One Being gave himself the name Maa Ngala.*
> *Maa Ngala wished to be known.*
> *So, he created Fan, a wondrous egg with nine divisions,*
> *and into it he introduced the nine fundamental states of existence. (p. 169)*

Bâ then goes on to explain that after the egg hatched, "it gave birth to twenty marvelous beings that made up the whole of the universe" (p. 169). But Maa Ngala still was not happy with what He had created. So He went on to create human beings by first mixing the twenty existing creatures and then by "blowing a spark of His own fiery breath into the mixture ... to whom He gave a part of his own name: Maa" (Bâ, 1981, p. 169). This being, because he was named after God and was given life through God's own breath, contained something of God Himself (Bâ, 1981, p. 169).

Creation of Divine Speech

After creating Himself by first naming Himself, and then humanity, God invented speech to communicate with humans. Bâ explains how this was done:

> Once Maa Ngala had created ... Maa, he spoke to him and at the same time endowed him with the faculty of replying. A dialogue was begun between Maa Ngala, creator of all things and Maa.... As they came down from Maa Ngala towards man, words were divine. (p. 170)

Because words came from God and were used by God to create humans and to communicate with them, speech can be seen as a gift from God.

Speech in Humans as Creative Power

Having been created in the divine image of God, humans possess the power to create through the use of speech. In fact, it is speech that puts everything into motion, even the divine potential in humans. Because God created the world through speech, then everything is speech in form. Bâ explains that "everything in the universe speaks: everything is speech that has taken on body and shape" (p. 170).

Not only is everything speech in form, but speech also serves another function—to strengthen. According to Ba (1981) "the Supreme Being conferred strength on Kiikala, the first man, by speaking to him. 'It was talking with God that made Kiikala strong'" (p. 170).

Heart, Mind, and Tongue

In *Selections from the Husia*, Karenga (1989) indicates that the ancient Kemetians taught that "Every word of God came into being through that which the heart and mind thought, and the tongue commanded" (p. 6). God is, therefore "within everybody as *heart and mind* and within every mouth as *tongue*.... What the heart and mind think, *and wish* is declared by the tongue" (Karenga, 1989, p. 6, italics his).

Good Speech Is Divine

Jacob Curruthers (1995) in *Divine Speech*, informs us that "the proper designations of the deep thought of ancient Kemet are *mdw ntr* 'Medew Netcher' (God Speech) and *mdw nfr*, 'Medew Nefer' (Good Speech)" (p. 39). However, there was no real distinction between good speech and God speech. "Only Medew Nefer was in accord with Medew Netcher. In fact, it is through the consistent practice of Medew Nefer [Good Speech] that human beings finally attained Medew Netcher [God Speech]" (Curruthers, 1995, p. 40). Good Speech is therefore divine.

Communication Fundamentals

To engage in good speech, it is important to know some fundamental things about communication including the different types of talking and listening, effective talking and listening, processing styles, and gender differences in communication.

Talk

As already indicated words are powerful. Your words can strengthen your partner or they can weaken or break them down. Good communication not only strengthens your partner but also strengthens you and your relationship. Communication that weakens or breaks down your partner serves to weaken or break down your relationship and can potentially destroy it. Good communication depends on consistency between two types of talk: *inner talk* and *outer talk*, and the spirit behind our words.

Inner talk is the internal conversations that occur. As Curruthers (1995) explains, "One thinks in speech. Even when one only 'thinks' about thinking, one thinks through (silent) speech" (p. 44). There are two types of inner talk:

- *Heart Talk*—The heart is the innermost part of our being and is the center of our emotions. It, therefore, speaks to our feelings. It is the heart that tells us what we are feeling.
- *Mind Talk*—The mind is the center of our thoughts and perceptions. The mind tells us what we are perceiving and what we are thinking.

Although heart talk speaks to how we are feeling, as with mind talk, we only understand these feelings through words. Inner talk leads to outer talk.

Outer talk is external expression that reflects inner talk. There are two types of outer talk:

- *Word Talk* is the verbal content of external expression. It is the actual words we use.
- *Body Talk* is the non-verbal content of expression. It is how we use the body to express what we are saying. Body talk includes how we use our voice, facial expressions, gestures, hand movements, body posture, position, and orientation.

Spirit behind words—The spirit of the message has to do with the intent behind it. Every outer expression is a reflection of our intentions. The types of talk are shown in *Figure 10.1*.

Figure 10. 1
Types of Talk

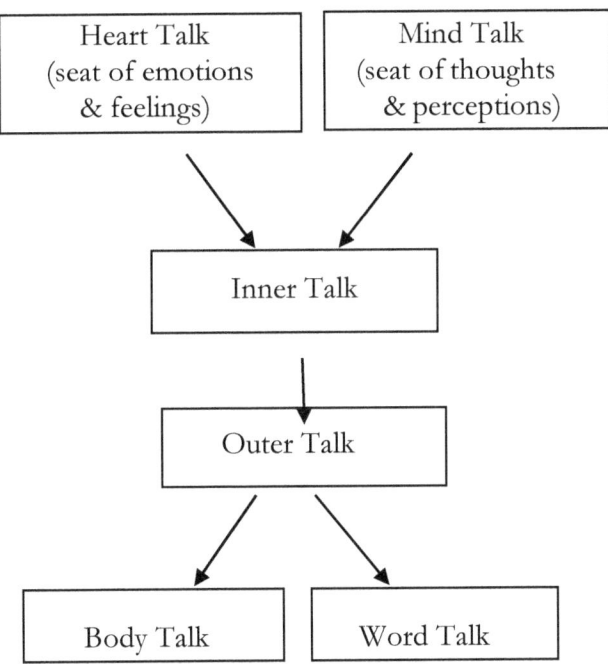

Thus, when one sends a message, this message consists of four components: the emotion behind it; the spirit of it, which gives off vibrations; word talk—what one says, one's actual verbal expressions; and body talk—how one says it, one's nonverbal expressions.

Words for Thought

We listen with our eyes. That is, we typically pay more attention to body talk than to word talk. Body talk, therefore, carries more weight. Research has found that how one talks, rather than what one says, carries about 65% of the message. Words for thought:

- The spirit behind what you say can have a great effect on your partner. He or she can feel vibrations and may respond to this more than to what you say.
- We all have unique ways of communicating. Some of us are passionate and dramatic when we speak using a lot of space and body movement, while others are more reserved, using very little space with little or no body movement. Some of us are primarily inner talkers and do not have much to say at all, outwardly, while others are outer talkers and have a lot to say outwardly.
- Word talk is irreversible. Once spoken, words cannot be taken back, changed, or undone. It is, therefore, important to think about what you are going to say before you say it.
- Words can wound a person for life. If it is true that we will be held accountable for all words and deeds, the words you speak can hurt you for eternity.

Effective Talking and Listening

Words take on significance based on the meanings we attach to them. Communication between two people means that at different points one person will be talking and the other will be listening. The talker is the person sending the message and the listener is the person receiving the message. As shown in *Figure 10.2*, communication is effective to the extent that: (a) the talker talks in a way or uses language that is constructive, and shows consistency between the various types of talk, and (b) the listener receives the message as was intended by the talker. Thus,

- Effective talking depends on how the message is sent by the talker, which depends on the use of constructive words and consistency between word talk and body talk.

- Effective listening depends on how the message is received by the listener, which depends on how accurately the listener interprets the intended message.

Figure 10.2
Effective Talking and Listening

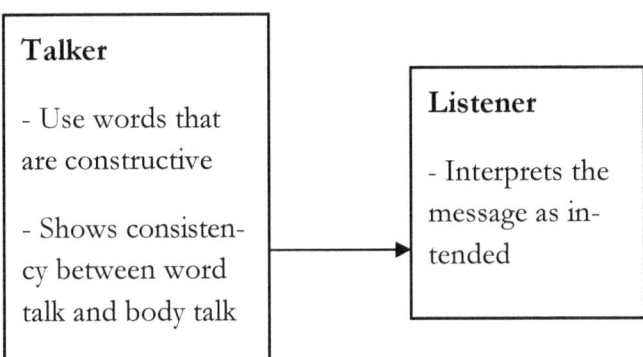

Ineffective Talking—A message is ineffective if there is an inconsistency between word talk and body talk. For example, a person may be saying one thing from their mouth, but their body talk indicates that their inner talk; either mind talk, or heart talk is different. Ineffective talk is words that hurt or wound in some way. Ineffective talk also includes destructive word and body talk. Examples of destructive word and body talk are below.

<u>**Destructive Word Talk**</u>
- Attacking by name-calling, belittling, criticizing, or judging
- Blaming/accusing a person of something
- Questioning a person's trustworthiness or credibility
- Disapproving of or showing contempt or disgust for the person
- Commanding, demanding, or attempting to boss a person around

Destructive Body Talk
- Facial expressions—frowning, looking disgusted, avoiding eye contact
- Gestures—pointing fingers or looking like you are telling someone off
- Body—orienting the body away from the person as if you are not paying attention, standing in a way that indicates that you do not care, with your hands on the hips, jumping up and down while yelling, approaching your partner in a threatening way
- Voice—volume, speed, tone, and pitch that sounds loud, fast, and/or threatening and emits negative vibrations

Ineffective Listening—How the listener receives a message is determined by their attitudes and beliefs; whether they think the talker is trustworthy or credible; their perceptions, which may have to do with their past and present experiences in general and with the talker, and whether there are unmet needs, wants, goals, or expectations. If the listener is having negative thoughts or feelings it may diminish their ability to listen effectively.

Effective Talking—Talking effectively means ensuring consistency between word talk and body talk and avoiding destructive word and body talk. It also means communicating in ways that show that you believe the person is worthy of your consideration and respect.

Effective Listening—Listening effectively means communicating to the person that you are listening and are interested in what they have to say. A strategy for effective listening is to indicate that you have heard them and understand what they have said. To engage in effective talking and listening, it is important to understand communication and connection.

Communication and Connection
Although there are many reasons for communication, a purpose for communicating in relationships is for the individuals to connect with

each other. The two types of connections are surface-level are surface level and deep level

Surface-Level Connection is the kind of connection we have with coworkers, acquaintances, and other associates. Much of the talk is surface level, which may or may not affect us deeply. When individuals get to know each other on a deeper level, they have a deep-level connection.

Deep-Level Connection is the connection between relatives, friends, and intimate others. Individuals can be affected more by the communication because they are deeply connected.

Our communication is designed to connect either on a surface level or a deep level. The type of talk will dictate the type of listening that is required. Although the types of talking and listening can be classified in many ways, we are classifying them as follows: (a) Functioning, (b) problem solving, (c) sharing (thoughts/feelings, experiences), and (d) exchanging ideas. Some talk only requires surface-level listening while others require deep listening. They are described briefly in Table 10.1 below.

Table 10.1 Connection and Communication

Type of Communication	Examples of Talking	Type of Listening
Functioning/ Informational	"The plumber will becoming today."	Surface to indicate that you heard them.
Problem-solving	"I am trying to figure out how to approach this matter."	Deep if the individual is sharing information that they need help on.
Sharing Experiences Feelings Thoughts	"My day at work did not go so well." "I don't think I like my job anymore." "I was thinking maybe I should consider looking for another job."	Deep if the individual is disclosing or sharing past or present experiences that cause deep feelings. Increases intimacy and relationship quality.

| Exchanging Ideas | Can include numerous topics, for example spirituality. | Deep and is expansive in that it helps individuals to grow. |

Processing Styles

Some people experience the world more inwardly, have a more inner orientation, or are more introverted, while others experience the world m

ore outwardly, are more outwardly oriented, and are more extroverted. Because we have different ways in which we experience the world, we also have different ways in which we process our thoughts and feelings. People can therefore be categorized as *inner processors* and *outer processors*. There are also *avoiders*, those who avoid dealing with their thoughts and feelings at all.

Inner processors are individuals who need to work through their thoughts and feelings before talking about them. In some instances, such individuals may distance themselves until they work through the problem. After they have finished processing their thoughts and feelings, they are then ready to talk. If you find that you are with an inner processor, you may need to give them the space they need to process through their thoughts and feelings. Equally important is that if you are an inner processor you should communicate in a positive way that you need time to think about things, and that you will be available to talk once you are finished working through your thoughts and feelings.

Outer processors are individuals who need to talk about their thoughts and feelings as they work through a problem. Individuals like this may talk to their partner, relatives, or friends until they feel that they are comfortable with how they feel about what they are experiencing. When a person is an outer processor, they may have to discuss an issue or problem immediately. Some outer processors cannot move on, rest, or sleep until they have talked about the problem.

Avoiders are people who do not deal with problems at all; internally or externally. Because working through their thoughts and especially their feelings might open wounds, cause them to have to deal with themselves and/or the other person, they may avoid problems altogether. Avoiders might also be in denial about reality and/or might be irresponsible.

Gender Differences

The popular works of Deborah Tannen, *You Just Don't Understand* (2007), and John Gray *Men Are from Mars and Women Are from Venus* (2012), provide insight into gender differences in communication. In these works, the authors describe the sources of gender differences, the values underlying them, and some of the behaviors. According to Tannen (2007), much of the style of communication of males and females begins with early socialization, which stems primarily from play and interaction. Although they often play together, boys and girls typically play in same-sex groups. This means that the games they play and the language they use are different.

As shown in Table 10.2, boys typically play in large groups with a hierarchy, an elaborate system of rules, and a group leader who gives orders. For boys, the game itself is the priority. The play is competitive; it has winners and losers and is based on status, which has to do with who is more skilled or best at what. Girls, on the other hand, typically play in small groups or pairs, where friendship, being liked, and closeness are important. It is not about who is better at what. Their games are more focused on making sure everybody gets a turn. Communication for boys is a way to achieve status, which is done by taking center stage and telling stories or jokes or by challenging others. Communication for girls is not about jockeying for status; it is about sitting together and talking.

Table 10.2 Gender Differences in Communication

	Boys/Men	Girls/Women
Socialization/ Early Play	Competitive—large groups with rules, focused on status, and who is best at what	Sharing—small groups/pairs, based on friendship, being liked, and closeness
Values	Skills/competency, status, independence	Relationships, connections
Communication Motivation	To maintain position in hierarchy; to preserve independence; to avoid being pushed Around	To maintain closeness; preserve intimacy; to avoid being isolated or pushed away
Communication Styles	*Report* talk—do better in public conversation where they hold center stage	*Rapport* talk—do better in private conversation where they do not have to worry about being judged

These early forms of play emerge in the values that men and women eventually adopt; what is important to communicate about and how they do so. Although relationships are important for men, status, skills, and competency tend to be valued even more. Although status and being skilled and competent may be important for women, relationships tend to be more valued.

For women, the primary goals of communication are to maintain closeness and connections, to preserve intimacy, and to avoid isolation and being pushed away. For men, the motivation in communication is to maintain their status in what is perceived as a hierarchy, to maintain the upper hand in order to not be put down or pushed around, and to preserve independence. A major difference in communication styles for men and women is that for men communication is *report* talk while for women it is *rapport* talk. Many men do better in public conversation in which they are the center of focus, while women do better in private conversation and do not like to engage in public conversation where they will be judged by others. What men and women communicate about is another area in which they may differ. Since women are more private-talk focused, and as girls usually had a best friend; someone with whom they shared their secrets, the details of their day, and their fleeting thoughts, they are used to talking about these kinds of things. For men, their secrets, the details of their day, and their fleeting thoughts and feelings may seem unimportant. This may be why some men do not talk about these kinds of things, and why they do not understand what women want from them when they talk about them. Because men use communication to preserve their independence and to avoid being pushed around, they may see women who seek intimacy through talking as trying to manipulate them or control their independence.

How men and women process their thoughts and feelings under stress is another difference. Gray (2012) indicates that women generally cope with stress by talking about problems, while men cope with stress by going inward. A major reason men cope with stress inwardly is because of the importance of being problem solvers. Because masculinity includes being capable of fixing things, men feel pressure to be problem solvers. When a problem arises, they may feel that they are supposed to be able to solve it and generally will not talk about it until they have found a solution.

Women, on the other hand, are not under the same pressure as men to be problem solvers. They do not have to be capable of fixing things to be feminine. Women typically need to talk to work through their thoughts and feelings while problem-solving. Talking through problems helps them to work through their feelings and is something they may be more efficient at because they have been doing it since childhood.

Many men are not adept at dealing with or talking about their emotions or feelings. Thus, if a problem or issue arises that requires them to have to deal with their emotions since it is supposedly unmasculine for men to be emotional, this may make communication difficult. Also, because of physiological differences that trigger the fight, flight, or freeze responses, if the communication becomes too intense, some men may become violent, flee—by exiting the situation, or shut down and not communicate at all. If a problem persists over time, they may seek to emotionally distance themselves to cope.

Overall, because men and women often do not know their different motivations for communicating and differences in communication styles, this can sometimes lead to communication break-down and unnecessary power struggles.

TALKING AND LISTENING WITH CARE

Talking and listening with care (TLC) consists primarily of three components: (1) talking, (2) listening, and (3) caring. TLC is the merging of the three components: effective talking and listening with a caring attitude.

A Caring Attitude

When communicating, our attitude reflects our perceptions of and how we feel about the person with whom we are communicating. It reflects whether we think they are important and whether their position or opinion about a matter counts. We can adopt one of two attitudes:

> *"You are not a person of worth—your thoughts and feelings are not important to me."* This can translate into: *"I don't care about you."*

> *Or*

> *"Being created in the divine image of God, you are worthy. I honor and respect you and therefore value your thoughts and feelings."* This can translate into: *"I do care about you."*

Our attitudes may be influenced by past experiences with others, including caregivers, friends, and intimate partners. Since words can create or destroy, what we say can have a boomerang effect which often comes back rather quickly in conflicts. We must also take into consideration how our values influence how we think about things and the things we think are important. Because we see the world and experience it through our value system, when someone does not share these same values, it may distort our perceptions of them. Such perceptions are often reflected in the spirit of our communication. This spirit is reflected in what we say and how we say it.

Extended/Expanded Self or WEUSI

A way to develop a caring attitude is to see your partner as an extension of yourself. Since we all are connected through spirit to the Divine, and we are an extension of the Divine, our communication with one another should reflect this. This is referred to as the *extended self* (Nobles, 1976), *expanded self* (Karenga, 1999), and *WEUSI* (Asante, 1980; Williams, 1981). In communication, the extended or expanded self says, "When I am talking to you, I am talking to myself. I am you and you are me. I should talk to you in the way that I want to be talked to." By incorporating the expanded self, extended self, or WEUSI in our communication, we develop an attitude that conveys: "I" want to communicate in a manner so that "WE" can feel good and strengthened within ourselves and in our relationship. This benefits "US" which includes our children, our families, our communities, our nation, and the world. More fundamentally, you can develop a caring attitude by communicating in a way that shows that you honor and respect your partner and that you honor and respect yourself. To develop a caring attitude, you should also focus on the three Cs of caring.

The Three Cs of Caring

The three Cs of caring are consideration, concern, and commitment.

> *I consider you* a person of value, worthy of my consideration since you have been created in the divine image of God.

> *I am concerned about you* and your happiness and well-being, my own happiness and well-being, and the happiness and well-being of our relationship. I am concerned that you are able to meet your needs, wants, goals, and expectations, and I am able to meet my own.
>
> *I am committed to you* and our relationship.

Incorporating the three Cs in communicating with your partner helps both of you to communicate in ways that honor and respect each other. And honor and respect are necessary to maintain a good relationship.

CONFLICT

We all have needs, wants, goals, and expectations. It is important to distinguish clearly between them:

Need—a condition or situation in which something is necessary

Want—a great desire or a wish for something

Goal—a purpose toward which an endeavor is directed; an objective

Expectation—anticipation of something; to look forward to the probable occurrence or appearance of something

Generally, an issue or problem arises when there is an inconsistency between what we need or want and what we are getting; someone or something is interfering with a goal or an expectation. In essence, an issue or problem arises when our wants, needs, or goals are not being met, or when something or someone falls short of what is anticipated. When this occurs, it may lead to conflict. There are some factors, however, to consider about conflict:

It is inevitable—To be human is to have conflict. We all have different needs, wants, goals, and expectations at different times. No two people are going to share the same needs, wants, or goals at the same time. Therefore, no two people are going to be on the same accord 100 percent of the time.

It may be a blessing—Conflict can be seen as a curse and responded to accordingly, or it can be seen as a blessing. A conflict may be a wake-up call, a message from the spirit world that something is wrong in our lives, or something is going in the wrong direction in our relationship. It may indicate that something needs changing. Conflict may lead you to take steps to make the changes necessary to preserve the relationship.

It is necessary because it:
-Helps you to clarify your own wants, needs, goals, and expectations, and the values underlying them
-Helps you to grow as individuals
-Helps you to grow together.

It is how you handle conflict that matters. Having communication competencies is necessary to resolve conflicts effectively. The goal is to make sure each of your needs, wants, goals, and/or expectations are met, while simultaneously maintaining the integrity of the relationship.

Problems or Issues

Some problems can be resolved and some cannot. It is estimated that close to 70 percent of problems in relationships can- not be resolved. Typically, unresolvable problems are those that stem from differences in worldview and/or values, or deeper issues like trust. It is important to distinguish between the problems that can be resolved and those that cannot be resolved. Then develop strategies to resolve those problems that can be resolved and strategies on how to heal and/or coexist with those that cannot be resolved.

Offensive and Defensive Talk

Conflict resolution consists of trying to resolve a problem or come to some resolution about an issue. Often, when attempting to resolve conflict, we do so by engaging in talk that is offensive and defensive.

Offensive Talk—Although the intent may not be to offend, individuals often have few skills to express their discontent or dissatisfaction when their needs, wants, goals or expectations are not being met. This dissatisfaction combined with a lack of effective skills can lead to communication that can be offensive. Other times because the person has felt disregarded or disrespected in some way, they do intend to offend. The individual wants the other person to feel or experience what he or she is feeling or experiencing. They, therefore, communicate by lashing out, where they hurt, wound, or inflict the same discomfort that they perceive the other person is causing. When one communicates in this manner, they typically put the other individual on the defense.

Defensive Talk—An individual who communicates in an offensive mode may trigger the other person to go into a defensive mode. This defensive mode protects the other person from words that wound or hurt. The other person may also go into an offensive mode by lashing back at the offensive person in an attempt to wound or hurt back. Alternatively, the defender may just shut down emotionally to ward off attacks and say nothing.

Using offensive-defensive talk, neither of the parties is listening; both are talking to defend their respective positions or themselves from attacks by the other. By resorting to this form of communication, they get nowhere. In offensive-defensive talk, one or both partners get hurt. The objective is to get to a place where partners can resolve conflicts respectfully and where the needs, wants, goals, desires, or expectations of both can be met.

Conflict Styles

There are generally three styles that couples use to resolve conflict, all of which may have positive and negative outcomes. As shown in Table 10.3, one or both partners may seek to resolve a problem, but because they lack communication skills, it leads to misunderstandings.

Table 10.3 Conflict Styles

Conflict Style	Both Seek to Resolve Conflict	Neither Seeks to Resolve Conflict	One Seeks to Resolve Conflict; the Other Seeks to Avoid it
Outcome: Positive	Using skills can lead to a healthy resolution	Live with it and just move on	
Outcome: Negative	Without skills, can lead to misunderstandings; may be resolved or left unresolved	Can lead to a buildup of resentment, and eventually, emotional distance	Breeds frustration, resentment, negative perceptions, and eventual emotional distance

If both partners seek to resolve the issue and have communication skills or competencies, they may be able to come to some resolution so that both feel heard, understood, respected, and the relationship is left intact.

In some instances, neither partner may seek to resolve problems or issues. Some couples resort to this when they find that they are unable to resolve problems without things escalating and getting out of control. They may leave the issue unresolved and just move on and continue to have a healthy relationship. On the other hand, avoiding conflict may lead to a buildup of resentment on the part of one or both partners. This may lead one or both to become emotionally distant.

If one partner seeks to resolve problems while the other seeks to avoid them, this may breed frustration on the part of the one who wants to resolve them. He/she may become resentful and subsequently emotionally distant. When either partner begins to disengage from the other emotionally, it may eventually lead to the dissolution of the relationship.

TLC—Three-Step Program

Working through problems or resolving conflicts using TLC includes three steps: (1) Inner talk, (2) Outer talk, and (3) Co-action.

STEP 1. Inner Talk

Inner talk begins with going inside yourself to think about the problem first. What you want to do is: (a) be clear about what is causing the problem or issue; (b) identify exactly what the problem/issue is; (c) work through your thoughts; (d) work through your feeling; and (e) make a decision about what to do.

What is causing the problem/issue? It is important to identify what happened or did not happen that caused the problem/issue to emerge. What need, want, goal or expectation was not met? Be clear and specific about this.

What is the problem or issue? After identifying what caused the problem, the next step is to clearly identify it. It is important to name it; to clearly state what the issue is.

Questions to Consider

- Your interpretation—Is the problem as bad as it seems? Does something need to change, or do you need to change your perceptions?
- Are there things in your past that might be distorting your perceptions?
- What are the underlying factors?
- If it is something that someone is or is not doing, what do you think is motivating it? Is the person aware of it? What might the individual be experiencing that you are not aware of?
- If the individual is aware of it, what might be motivating it?

What are your thoughts? In working through your thoughts, it is important to differentiate how your focus can influence your perceptions. There are two types of focus you can take in thinking about and ultimately approaching an issue.

> *Other-focus* means you focus on the other person. You focus on your thoughts and feelings about the other person. This could lead you to communicate in a manner that blames, criticizes, or judges, which means that you may attack your partner rather than address his/her behavior.
>
> *Self-focus* means you focus on yourself, which may include how you are being affected by the problem. This means your communication will focus on the *effect* your partner's behavior is having on you.

It is important to distinguish clearly between a need and a want. As indicated previously, a need is something that is necessary. In most instances, one may have a difficult time living without it. A want is a desire or wish for something. Because wants are often thought to be needs, this may influence one's perception of the issue or problem, which may also affect one's approach to a resolution. If a want is perceived as a need, individuals may feel they cannot live without what it is that is desired. They may, therefore, become entrenched in their position. Being entrenched can lead to unnecessary power struggles, which can ultimately lead to a break in the relationship. Therefore, it is important to distinguish clearly between a need and a want.

What are your feelings? Feelings stem from the kinds of emotions the issue evokes. Six major emotions include anger, fear, disgust, sadness, surprise, and happiness. You may also experience variations of these emotions or feelings. Emotions and feelings are physiological reactions to our experiences. For example, anger may evoke physiological changes, such as a more rapid heart rate, the rise of adrenaline in the blood, and increased blood pressure. Such a physiological response might trigger a fight, flight, or freeze response. Although it is natural to feel emotional, and they are a natural response to our experiences, many of us are not adept at expressing them. Expressing feelings may be especially difficult for some men since men are not supposed to be weak.

Avoiding dealing with feelings can lead to being physically, emotionally, psychologically, and spiritually unhealthy. Repressing emotions like anger can lead one to experience a host of physical problems stemming from too much adrenaline in the body over a long period of time. Other repressed emotions can lead to a negative outlook on life and make one sick. Not expressing feelings can lead to relationship deterioration because it can:

1. Lead to a build-up of resentments, which can increase conflict and erect invisible walls between partners. One or both individuals may then begin to emotionally distance themself from the relationship;
2. Distort perceptions, where words and behaviors of partners are interpreted more negatively, even when the intent is good;
3. Prohibit productive relationship work, which includes resolution of relationship problems.

It is, therefore, important to develop the skills necessary to express feelings. As indicated, when an experience brings about an emotion or feeling, it is natural for the body to seek to restore balance. The experiences or sensory perceptions that give rise to our emotions or feelings urge us to take action. The next step, then, is to act.

What action will you take? At this point, you will decide whether to: (a) let the problem/issue go or (b) approach your partner so that you can discuss the issue/problem. An important fact to note about inner talk is that you may do it not only while you are awake, but while you are asleep. Sometimes a person may sleep on a problem and by the next day, become clearer about it. What may happen in some instances is that your mind continues to work on the problem subconsciously. Also, your spirit visits other interdimensional realms while you are asleep to seek answers. Thus, when you awake, the answer is clear.

By using inner talk and the guidance from other realms to help you process and sort through your thoughts and feelings about an issue, you may resolve it yourself, or you may decide that it is not as big a deal as you originally thought it was. You may, therefore, have no need to consider it further. If, on the other hand, you find that it is a problem that you cannot work out alone, you may decide that you need to discuss it further with your partner. If you decide you need to talk about it, then the next step is outer talk.

STEP 2. Outer Talk

Outer talk consists of: (a) approaching your partner in a respectful manner; (b) planning to work through the issue; (c) issue talking and listening with care (ITLC), and (d) resolution talking and listening with care (RTLC).

Approaching your partner—Factors to consider when approaching your partner include:

- *Hard approach versus soft approach*—A hard approach is one in which you attack, blame, or accuse, disapprove of, or command your partner. A soft approach is when you do not attack, blame or accuse, disapprove of, or command your partner. You do not want to be offensive; otherwise, it will put your partner in a defensive mode. This can potentially turn the talk into an offensive-defensive match, and nothing gets resolved.
- *Your emotional state*—Are you too emotional or heated about the problem to be able to approach your partner in a way that would avoid hurting his/her feelings or putting him/her on the defense?
- *Timing*—Is this the right time to bring up the problem or issue or might another time be more appropriate? Is it late at night when your partner is too tired to be receptive to you?
- *Difficulties your partner are currently undergoing*—What types of issues might he/she be experiencing that could prohibit him/her from being receptive to your approach in a positive way?

Plan to meet—You will agree on a date and time to meet to talk about the issue. You should decide whether you will discuss it at the time the issue is brought up, or whether another time would be better. It is important to set a date and time that works for both of you.

Issue talking and listening with care (ITLC)—Using the talking and listening with care skills, talk through the problem. Remember:

When
> your partner talks—*you listen* with care and reflect back what he/she has said.

When
> you talk—*your partner listens* with care and reflects back what you have said.

Talk and listen with care remembering that you care about your partner; you are concerned that his/her needs, wants, goals, or expectations are met as well as your own, and that you are committed to the relationship. You should continue to talk and listen, taking turns until both of you have thoroughly shared your thoughts and feelings about the specific issue or problem. Make sure you both have said everything you need to say and have heard and understood everything the other had to say.

Talking Strategies

Use "I" statements versus "you" statements—When using "you" statements, the listener might take it as blaming. This may put him/her on the defensive. Once in the defensive mode, he or she is now in the position to block out what is being said, making it difficult for you to be heard. For example, saying "I feel unloved" versus "You don't love me," does not blame.

The extended self means "I" am also "you"—The objective here is to become each other. Try to see the world from each other's vantage point. Each person should talk to the other person the way they would like to be talked to. Do not offend or hurt.

Focus on your partner's behavior rather than him or her—Be careful not to make attacks on your partner's personhood by name-calling, belittling, criticizing, or judging; accusing or blaming; questioning his or her trustworthiness; disapproving of or showing contempt or disgust, or commanding. People typically will not respond positively if they perceive that they are being attacked. Rather than deal with the issue, they will attempt to defend themselves.

Stay on the subject—Be careful to not stray to extraneous subjects that have nothing to do with the subject at hand.

Do not bring up past issues—Especially if they are not relevant to the problem at hand.

Do not argue over facts—Instead of saying, "You said you would ... " say, "It was my understanding that you would ..."

Avoid statements like "always" and "never"—These statements might lead your partner to focus on the fact that they do not "always" or "never" do something, rather than the real issue.

Listen for and outline the underlying issues that were not so apparent—Decipher and break down the issue(s) and resolve them one by one. You may decide to talk through the underlying issues during the current discussion, or you might decide to meet at another time to talk through the issues that have emerged.

Listening Strategies

Focus on the extended self—This entails trying to understand the thoughts and feelings of your partner. By focusing on the extended self, you become him. Becoming your partner helps you to understand what he may be experiencing. It also helps you to see the world from his vantage point. If your partner feels you care enough to consider what he is thinking and how he is feeling, and that you are trying to see things from his point of view, it makes him feel more comfortable talking to you.

Paraphrase what your partner said—Essentially you should rephrase what your partner has said or what you think she is trying to say. Sometimes it may be good to repeat what she has said, other times rephrase your partner's words using your own words. Be sure the content and meaning are consistent with what she has said.

Reflect what your partner is feeling—To reflect what your partner is feeling means thinking about how you would feel if you were in his/her position. It also means showing empathy. Some examples include:

"So, you feel hurt that I ..."
"You feel disappointed by ..."
"This makes you feel ..."

Resolution talking and listening with care (RTLC)— Using RTLC, both of you should participate in generating possible solutions. There are several steps you can take to reach a resolution.

1. Work to arrive at a possible resolution, putting your ideas on paper.
2. Decide which solutions you cannot live with and eliminate these from the list.
3. Decide on the solutions you can live with.
4. Select the solutions you can live with. It is important at this step to find common ground. Review the list and circle those solutions that you agree are possible, selecting at least three. It is important for you to come to a resolution by compromising: give something to receive something.
5. Select the resolution that is the best fit for both of you.

Checklist for the Resolution

Knox and Schacht (2016) identify five questions to consider in determining whether a resolution is a good one.

1. Is the resolution mutually satisfying for both of you?
2. Is the resolution specific? Are both of you clear about what you are to do, when, where, and how?
3. Is the resolution realistic? Can both of you achieve what has been proposed?
4. Have you specified what will be done if the problem or issue recurs?

5. What strategies have been included to prevent the problem or issue from recurring? (p. 236)

STEP 3. Co-Action

Co-action includes acting together to do the following:

Initiate and carry out the resolution—The solution will actually be implemented. Both of you must remain committed to what you said you would do.

Meet again to evaluate the outcome—Find out whether you have been willing and able to follow through on the resolution, and whether the desired outcome has been achieved.

Factors to Consider

Things might not turn out the way you expect them to—Often our plans seem achievable in the ideal but are not realistic.

Old habits die hard—It is important to incorporate strategies to help you get back on track should either of you fail to follow through on the agreement. This is particularly the case when the resolution involves breaking a habit. Strategies may include ways in which you will remind each other, for example, reminder notes, a gesture, or a statement when one partner forgets.

Whatever strategies you use to help break old habits should be agreed upon by both of you beforehand. Even though you agree on strategies, each of you should be responsible for changing your behavior. If there is a need to revise the strategies, you should use TLC. You may have to revisit the plan if you find that you need to repeat the ITLC and RTLC steps under the TLC three-step program.

HELPING YOUR PARTNER TALK THROUGH A PROBLEM USING TLC

There are instances in which your partner may have a problem or needs to work through his or her thoughts and feelings about an issue. What he or she needs to talk about may have nothing to do with you. It may have to do with work, family, friends, or making a decision about something. In other instances, he or she may need to vent frustration or use you as a sounding board. When we find ourselves in such a situation, our natural response is to help. This leads us to engage in listening and responding that, although the intent is to help, gets in the way.

Carl Rogers, a noted psychologist, found that 80 percent of communication between individuals to be evaluative, interpretative, supportive, probing, and understanding - in that order (Johnson, 2000). How do these methods of listening and responding and the roles we assume to help, hinder us from helping our partners?

Evaluative—When giving an evaluative response, often the individual assumes the role of an adviser. Advising can be helpful in some circumstances, and people may even ask for it in some cases. However, giving advice can be threatening, putting the individual on the defense, particularly when she is just seeking to express her thoughts and feelings. When telling your partner what she ought to do, you are assuming that she does not already know what to do. It can also be perceived that you are being judgmental because it may indicate that your partner has failed at or is not doing something she should be doing. It can also suggest that you know more about the issue than your partner, with the ultimate effect of making her feel inferior.

Interpretive—When giving an interpretive response, many of us assume the role of the therapist. Although many people need psychotherapy, there are professionals for this and a time and place for it. When you assume the role of a therapist, you may start telling your partner what his problem means, his motivation behind it, or what is really going on with him. This may communicate to him that you know more about his motivations than he does. The interpretive response can also be threatening and put your partner on the defense.

Supportive—Although for many, their intentions are to be supportive of their partner, when they are experiencing a problem, what often happens is they end up minimizing what they are feeling. This happens when you say things that seem to indicate that you lack interest, understanding, or empathy. For example, your partner might express that she feels bad or hurt about something and you make statements like, "That's life," or "You got to take the bitter with the sweet." You may also minimize her feelings when making statements like, "You need to snap out of it," or "You need to get over it and move on." These kinds of responses have the effect of saying to your partner, "You should not feel the way you are feeling"; they can be threatening and even hurtful.

Probing—Although asking questions can make your partner feel that you are interested in what he is saying and deepen your understanding, it can also get in the way of effective communication. If you are going to ask questions for clarity, it is important to ask open-ended questions. This allows your partner more freedom to talk about his thoughts and feelings. Also, it is important to not ask "why" questions, because most people cannot explain the reasons that they do things. It may make your partner defensive, because asking him why he did something may communicate disapproval or criticism. Because some "why" questions may put your partner in the position to have to justify his decision, it may prohibit him from further exploring his thoughts and feelings about the problem.

Understanding—An understanding listener, listens to his/her partner with care, and reflects what he/she has said. This communicates to your partner that you are interested in helping him/her process through his/her thoughts and feelings about a problem or issue.

All of these communication techniques may be useful at some time or another and can be effective when used under the right circumstances. None of them are good or bad; it is the failure to recognize which listening technique is most appropriate that interferes with our communication and the building of a quality relationship.

In addition, overuse of any of the methods can be a barrier to effective communication. It has been found that "When a person uses one category of response as much as 40 percent of the time, then others see them as *always* responding that way" (Johnson, 2000, p. 232). By using caring and understanding listening strategies discussed here, one would simply reflect what one's partner has said. Let us take Kenya and Kenyatta, for example, looking at how Kenyatta might respond to Kenya as outlined in Table 10.4.

Kenya expresses:

"I am so overweight. I need to go on a diet. I feel so unattractive. Ugh, I can't stand the way I look. It makes me feel bad about myself."

As shown in Table 10.4, by being a caring and understanding listener, Kenyatta has allowed Kenya to talk about what she is thinking and how she is feeling without having to feel guilty about her feelings, answer a lot of questions, defend herself, or be told what is wrong with her. Kenya feels good that she has someone who will listen and understands her. Also, because Kenyatta used caring and understanding listening, it helped Kenya feel connected to him; and therefore, she feels closer to him. This helps in the building of a quality relationship.

Table 10.4 Kenyatta Helping Kenya Talk Through a Problem

Kenyatta's Responses	Effect on Kenya
Evaluative: I did not want to say it, but I think you should be concerned about your weight. Maybe you should think about joining the gym.	Although Kenya thinks that she has a weight problem and feels unattractive, she may have not known that he also sees her as unattractive, which makes her feel worse.
Interpretive: Your problem is that	This statement might put

you are too focused on your physical appearance. Maybe you should get help with your self-esteem instead of your weight.	Kenya on the defense. She may now feel compelled to defend his accusation that she is too focused on physical appearance and that she has issues with self-esteem.
Supportive: You should stop feeling bad about your weight and look at the blessings you have.	This statement might communicate to Kenya that she should not feel the way she does. It may undermine how she is feeling.
Probing: Why do you think that you are overweight?	Kenya has to explain what she is thinking and how she feels about her weight.
Understanding: So, you think you are overweight. You feel unattractive. Is there anything I can do to support you or make you feel better? Or he could also just simply say, "I love you the way you are"	Kenya feels heard, understood, loved, and supported.

In conclusion, communication is essential to our survival. TLC includes communication competencies in talking, listening, and showing a caring attitude. Effective talking includes using constructive word and body talk and being sure they are consistent. Effective listening is listening with care and understanding. It means filtering out negative perceptions so that they are not reflected in your attitude. Showing a caring attitude includes focusing on the three Cs: consideration for your partner; showing that you are concerned that his/her needs, wants, and goals are met as well as your own; and showing commitment to the relationship. The TLC three-step program includes working through inner talk (your thoughts and feelings), outer talk (using strategies to approach your partner, ITLC, and RTLC), and co-action (moving together to carry out the resolution). By developing an understanding of how to communicate effectively and developing competencies in these areas, you can work through your individual issues, and solve problems you share mutually.

When you are able to navigate through lower levels of communication, solving problems that are individually or mutually shared, you can spend more time and energy on higher levels of communication—that which is mutually expansive. Exchanging ideas helps you to merge and become one. Expansive communication is the key to spiritual growth, and spiritual growth is the key to a satisfying and fulfilling life together. With good communication skills, more energy and time can be devoted to carrying out your purpose for this lifetime and your spiritual evolvement.

Chapter 10 Exercises

> # *Talking and Listening With Care*

These exercises are to help you and your partner increase awareness of your communication styles, and to improve how you communicate and resolve conflict. They include an exercise to help you talk and listen through an issue using the TLC three-step program.

> **EXERCISE 10.1** *Caregivers Communication & Conflict Styles*

1. Write M (me) for yourself, and MP (my partner, if you have a partner) on the line that best describes your parents/caregivers' communication, conflict resolution, and relationship styles.

_____They argued passionately. However, they were still able to resolve their conflicts.

_____They discussed issues in a controlled and calm manner. They disagreed but agreed to disagree. They generally let each other know their opinion but did so respectfully. They validated each other and showed that they valued each other's opinions.

_____One parent would argue, dominating the conversation, while the other parent would say little or nothing, tune him/her out, or just leave.

_____They engaged in offensive and defensive arguments where they would talk at the same time, with one or the other yelling. One or both of them would attack the other, blame, call names, accuse, and/or belittle.

_____When a problem or issue arose neither sought to discuss it. They just believed that it would eventually work itself out and/or that if they prayed on it, it would resolve itself.

_____I was raised by one caregiver. This does not apply to me.

_____Other _____

2. In the space below, expand on how your parents communicated and resolved conflict, the type of relationship they had, and your thoughts and feelings about it.

_____
_____
_____
_____
_____

> **EXERCISE 10. 2. *Your Communication & Conflict Styles***

1. Check the box that best describes the way you and your partner usually communicate and resolve conflicts.

☐ We argue passionately. However, we still respect each other and can resolve our problems.

☐ We discuss issues in a controlled and calm manner. We disagree but agree to disagree. We generally let each other know our opinion but do so respectfully. We validate each other and show that we value and respect each other's opinions.

☐ One of us does most of the talking, essentially dominating the conversation, while the other says little or nothing, tunes the other out, or just leaves.

☐ We engage in offensive and defensive arguments where we talk at the same time and one or the other yells. One or both of us attacks the other, blames, calls the other names, and/or puts the other down.

☐ When a problem arises, neither of us seeks to discuss it, and this is acceptable to us. We believe that things will eventually work themselves out. One or both of us may believe that if we turn it over to God, He will take care of it.

☐ Other_____

2. In what ways are your communication and conflict styles similar to or different from your parents?
_____
_____
_____
_____
_____

3. Put a circle (and a square if you have a partner) around the number that corresponds to how often you do the following when attempting to resolve conflict.

Style of Communication	Very Little Very Often
a. Attack by name-calling, belittling, criticizing and/or judging	1 2 3 4 5
b. Blame and/or accuse	1 2 3 4 5
c. Question the other's trustworthiness or credibility	1 2 3 4 5
d. Disapprove of, show contempt, or disgust	1 2 3 4 5
e. Command, demand, or attempt to boss the other person around	1 2 3 4 5
f. Frown, look disgusted, and/or avoid eye contact	1 2 3 4 5
g. Yell and/or scream	1 2 3 4 5
h. Approach in a threatening way	1 2 3 4 5
i. Use other negative body language, e.g., act like do not care, not paying attention, etc.	1 2 3 4 5

4. Put a circle (and a square if you have a partner) around the number that corresponds to how you feel when you attempt to communicate and resolve conflict using the methods in the table below.

When we attempt to communicate and resolve an issue, I/my partner generally feels ...	Not at All				A Lot
	1	2	3	4	5
Disrespected	1	2	3	4	5
Disregarded	1	2	3	4	5
Belittled	1	2	3	4	5
Invalidated	1	2	3	4	5
Criticized	1	2	3	4	5
Blamed	1	2	3	4	5
Judged	1	2	3	4	5
Misunderstood	1	2	3	4	5
Anxious/worried	1	2	3	4	5
Hurt	1	2	3	4	5
Sad	1	2	3	4	5
Angry					

5. Describe further how you generally communicate and how it makes you feel.

_____
_____
_____
_____
_____

6. Check the boxes that correspond with what you wish your partner would do more or less of, and what your partner wishes you would do more or less of when communicating and/or resolving conflict.

I wish my partner would...	*My partner wishes I would...*
☐ Talk more	☐ Talk more
☐ Listen more	☐ Listen more
☐ Be more open with his/her feelings	☐ Be more open with my feelings
☐ Be less sensitive	☐ Be less sensitive
☐ Lighten up some and not take things so seriously	☐ Lighten up some and not take things so seriously
☐ Have more of a sense of humor	☐ Have more of a sense of humor
☐ Not take what I say so personally	☐ Not take what he/she says so personally
☐ Value my advice	☐ Value his/her advice
☐ Respect my opinion	☐ Respect his/her opinion
☐ Stop trying to force his/her opinion on me	☐ Stop trying to force my opinion on him/her
☐ Not get upset when I do not agree with him/her	☐ Not get upset when he/she does not agree with me
☐ Stop trying to control me and/or the conversation	☐ Stop trying to control him/her and/or the conversation
☐ Not punish me if I do not agree with him/her	☐ Not punish him/her if he/she does not agree with me

7. Discuss what you would like to change about how you communicate and resolve conflict.

_____
_____
_____
_____
_____

> **EXERCISE 10. 3. *Your Processing Styles***

1. For the statements below, put a circle (and a square for your partner) around the number that corresponds to how often this

method is used to work through your thoughts and feelings when a problem or issue arises.

When an issue or problem arises I/my partner usually…	Not Often				Very Often
	1	2	3	4	5
a. Talk about it with my family members, friends, or someone other than partner first	1	2	3	4	5
b. Pray and/or really think about it before talking about it	1	2	3	4	5
c. Do not like to talk about it until a solution is found	1	2	3	4	5
d. Talk about it with partner as soon as it arises	1	2	3	4	5
e. Spend a lot of time thinking about it first before talking about it with partner	1	2	3	4	5
f. Do something to forget about the problem or issue, hoping it will just go away	1	2	3	4	5
g. Need space to reflect on thoughts and feelings	1	2	3	4	5
h. Do not bother with or think about it	1	2	3	4	5
i. Just let the problem work itself out	1	2	3	4	5

Question	Processing Style
b, c, g	Inner processor
a & d	Outer processor
f, h, i	Avoider
Mixed	May process some things internally and other things externally, and some things may be avoided

2 Based on your responses to the questions above, describe which processing styles best characterizes you and your partner?

_____
_____

3. Describe how you generally process problems or issues.
If a problem or issue arises, I usually... while my partner usually...

_____
_____

4. If your processing styles are different, describe how you usually deal with it. How do you feel about the way it is dealt with and if something needs to be changed, what will you do?

_____
_____
_____
_____

EXERCISE 10. 4. *Resolve a Conflict Using TLC*

Use the TLC three-step program to solve or work through an issue you are currently experiencing.

1. Step One: Inner Talk
i. Identify the issue/problem: Exactly what is the problem?

_____
_____
_____

ii. What caused the problem? What occurred or did not occur that led to the problem?
_____
_____
_____

iii. Mind Talk: What are your thoughts?
   <u>Self-focus:</u> *(Focus on your thoughts of how your partner's actions affect you rather than what you think about him/her)*
   <u>My thoughts are</u>. . . *and my partner's thoughts might be…*
_____
_____
_____

iv. Heart Talk: What are your feelings?
   <u>Self-focus:</u> *(Focus on how your partner's actions make you feel rather than how you feel about him/her)*
   <u>My feelings are.</u> . . *and my partner's feelings might be. . .*
_____
_____
_____

2. Step Two: Outer Talk

i. Approach your partner (if you are not already doing this exercise together).

   a. <u>Soft Approach</u>: *(Using a soft approach, construct what you will say when you approach your partner)*
   _____
   _____

ii. Plan to work through the issue. However, before approaching your partner, consider whether this is the appropriate time to bring up the problem.

    a. My/my partner's emotional state about the issue is. . . and the best time to bring this up might be. (i.e., when you are less emotionally charged about the issue or after you have had some time to think about it).

    _____
    _____

    b. Difficulties I/my partner am/is facing now. . . and the best time to discuss this might be. . . (i.e., when you/your partner are/is feeling better)

    _____
    _____

iii. You should agree to a date and time to discuss the problem. We will meet and discuss the issue on *(date and time)*

    _____

iv. Issue talking and listening with care (ITLC)

    c. Identify and describe at least three *talking strategies* you will use:

    _____
    _____
    _____

    d. Identify three *listening strategies* you will use:

    _____
    _____
    _____

    e. After discussing the issue using ITLC, describe the underlying issues that emerged:

    _____
    _____
    _____

v. Indicate when you will deal with the issues that emerged.

Issue		
a. _____ _____	☐ Now	☐ Another time _____ Date/Time
a. _____ _____	☐ Now	☐ Another time _____ Date/Time
a. _____ _____	☐ Now	☐ Another time _____ Date/Time

iv. Resolution Talking and Listening with Care (RTLC)—indicate your and your partner's needs, wants, goals, and/or expectations in the spaces below.

    f. *Your* wants, needs, expectations, and/or goals

_____

_____

    g. *Your Partner's* wants, needs, expectations, and/or goals

_____

_____

Possible Solutions

    h. Brainstorming - write down possible solutions

_____

_____

    i. Write down solutions you/your partner *cannot* live with

_____

_____

    j. Write down your final solution

_____

_____

3. Step Three: Co-Action

i. Your plans *(write down exactly what each party will do)*:
_____
_____
_____

ii. Possible reminders for change *(put a star by the ones you actually use)*:
a._____
b._____
c._____

iii. What are your plans if the solution needs to be revised?
_____
_____

iv. <u>Solution checklist</u>: Check the boxes if your solution meets those criteria. If it does not meet all the criteria below, you may need to revise it. The solution:
- ☐ Is mutually beneficial to both of us and the relationship
- ☐ Is specific; we are both clear on what each is to do—when, where, and how
- ☐ Is realistic; both of us can achieve what we have proposed to do
- ☐ Includes strategies to keep the problem from recurring
- ☐ Includes ways to remind each other of what we are supposed to be doing

---

EXERCISE 10.5. *Communication Narrative*

---

1. Describe additional things about the way you and your partner communicate and resolve conflicts and changes you would like to make.
_____
_____
_____
_____
_____

Additional Notes

11

Sexual Healing and Bliss

Big screen, smart televisions, computers, internet, and other technology of the information/experience age, enables us to manufacture many of our experiences. Although technology provides us with many benefits including the opportunity to transcend our own worlds and engage with the worlds of others, the question is what worlds are we engaging in and what effect are they having on our physical, psycho-emotional, and spiritual health? More importantly, what effect are they having on our sexual health?

Living in societies in which many of our experiences are manufactured may make us feel compelled to repress certain aspects of ourselves so that we are not only able to survive but thrive. But just as our experiences are manufactured, we may manufacture a personality to fit in. Yao Morris (2008) in his book, *Awakening the Master Feminine Principle,* refers to this as the *counterfeit personality.* According to Morris, a primary factor in being able to fit into market-driven societies based on money, power, and scarcity is the repression of our natal masculine and feminine principles, physically, psychically, and *energetically*. The degree to which these principles are repressed may be the extent to which the counterfeit personality has taken residence. The degree to which the counterfeit personality has taken residence may mean that we have shut down not only the masculine and feminine principles but the natal blueprint for why we incarnated this time. And when we broadcast to the world our counterfeit personality, we begin to attract others who are living through their counterfeit personality. When two counterfeit personalities get together, a great deal of time is spent working through the stuff this is made of. Some of this gets played out in our interaction styles including in the bedroom.

Modern technology has also bought hand-held computers in the form of iPads and smartphones. These products provide us the opportunity to stay connected to the world around us. But while we are staying connected to the world, we are disconnected from those immediately around us. More importantly, we are disconnected from ourselves. One of the places in which this disconnect may also play out is in the bedroom.

To move towards sexual health and healing, it is important to first examine societal ideas about gender; how these ideas affect how we develop physically, psychically, and energetically; the factors that have caused the counterfeit personality to take resident; how these factors may be preventing us from being our authentic selves; how this may undermine our health including our sexual health; and how all this may affect our sexual interaction. Once we understand these factors, we can move towards healing so that our authentic selves can emerge; this is necessary for sexual health. When sexual healing takes place, it can lead to health in all aspects of our lives, which is necessary for relationship health.

SEX & GENDER

The counterfeit personality reveals itself in the areas of sex and gender. In societies that bombard us with market-driven ideas about masculinity and femininity particularly when those ideas are not healthy, may not only cause us to have an unhealthy approach to gender but cause us to shut down our natal masculine and/or feminine faculties. Shutting down these faculties may also mean that we are repressing the blueprint to express ourselves fully.

Although there are many ideas about sex and gender, there are generally four primary components to what it means to be a man or woman in a given society. These include sex—based on the biological distinction of being male or female; gender—which are socially defined ideas of masculinity and femininity; gender identity—how one identifies, e.g., man or woman; and gender roles—socially prescribed roles based on the previous three. Although gender studies indicate that the biological distinction of sex—male and female is distinct from gender—masculinity, and femininity; and that the latter is socially constructed, the question is, to what extent are Western constructions around gender manufactured by limited material based (biology) understanding of these principles? Do biological distinctions lay an energetic foundation for a natal blueprint for how the feminine expresses itself? Is there a natal blueprint for how the masculine expresses itself? And if this is the case, how do we nurture these expressions so that these two polarities may join for maximum expression and experience?

Indigenous societies, particularly traditional African societies, may provide some clues. Among the Dogon of West Africa, when a child is born although it may have the biological distinctions of male or female, energetically, it is possessed with both the masculine and feminine principles. These principles are rather fluid, making the child for all practical purposes androgynous; moreover, as the child possesses both principles, this makes him/her rather unstable. It is through rituals of rites of passage that the child is physically, psychically, and *energetically* nurtured or socialized to their outward biological expression as a boy or girl. Rites of passage helped to eliminate confusion around gender identity, which is particularly important for a society and its members to function healthily. In other cultures, for example, among the Dagara of West African, when a boy or girl has strong masculine or feminine proclivities opposite to their sex, despite efforts to make them socially a boy or girl, they are believed to be special people because they have the ability to access both the masculine and feminine principles in ways that most people are not. These individuals are considered gatekeepers, people who are comparable to shamans in many cultures because they have access to both the physical and spiritual worlds and are seen as mediators between the two genders. The same is the case for some Native American peoples. Such individuals were referred to as "two spirit," and were given the status of shamans. So, although we generally want to classify people into discreet categories of boy and girl, there are those who are somewhere in the middle or who possess both; they are referred to as the "third" sex or transgendered in the West; although such descriptions are not based in spirituality. Whatever the case may be, people need to be all of whom they are to have the maximum sexual experience and be the best of who they can be.

Puberty

Puberty is when the secondary traits of the biology of the male and female begin to manifest. Puberty is initiated when the hypothalamus gland releases signals to the pituitary gland which releases luteinizing and follicle-stimulating hormones. These hormones stimulate the production of the sex hormones by the gonads; estrogen for girls and testosterone for boys, which causes physical changes leading to sexual reproduction maturation. While the hormones are awakening the masculine and feminine principles psychically and energetically, the boy and girl are also receiving messages from society about what it means to be a boy and girl and what it means to be masculine and feminine.

Although in the US masculinity and femininity are multidimensional, fundamentally, masculinity is associated with strength, and femininity is associated with beauty. Where they feel they are on the hierarchy of strength (boys) and beauty (girls) will affect their feelings of adequacy in these areas and ultimately their sexual maturation and development. In addition, if other messages from the family, community and the broader society around gender and sexuality are negative and not conveyed in healthy ways, the boy or girl may begin to shut down the master feminine/masculine faculty for continued healthy sexual development.

Market Masculinities and Femininities
Overvaluation of the Masculine
In cultures throughout the world, particularly in the West, including those that have been greatly influenced by the West, masculinity is

more valued. The fact that in Western-based world religions, e.g., Judaism, Christianity, and Islam, God is masculine and there is a lack of the feminine speaks to the high value placed on masculinity in these cultures. But although masculinity is highly valued, constructions of masculinity are not necessarily healthy for men. Manufactured ideas of masculinity are shown in popular media where men are portrayed as wealthy, powerful, violent, and disrespectful to women (which reflects the low value placed on the feminine). In superhero representations, for example, men are portrayed (and now women) as violent and destructive and these themes get played over and over again. Because the masculine is so highly valued, it is not surprising that both men and women focus more on the masculine aspects of themselves and suppress the feminine.

Suppression of the Feminine

As indicated, femininity at its most fundamental level is associated with beauty. If a girl feels that she is not beautiful, it is going to affect how she feels about herself early in her development and how she grows into a woman. A factor in the construction of gender is the fine line between femininity and sexuality; U.S. culture has difficulty distinguishing between the two. This particularly shows in consumer capitalism, where sex, which is often sold by peddling images of women and their body parts, is used to sell just about everything. Because of the merging of materialism, femininity, sexuality, and women's bodies, some women feel that they cannot be feminine without broadcasting sexuality, which they want to avoid, to avoid being perceived as a whore, or other culturally specific negative epithets, like "hoochies," "hos," and "freaks" that are used to describe African American women. In addition, misogynistic overtones and violence against women exist throughout the world. Women shut down their feminine sides to avoid potentially putting themselves in harm's way. Additionally, is the difficulty women find with expressing their feminine side when it is not being nurtured. When a woman has to express masculine traits to survive in a male-dominated world, without material and emotional support, it is difficult to express her feminine side. The result is that the feminine becomes suppressed and so does her sexuality.

Sexual Repression Myths

U.S. society experiences sexual schizophrenia. Sex is pervasive and used to sell just about everything, but then we are taught to feel shame and/or guilt about it. Sexual repression began with myths in early America. During the Victorian period, women were seen as not having a sex drive and were expected to be pure, chaste, and modest and to help their husbands control their own passions for the sake of society.[1] In the early 20th century, Sigmund Freud helped to debunk the notion that women were passionless creatures without a sex drive by finding that they have two types of orgasms: clitoral and vaginal. However, he continued to perpetuate repressive myths by determining that the clitoral organism crippled women, rendering them indifferent to intercourse, and men were encouraged to stay away from it.

The sexuality of men was also repressed. Men were taught that one ounce of semen was equivalent to 40 ounces of blood, and the loss of too much semen could cause debilitation, disease, and death. It was thought that every time a man ejaculated; he ran the risk of disease of the nervous system. A host of diseases were thought to result from masturbation including dementia, insanity, blindness, pimples, hair loss, and suicidal tendencies. Foods suggested to help extinguish sexual desire and curtail masturbation were Graham crackers and Kellogg's cornflakes.

As Victorianism eroded, it gave rise to a new cultural ethos, and views about sexuality began to change. For men, the values of sexual continence and control were replaced with sex as recreation. For women, Masters and Johnson's found that they were not only as excitable as men and could reach an orgasm just as quickly, but that they were capable of multiple orgasms. It was also found that women could have vaginal orgasms through stimulation of the Grafenbergh

---

[1] The Victorian era is a period in England between 1837 and 1901 (during the reign of Queen Victoria), where emphasis was placed on strict moral standards, modesty, prudishness, and sexual restraint.

or G-spot, an area just under the hymen. The birth control movement, advancements in reproductive technology, women's movements, and the feminist movement all contributed not only to the liberation of women in general but also to the liberation of their sexuality. Despite how views have changed, myths still linger, and many men and women are still affected by them.

Body Esteem

As indicated, beauty underlies femininity in the construction of gender for women. A major factor in how women feel about sex is how they feel about their bodies. Because of the commercialization of women's bodies and body parts, many women feel uncomfortable with sex because they do not feel good about how they look. Women are bombarded with market-driven ideal standards of beauty. If they are not thin or if they do not have a Coca-Cola bottle shape, they may not feel good about themselves. Men are also bombarded with idea standards and if they are not tall, muscular, or have big phalluses, they may not feel good about themselves either. If we do not feel good about our bodies and/or have low body esteem, it can have a deadening effect on our sexuality. It is important to feel good about our bodies to feel good about sex and sexuality.

Past Experiences

Both men and women are victims of sexual abuse. Those who have not personally had such experiences may have family members and other loved ones who have been victims of such abuse. Such experiences can leave deep wounds. Both men and women have also undergone a cycle of entering and out of relationships causing them to experience a great deal of pain. Such experiences can cause them to shut down emotionally and sexually. It is important to explore childhood and adult experiences to discover how these experiences may be affecting one's ability to have a healthy sexual attitude and a healthy sex life.

Sexual/Reproductive Dysfunctions

What potentially are the outcomes of negative social conditioning and past experiences on sexual and reproductive health? In combination with the unnatural ways in which we try to fit into the machine culture, including the food we eat, and the air we breathe, the physical and psycho-emotional manifestations reveal themselves in some of the sexual dysfunctions experienced by men and women briefly shown in Table 11.1 below.

Table 11.1 Sexual/Reproductive Dysfunctions

Women	Men
-Premenstrual syndrome (PMS)	-Rapid ejaculation—caused by problems in the parasympathetic nervous system
-Menstrual cramps	
-Heavy bleeding	
-Fibroid tumors	-Erectile dysfunction
-Early menopause	-Lack of interest in sex
-Dyspareunia (painful sex)	-Impotence
-Lack of Interest in Sex	
-Unable to Lubricate	
-Difficulty achieving an orgasm	
-Infertility	

SEXUAL HEALING

Being clear about how all the factors outlined above have affected our sexual health is necessary to start the healing process. Moving forward, however, starts with being able to communicate openly and honestly about sexuality, and being aware of and engaging in practices that promote healing.

Communication

Sex is a form of communication and is merely another way of expressing ourselves. However, because we live in a society that sends conflicting messages around sexuality, and because sexual repression makes us feel shame and guilt about it, some people have difficulty communicating about sexuality in healthy ways. Patricia Love and Jo Robinson in *Hot Monogamy* (2012), note that most people do not talk directly and honestly *about* sex (p. 43). They talk *around* sex (p. 43). The self-defeating ways in which we talk around sex can be summarized as follows:

How we communicate our interest—Many couples use "veiled comments, euphemisms, winks, sighs, gibes, jokes, put-downs, lies, and code words" to express their interest in sex (p. 43). Others use impersonal overtures saying things like "I'm horny" or "I want some," rather than letting their partner know they are interested in them, by saying things like "I want to make love with you (pp. 45-46)."

How we communicate our disinterest—When one partner may not be feeling up to sex, some ways in which they may communicate about it includes saying things like, "You need to get some sleep," or using excuses and/or preconditions that have to be met for sex. For example, saying things like, "When the kids are asleep," "When I am not feeling fat or bloated," "When Monday night football is over," "On the weekend," etc. (pp. 45-46).

Not communicating at all—Some things we fail to communicate includes our unhappiness about an aspect of our sex lives, e.g., frequency differences, our partner's level of interest or disinterest, and how we feel about it, what we like or do not like, and what feels good and does not feel good. We may also avoid topics that are uncomfortable to talk about like the inability to achieve an orgasm, oral sex, masturbation, sexual fantasies, HIV, a partner's hygiene, etc. Failure to communicate about issues around sexuality may stem from wanting to avoid hurting our partners' feelings, or because we feel embarrassed or ashamed about some aspect of ourselves or sexuality (pp. 47-48).

Communicating in hurtful ways—When we allow our frustrations to build up and come off as being critical or sarcastic it can be more even more hurtful (pp. 52-54).

If we are unable to talk openly and honestly about sex, it makes it difficult to have a good sex life. To move towards sexual health, it is therefore important to be able to talk openly and honestly about sex.

Second Puberty

According to Morris (2008), healing many of the sexual dysfunctions we experience can begin with setting into motion practices to awaken the natal blueprint—that is recall the program in our DNA for expression of the masculine and feminine principles. The sex gene that distinguishes males from females and the aspect of consciousness that awakens them is the master masculine and feminine faculties. Second puberty is awakening the master and feminine faculties that may have been shut down during and after puberty. This awakening can begin with deconstructing the counterfeit personality and employing energy practices from Tantra and Traditional Chinese Medicine (TCM).

Deconstructing the Counterfeit Personality

The counterfeit personality is defined by Morris (2008) as the difference between the personality attributes we have developed and those we were born with. It is a structure that gets lodged into the auric field and controls the energy core and ranges from mild to acute, to chronic, to severe. In the mild or acute stages, aspects of our authentic selves are still present, and the counterfeit aspect of ourselves interferes in our relationships. When it is chronic or severe, the counterfeit personality has taken over and we are standing on the sidelines.

If you recall, when there is a wound to either of the physical, emotional, or mental bodies, it leaves an energetic wound, in the form of a crystal that is recorded at the cellular and potentially DNA levels. Thoughts and emotions around dogma and manufactured and/or false belief systems can also leave lasting energetic imprints. Deconstructing the counterfeit personality entails healing from negative experiences and trauma, overcoming hang-ups around sexuality including stereotypes and myths, and misperceived notions of body type and beauty standards, and letting go of manufactured, narrow, and rigidly defined dogma, ideas, and belief systems, including those around gender. Deconstructing the counterfeit personality is necessary for the authentic self to emerge. When the authentic self emerges, it can lead to sexual health and a fulfilling sex life.

Tantra

Tantra, a Sanskrit word, means to weave, stretch, and expand. The practice of tantra is thought to have originated with the Dravidians (Black African descendent people) who flourished in the Indus valley in India some 6000 years ago. It evolved to include spiritual practices of yoga, meditation, and mantras to promote health and increase consciousness. In the West, Tantra or Neotantra has come to be associated with techniques for cultivating a more fulfilling sexual relationship. For the purposes of this work, Tantra is the science and practice of awakening the higher sexual attributes from their dormant state. It includes diet and exercise, meditation, energy healing, reflexology, and other practices. Ultimately the goal of Tantra is to awaken one to the natal blueprint in their DNA; their authentic self, so that they can relate to their partner as the highest and best version of themself, which can lead to sexual bliss and spiritual evolvement.

Yin and Yang

To begin the process of sexual healing it is important to understand the principles of yin and yang. In one of the oldest doctrines from Egypt, the creator finding nowhere upon which to stand, created itself, and then goes on to create all forms. When creating itself, it first makes two; creating duality with two polarities that are complementary to each other and are thought to be the basis of all of life. This duality is referred to as yin and yang in Traditional Chinese Medicine (TCM) and is complementary and opposing forces that are interdependent and in constant motion. Some of the ways in which these forces express themselves are shown in Table 11.2.

Although yin is generally associated with femininity and yang with masculinity, the reality is that all of life including men and women possess both yin and yang and these principles are present throughout the entire body system, both physically and energetically. Although they are female in their physical make-up, some women may naturally have more yang psychically and energetically. Some men may have and exhibit more yin. The problem is when society places more emphasis on the yang than the yin side of life, so that one's natural inclination may be repressed, and now there are more masculinized or yang men and women. If a woman is expressing her yang side, but it is her destiny to attract a yang-dominated male, then because she is broadcasting her yang side, she may be repelling what it is she needs and wants to attract. It is necessary to balance the yin and yang so that whatever is programmed in one's DNA or natal blueprint, can express itself so that one can attract the right person.

Table 11.2 Yin and Yang

	Yin/Feminine	Yang/Masculine
Cosmic Body	Moon	Sun
Direction	Inward	Outward
Element	Water	Fire
Temperature	Cold	Hot
Disposition	Receptive	Arousal
Brain Hemisphere	Right	Left

Diet & Exercises

Proper diet and exercises are necessary to resume second puberty and awaken the master faculties for sexual health. Dietary practices include foods, herbs, and vitamins to help cleanse and strengthen those body functions that need healing. Although a proper diet, in general, is necessary, some foods that help restore sexual health are outlined below (Morris, 2008).

- ***Vitale water***—a gallon a week of $H_{12}O_6$ water, with an Alkaline pH of 6.8 to 7.8. This is necessary for the kidneys to neutralize and stabilize waste in the blood. Mineral drops can be purchased to

add to water; also, there are pH Alkaline strips that can be purchased to check the alkaline levels in the water.
- *Vegetable drinks*—with an emphasis on roots, e.g., beets, radishes, carrots
- *Vitamins*—C-4000-6000 mg & iron
- *Oils*—foods with Omega oils, flaxseed, etc.
- *Amino Acids*—to help restore depleted essence or Jing (discussed in more detail in this chapter)

Meditation
Meditation should also be practiced. The goal of meditation for purposes of sexual health is focused on shutting down left-brain thinking and opening channels so the energy can flow to the right brain. This helps to open the channels in the meridians so that sexual energy can flow through.

The Energy Body
Energy work entails a number of healing modalities to help un-block energy so that the vital force or qi can flow. The energy practices outlined in previous chapters should be employed regularly and consistently. However, for the purposes of sexual healing, energy healing focuses on qigong, reflexology, table work, and other practices. The energy body consists of seven chakras, seven layers of the aura, the endocrine system, and the core energy body. There are two types of energy. The first type is vital energy referred to as vital or life force. This energy flows through the body through the seven chakras, 12 major meridians, and 72,000 nadis (in Tantra).

There are three main nadis: Ida, Pingala, and Sushumna. The Sushumna Nadi is around the central nervous center and connects the root chakra to the crown chakra. Pingala lies to the right of the spine, relates to the sympathetic nervous system, and represents male, yang, or positive energy. Ida lies to the left of the spine relates to the parasympathetic nervous system, and represents female, yin or negative energy.² The serpent energy or what is referred to as Kundalini, is the energy that sets at the base of the spine in a coiled-like fashion. When it is awakened properly and slowly through the seven chakras, it can lead to an expanded state of consciousness, bliss state, and liberation.³ The energy body is briefly defined below.

Seven Chakras—include the root, sacrum, solar plexus, heart, throat, brow, and crown. The chakras that are the focus for tantra work are the sacrum and heart chakras.

Twelve Meridians—include the lungs, large intestine, stomach, spleen, heart, small intestine, bladder, kidney, pericardium, triple warmer, gallbladder, liver, conception vessel or ren, and the governor vessel. Most energy work in Tantra focuses on the kidney/bladder, and heart/pericardium meridians.

Auric Field—has seven layers that correspond to the seven chakras and reflects them.

The Endocrine System—the seven major glands are the interface between the core energy body and the chakras. They include the adrenal glands (root chakra), ovaries and testes (sacral chakra), pancreas (solar plexus chakra), thyroid (throat chakra), thymus (heart chakra), pituitary gland, (third eye/brow chakra), and pineal gland (crown chakra).

The Energy Core—the central tower controls the energy body. It has two components: operation and architecture. The operations include the lifestyle practices we engage in to control its operations.

---

[2] The caduceus symbol in modern Western medicine is what the Kundalini rising looks like. The caduceus is thought to be derived from ancient Egypt and represents the staff of Tehuti (Egyptian god of wisdom—later represented as Hermes in Greek esoterism). The two serpents (symbols of wisdom and protection in ancient Egypt) represent the slow rising of the two polarities of masculine and feminine energies (through the Sushumna, Ida, and Pingala—pathways in Tantra) around the seven major chakras. The bird at the top of the caduceus represents liberation of the soul.

[3] If the Kundalini energy is awakened too quickly, which can occur during intense yoga exercises, mental trauma, stress, accidents, and near-death experiences, etc. it can lead to what is referred to as a Kundalini crisis, which can subsequently lead to physical and/or psychological problems. One would be wise to work with a teacher to assist with the proper awakening of Kundalini energy.

The architecture is the structure of the energy core, which is the subconscious mind which can be restructured through conscious intent to control the information we take in through our conscious mind. The energy core is where the work is done to deconstruct the counterfeit personality (Morris, 2008).

The Endocrine System & Hormones

In *Conversations with Ogotemelli*, Marcel Griaule (1970), indicates that the Dogon of West Africa believed the sex organ [to be] the high altar of a man's foundation. . ." (p.159). According to Dr. Stephen T. Chang in *The Toa of Sexology* (1986), the sexual organs and glands are considered the 'stove' of the body. The sex glands produce the hormones—the 'fire' which helps rejuvenate cells and tissues. If the sex glands are not functioning properly, it can lead to improper functioning of cell and tissue generation which can lead to improper functioning of the rest of the physical body and subsequently the mental, emotional, and spiritual bodies.

The endocrine system includes the seven major glands around the chakras. A properly functioning endocrine system is important because the glands are the interface between the energy body and the physical body. Although all glands must be functioning properly, the three that play a primary role in sexual health are the hypothalamus, pituitary, and sex glands. The hypothalamus secretes a releasing factor into the bloodstream. It then stimulates the pituitary gland to release sex hormones, gonadotropins to the gonads, ovaries for women, and testes for men. This in turn prompts the gonads to release their own hormones into the bloodstream, estrogen, and progesterone for women and testosterone for men (and women). If there is a leakage or blockage of vital force in one gland, it will affect the rest of the system. Since the sexual glands are the foundation "fire" or "stove" that fuels the rest of the glands, they must be functioning properly (Chang, 1996, p. 18). There are blood tests to check whether the glands are producing the level of hormones necessary for good health.

Hormones in Gender Differences in Desire

It is common knowledge that generally, men have more interest in sex than women. When a woman with a high sex drive is paired with a man with a normal sex drive, they usually have a good sexual relationship. However, when there are differences in levels of desire, it can create friction in the relationship. Testosterone, which is the hormone that fuels the sex drive in both genders, may explain some of the differences in levels of desire in men and women. Although testosterone is commonly thought to be a "male" hormone, both men and women have it. However, men have higher levels of it, about 10 to 20 times more than women. While a man's testosterone level may fluctuate, with the level being double in the morning, and decreases throughout his life, for women it may decrease to critical levels throughout the 28-day menstrual cycle, causing them to have little or no interest in sex.

A women's sex drive may fluctuate more dramatically and for longer periods of time during pregnancy, lactation, and menopause. During pregnancy, women may experience increased desire. While they are nursing, some women experience a dramatic drop in interest in sex, which may have to do with the rise in prolactin (the hormone that stimulates milk production), or a decrease in testosterone. Decreased interest in sex may have been nature's way of creating space between children when mothers were nursing through breastfeeding so as not to endanger the life of the existing child. Finally, many women have *diminished* interest in sex during menopause when their ovaries stop producing testosterone. As they age, women may also stop producing or produce lower levels of estrogen, progesterone, and other hormones, while testosterone levels drop for men as they age. Stress, lack of exercise, and a poor diet further deplete hormones necessary for healthy sexual functioning.

Five Organ System & Qigong

The Five Organ System

The organs and how they correspond to energy might be best understood under Tradition Chinese Medicine (TCM). According to TCM the three treasures in life are jing, shen, and qi; there are three cavities in the body in which they are primarily contained. Jing is the physical essence of organic life in humans and can be found in the lower cavity. Shen is the spiritual essence of life and can be found in the upper cavity, and qi is where both Jing and Shen meets and comes from air and food and is the middle cavity. Under TCM there are five primary organ systems. Referred to as *Yang Fu*, all of the organs consist of both yin and yang. However, within the five-organ system, each pair of organs has a primary yin and yang function—one that receives, manufactures, stores and another that transports and/or cleanses. Each organ system has a corresponding meridian through which the qi flows and corresponds to an element and season. These are outlined under the Qigong section that follows.

Although healthy organ functioning is important to overall health, proper kidney functioning is vital to healthy sexual functioning. According to TCM, the kidneys are where our Jing or essence is stored. This essence or jing includes congenital energy— what we inherit from our parents and are born with and acquired energy— that which is acquired and influenced by what we consume. The kidneys are the foundation for all bodily processes, especially growth, development, and reproduction. The kidney essence is infused in the bone; the bone changes it to marrow which changes it to blood. An under-functioning kidney can lead to bone weakening, growth retardation, and blood deficiency diseases. The kidneys are also responsible for the movement of clean water that is vaporized and distributed to the lungs and removing unclean water through the bladder. In addition, they are crucial for the development of the essence of the sexual glands.

Qigong

Originating with TCM, qigong, are movements, sounds, and breathing practices that help to cultivate the life force or qi through balancing the yin and yang aspects of ourselves. Although the objective of qigong is optimal health in all aspects of the self, the focus is on balancing the qi of five major organ systems outlined below. Qigong works by the principle of four seasons and five elements/phases. As the veins and arteries are conduits for the blood, the meridians are conduits for qi or life force energy. Each of the four modalities of energy (qi), earth, air, fire, and water correspond to five pairs of "energy-organs" (Amen, 2009). Each pair of organs have a yin and yang function in the transmission of energy. When there is an imbalance, excess, or deficiency of the energy of the four elements it causes disease. Healing sounds (which help to expel negative emotions, stale or congested qi from the organs), and movements play a role in re-establishing the circulation of the qi by enhancing the function of the organ system that is related to each of the elements or stages in the transformation of energy ("Teach Yourself," n.d.).[4] General practice would focus on balancing the qi which is essentially balancing the yin and yang energy of the organs. Some systems focus on tonification practices for the yin or yang energy of the season, for example, for the fall and winter (inward period) one would focus on yin tonification practices, and for the spring and summer, yang (outward period) tonification practices. Other tonification practices focus on the 30-day cycle, while others focus on daily practice.

Since the kidney provides jing or essence to the sexual organs, the primary organ system of focus for sexual health is the kidneys/bladder system. Because certain times of the day correspond to when an organ system is at the height of its functioning, it is important to adhere to dietary habits for optimal health. For example, one would consume a light breakfast in the morning when the stomach and spleen are most active, the heaviest meal and

---

[4] Different sounds were found on the Internet. See: http://baharna.com/chant/six_healing.htm. The sounds here are the ones that were most common on the Internet including demonstrations on Youtube.

exercise in the afternoon when the body is the hottest and able to break the food down, and a light meal in the early evening when the body is cooling down. The organ associated with the season, element, and healing sound is outlined below. *Figure 11.1* shows the time of day when the organ system is most active. One can consult the Internet for numerous sources on how to do the sounds in conjunction with the movements. [5]

Figure 11.1
Chinese Body Clock

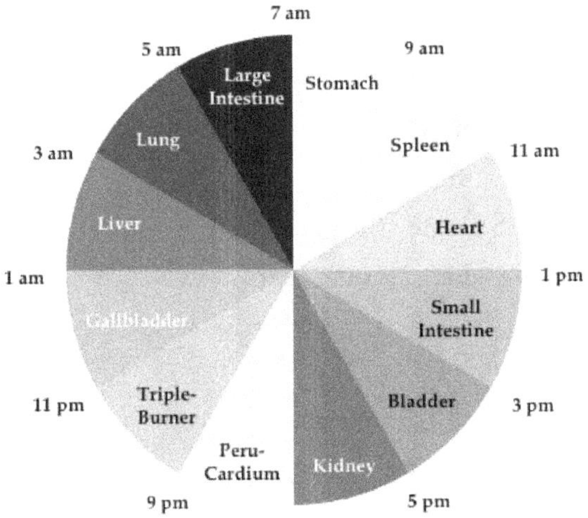

(Pie chart showing organ systems by time of day: Large Intestine 5am, Stomach 7am, Spleen 9am, Heart 11am, Small Intestine 1pm, Bladder 3pm, Kidney 5pm, Peri-Cardium 7pm, Triple-Burner 9pm, Gallbladder 11pm, Liver 1am, Lung 3am)

1. Kidneys/Urinary Bladder
- Element—Water (metabolism)
- Season—Winter (cold and moist)
- Governs—The foundation of the other organ systems, the yin and yang functions of all the other organs
- Energetically—constitution, growth, and development, physical vitality, and endurance

---

[5] For more extensive information on Qigong, see: Amen, R. U. N. (2009). *Qigong healing prescriptions.* Brooklyn, NY: Khamit.

- Energy Transformation Stage—Warming up
- Sound—Chui (Ch way)

2. Liver/Gall Bladder
- Element—Air (wood)[6]
- Season— Spring (hot and moist)
- Governs—Movement e.g., circulation of blood and qi that governs relaxation of the tendons and ligaments which control the muscles
- Energetically—Plans, decision making
- Energy transformation—Warming up functions
- Sound: Xu (Shooo)

3. Heart/Small Intestine
- Element—Fire
- Season—Summer (hot and dry)
- Governs—Circulation of blood which governs the heart
- Energetically—Warmth, compassion, empathy, good communication
- Energy Transmission—Hot function
- Sound—He (Haaaw)

4. Stomach/Spleen
- Element—Earth
- Season—All seasons
- Governs—Producing blood and qi—digestion, assimilation, and transformations of nutrients into body parts of the body
- Energetically—Harmonizing, earthing, centering, and reasoning)
- Energy Transmission—Warming up function
- Sound—Hu (Whooo)

---

[6] Air is replaced with wood in TCM

5. Lungs/Large Intestines
- Element—Earth/metal[7]
- Season—Autumn (cold and dry)
- Governs—Structured, crystallized movement and elimination
- Energetically—Breath and emotions
- Energy Transmission—Cooling down
- Sound—Si (Tzzz)

The sound Xi (pronounced SHeee) is done silently. Referred to as the Triple energizer or warmer; also called *San Jiao* is not associated with a physical organ but with the energetic pathways that run through the upper, middle, and lower cavities of the body. One of its main functions is to regulate qi and fluids surrounding the internal organs.

Deer Exercises

Deer exercises help to build up the sex tissues, organs, and sexual ability. According to Chang (1986), deer exercises originated by Taoist sages years ago after observing three animals, the turtle, crane, and deer, that were noted for their longevity. While observing the deer, they also found that it had strong sexual and reproductive abilities, which they believed had to do with exercising its anus through wiggling its tail. Out of these observations, the deer exercises were created. The steps for how to do deer exercises are outlined below.

Men

First stage
The first stage is to encourage semen production. It can be done standing, sitting, or lying down.
1. Rub the palms of the hands together to generate heat.

---

[7] Earth is replaced with metal in TCM.

2. Lightly cup the testicles with the right hand without squeezing (your partner can help by doing this).
3. Place the palm of the left hand one inch below the navel and turn your hand clockwise or counterclockwise 81 times.
4. Reverse the entire process, rubbing the palms of the hands together vigorously, cupping the testicles with the left hand and rubbing the stomach with the right hand, and in the opposite direction 81 times (Chang, 1986, pp 71-73).

Second stage

The purpose of the second stage is to draw the energy through the chakras to the pineal gland. This is done by drawing in the muscles around the anus up and in and then relaxing. This is done as many times as you can without feeling discomfort (Chang, 1986, p. 73).

Women

First stage

1. Cross your legs so that the heel of one of your feet is pressed against the opening of the vagina. If you have difficulty, then use a round object like a baseball or you or your partner can apply pressure to the vagina with your finger. If you use your finger, stroke the lips of the vagina in a clockwise direction.
2. Rub your hands together to generate heat.
3. Rub your breasts slowly in an outward, circular motion, with the right hand turning counter-clockwise and the left hand turning clockwise, 36-360 times. Avoid touching the nipples of the breast to avoid over-stimulating them. Rubbing the breast in an outward direction disperses energy and helps to decrease the size of large breasts as well as helps to prevent lumps and cancer of the breasts. Rubbing inward stimulates the breasts and helps to increase the size of small ones (Chang, 1986, pp. 104-105).

Second Stage

Tighten the muscles of your vagina and your anus as if you are trying to close both while drawing your rectum upward as if you were drawing it upward inside your body, holding them as long as you can and then relax. Do this as many times as you can, noting that at first it may seem difficult, but over time you will get better at it. Do these deer exercises in the morning and at night (Chang, 1986, p. 105),

Genital Reflexology

Reflexology is the practice of healing that focuses on applying pressure to zones or junction points that the 12 meridians terminate to facilitate the healing of organs, glands, and other systems of the body. These zones include the head, hands, feet, ears, and genitals.[8] For the sexual organs the male and female genitals are the inverse reflex of each other. If they are the same size, every part of the penis is a perfect match for the vagina. An erect six-inch penis is the perfect size for an average vagina. When the penis penetrates the vagina, if they are not matched, e.g., the penis is too small for the vagina the woman may feel dissatisfied, or if it's too long, it can lead to problems, e.g., bacteria penetrating the uterus. Since there are points on the vagina and penis that correspond to points in the entire body, when there is a match, the reflexology zones on the penis will match the reflexology zones on the vagina. This means that the zone that corresponds to the heart on the penis will be aligned with the zone that corresponds to the heart on the vagina, the lungs, with lungs on the vagina, and so forth. Thus, when the sex organs make contact with each other, sex can promote the healing of various parts of the body. See Chang's *The Tao of Sexology* for how different positions during intercourse can stimulate the reflex zones and promote different types of healing throughout the body.

---

[8] These zones can also be stimulated for sexual pleasure.

Sexual Bliss

Activating and Stimulating the G-Spot & Prostate

Activating and stimulating the G-spot for women and messaging the prostate for men can not only promote healing but sexual bliss. For women, it is well known that they can achieve multiple orgasms through clitoral stimulation. It is therefore important for the woman and her partner to learn techniques to stimulate the clitoris so that she can climax and reach multiple orgasms. Activating the G-spot may enhance the experience.

The G-spot is an erogenous zone located about 2-3 inches up the front wall on the interior of the vagina between the vaginal opening and the urethra. Although there is an ongoing debate about whether the G-spot actually exists, whether it is just part of the clitoral orgasm or whether its sensitivity has to do with being located near nerve endings around the urethral sponge, when stimulated, it can lead to arousal, intense orgasm, and ejaculation for some women.

To activate the G-spot one might begin by opening channels and/or sending energy to the gall bladder meridian. One would then insert 1-3 fingers with the knuckles facing the back including the middle (energy) finger into the vagina. Once the fingers are in then pull the G-spot forward for about 15 minutes. Once it drops, reach back and grab it. This would be followed by massaging the major reflex points in the vagina. Once the G-spot is activated, it develops a life of its own and awakens the vagina. Awakening the vagina helps to facilitate an entire body orgasm and expanded sexual response.

For a man, his sexual glands consist of the prostate and the testicles. Since the penis does not produce anything but serves primarily to ejaculate semen, it is not considered to be a part of the sex glands. The testicles produce the sperm and the hormones, and the prostate secretes prostate fluid (made up of nutrients, hormones, and vital energy) that helps to make up the seminal fluid.⁹ The function of the prostate is to secrete prostate fluid and propel the seminal fluid into the urethra through the penis during ejaculation.

The prostate is about the size of a walnut. To ensure that it is healthy it can be checked and massaged (for sexual pleasure) by inserting the finger into the anus and reaching up to the navel. This is followed by rubbing back and forth on it applying as much pressure as possible without causing pain. Many men, especially heterosexual males are reluctant to check or massage the prostate because it is associated with homosexuality. However, it is important to check its size and message it regularly to prevent disease.

Table Work and the Energy Orgasm

Energy healing/orgasm focuses on table work which includes practices to unblock, open the channels, and/or increase the qi flowing through the meridians with a focus on the heart and sex organs. In addition to unblocking channels that may be closed due to lifestyle choices, it entails channeling energy centers around the sacrum and heart chakras so that a connection can be made between the genitals and the heart, with the goal of an entire body orgasm. A factor contributing to low sexual health and satisfaction is blocked channels and a disconnection between the genitals and the heart for both men and women. This disconnect may occur for several reasons, but the goal is to connect them back. A Tantra energy healer uses various energy modalities to unblock and heal, including building up and siphoning Kundalini energy and projecting it and facilitating the rise of Kundalini within the person they are working with.

---

⁹ Seminal fluid is comprised of prostate and seminal vesicle fluids and carries the sperm.

The Expanded Sexual Response

In more recent research it has been found that not only can women experience multiple orgasms, but that they can also experience an expanded sexual response (ESR), which is defined as "being able to attain long-lasting and/or prolonged and/or multiple and/or sustained orgasms and/or *status orgasmus* that lasts longer and more intense than the classical orgasm patterns defined in the literature" (Sayin, 2011). For some women, this prolonged orgasmic state can last as long as an hour. Many of the techniques discussed throughout this chapter can facilitate a woman experiencing an ESR.

For a man to experience an orgasm that not only helps him to preserve his jing, qi, or life force energy but allow him to have an ESR he would need to practice withholding his semen which can be achieved if he learns how to *injaculate* rather than ejaculate (Chang, 1986). When a male ejaculates, he loses about one tablespoon of semen, which is a great loss of vital energy, which may explain why he is exhausted after sex. For the man to *injaculate,* the Jen-Mo point which is a small indentation between the testicles and the anus is pressed, when he feels he is about to ejaculate. When this is done, rather than the semen being released through the penis and vital energy being lost, it is retained in the prostate, absorbed in the bloodstream, and carried throughout the body which helps revitalize it. Also, rather than the seven glands being depleted because of the loss of semen, it is dispersed throughout the seven glands to energize them, giving the feeling of being reborn. In addition, the man can experience not only intense pleasure but because it may take the prostate five minutes or more to empty the prostate, it may result in an orgasm that lasts that long.

Variety

The healing modalities and techniques described throughout this chapter can be used to spice up your sex life by adding variety. Additional practices can also add variety. Love and Robinson (2012) note that many of us have only one lovemaking style and suggest four different styles that include:

- *Quickies*—lovemaking without going through all the preliminaries
- *15–30-minute sessions*—moderate time or effort, typically at the end of the day or the first thing in the morning
- *Leisure lovemaking*—longer sessions lasting 40 minutes to an hour with mood-setting via candles, aromas, massages, oils, and other forms of stimulation
- *Adventuresome lovemaking*—trying out new things and fulfilling fantasies, and adding some risk and playfulness to lovemaking (pp. 149–151)

Variety might also include:

- *Stimulating and massaging non-sexual parts of the body*—This includes other reflexology zones like the hands, feet, ears, head, eyes, neck, etc.
- *Dress up and role-playing*—In a survey, it was found that of all the things that turn men on, 92% said they were most turned on by lingerie (which for many women may be uncomfortable if they are not comfortable with their body image). Women also find it exciting when men come to bed with something different on. As for role-playing, some people find looking like someone else, and taking on different characters and/or personalities stimulating.
- *Romance stories/novels*—Reading erotica can be stimulating particularly for women.
- *Sex toys, sex games, and erotic films*—Provide variety, fun, and help to make lovemaking exciting.

In summary, being aware of the factors that shut down the natal masculine and feminine faculties that awaken our ability for maximum sexual expression is the first step towards sexual health. Making sexual health a goal not only lays the foundation for a healthy sex life but an extraordinary and fulfilling one. As the healing modalities and techniques outlined in this chapter become part of your practice and you continue to explore the limitlessness of sexual expression, you will discover sexual bliss, spiritual evolvement, and ultimately a life of bliss.

Chapter 11 Exercises

Towards Sexual Health and Bliss

These exercises are to help you explore factors that may be preventing you from having a healthy sexual relationship and to incorporate practices that can lead to a healthy sex life.

EXERCISE 11.1. *Sexual Background*

1. Describe and discuss and how the following affect your attitude and behaviors around sexuality:
i. Early childhood messages and experiences
ii. Messages from society around sex and gender (i.e. myths, stereotypes, etc.)
iii. Past relationship experiences
iv. Current experiences you are having (i.e. stress, role strain, etc.)

_____
_____
_____
_____
_____

2. Check the box below for fears or inhibitions you have around sexuality.

☐ Contracting an STD	☐ Passing on an STD	☐ Contracting/ passing on HIV
☐ Being seen as a Whore	☐ Getting pregnant	☐ Being taken advantage of
☐ Performance	☐ Being used	☐ Being exploited
Lack of experience	☐ Having too many Partners	☐ Stereotypes/myths
☐ Other _____	☐ Other_____	☐ Other_____

3. Using the chart below, check the box that corresponds to issues you are experiencing if any.

Women	Men
☐ Premenstrual syndrome (PMS) ☐ Menstrual cramps ☐ Heavy bleeding ☐ Fibroid tumors ☐ Early menopause ☐ Dyspareunia (painful sex) ☐ Lack of interest in sex ☐ Unable to Lubricate ☐ Difficulty achieving an orgasm ☐ Infertility	☐ Rapid ejaculation—caused by problems in the parasympathetic nervous system ☐ Erectile dysfunction ☐ Lack of interest in sex ☐ Impotence

4. Describe factors from 1 and 2 above that may be contributing to sexual issues/dysfunctions.

_____
_____
_____
_____
_____

EXERCISE 11.2. *Body Esteem*

1. Use the chart below to answer the questions that follow about how you feel about your bodies.

Face	Back	Legs
Neck	Torso	Calves
Shoulders	Stomach	Feet
Arms	Behind	Weight
Hands	Genitals	Height
Chest	Hips	Size

Breasts	Thighs	Shape
Color	Tone	

2. Describe and discuss:
i. What you do not like about your own bodies
ii. How the way you feel about your bodies affects your sexual relationship
iii. What you like about each other's bodies
iv. What you can do and/or say to make each other feel better about your bodies

a. *I do not like…* _____

b. *My partner does not like…* _____

c. *How we feel about our bodies affects our relationship…* _____

d. *What I like about my body…* _____

e. *What my partner likes about his/her body…* _____

f. *What I can say or do to make my partner feel better about his/her body* …
_____

g. *What my partner can say or do to make me feel better about my body* …
_____
_____

EXERCISE 11.3. *Practices*

Communication

1. Describe and discuss the following:
i. How you communicate interest in sex
ii. How you communicate disinterest in sex
iii. Things that you need to communicate with each other about
iv. What you will do to create more open and honest communication

a. *When I am interested in sex I usually...*_____

b. *My partner prefers me to...*_____

c. *When my partner is interested in sex he/she usually...*_____

d. *I prefer him/her to...*_____

e. *When I am not interested in sex, I usually...*_____

f. *My partner prefers that I...*_____

g. *When my partner is not interested in sex, he/she usually...*

h. *I prefer that he/she...*_____

i. *Things that we need to talk about but avoid...*_____

j. *Hurtful ways in which we communicate include...*_____

k. *What we will talk about and how we/will talk about it so that we can improve our sex life...*_____

Levels of Desire and Frequency
2. Discuss differences in levels of desire and frequency.
a. *We typically have sex (number of times per month/week/day)*

b. *I would prefer it if we have sex...*_____
c. *My partner prefers that we have sex...*_____
d. *The effect of our different levels of desire on our relationships...*_____

e. *What we can do to reconcile our different levels of desire ...* _____

Current Practices

3. Use the chart below for suggestions to complete the statements that follow for your current practices and what you would like to happen. You can use other practices, not on the chart.

-Kiss (passionately, my neck, breast, penis)	-Be (more spontaneous, open, gentler)
-Lick (chest, breast, all over)	-Engage in (more foreplay, after play)
-Stroke (penis, clitoris)	-Move (slower, faster)
-Play with (testicles)	-Hold (me tighter, penis)
-Talk (to me, dirty, sexy)	-Find (G-spot, prostate)
-Wear (lingerie, exotic clothes)	-Massage (body, prostate)
-Insert (fingers in vagina)	-Explore (different positions, role play)
-Use (sex toys, games, food)	-Perform (oral sex, anal sex)
-Rub (down with oil)	

a. *Things that I <u>do not</u> like that my partner does...* _____

b. *Things my partner <u>does not</u> like that I do...* _____

c. *I like it when my partner...* _____

d. *My partner likes it when I...* _____

e. *I would like for my partner to...* _____

f. *My partner would like for me to...* _____

4. Describe in more detail your current practices, what you would like to change about your sex life and your goals for doing so.

_____
_____
_____

EXERCISE 11.4. *Future Practices*

1. Describe and discuss practices discussed in this chapter that you/will incorporate in your lives to promote healing and enhance your sex life (e.g., Qigong, meditation, deer exercises, genital reflexology, table work, activating and stimulating the G-spot and prostate, etc.).

Additional Notes

12

Stairway to Heaven

To help us on our spiritual journeys, one of the most ancient people on Earth, the Kemetians (the Egyptians), etched on their sacred temples the Tree of Life to be a guide for our spiritual evolvement. Through living among the Canaanites and the 400 or so years that the Hebrews spent living among the Kemetians, the Tree of Life found its way into the Hebrew Kabbala; it has also been adapted to various other religious and spiritual traditions in the West, including mystical Judaism, Christianity, some Western Esoteric traditions, and New Age spirituality. We are using the Tree of Life as articulated by Ra Un Nefer Amen (1990) in the *Metu Neter* and the numerous other volumes that he has written, as a guide for you to follow. Since our use of the Tree of Life in this work is only a cursory overview of it, you are strongly urged to seek out the works of this author as well as others for increased understanding.[1]

The Tree of Life consists of 10 spheres of consciousness, light, or aspects of God. Each sphere also has deities, gatekeepers, and/or guards, which we are referring to as Universe Helpers as well as colors, gems, sounds, day of the week, month, etc. which can invoke their presence. If you recall from Chapter 1, most, if not all, spiritual (and religious) traditions identify Universe Helpers. The more widely known ones are:

---

[1] See Ra Un Nefer Amen's (1990) *Metu Neter Vol. 1* for the Kemetic (Egyptian) version of the Tree of Life, and Dion Fortune's (2009) *Mystical Qabalah* for the esoteric version of it for further explanation.

- Kemetic/Egyptian—*Neteru*;
- Judeo-Christian—*Angles/Archangels*;
- Islam—*Angels/Archangels*;
- Yoruba—*Orishas*;
- India—*Devas*; and
- New Age—*Angels, Archangels, Ascended Masters* (who once had earthly bodies and ascended).

As also indicated in Chapter 1, when the universe unfolded, it did so in 10 emanations. According to Amen (1990), in sphere 0, the Subjective Realm of reality, there was nothing, just unlimited energy/matter. In the first emanation sphere 1, the Universe Soul identifies with its unlimited time, space, and potential and brings forth awareness that it "is capable of being whatever it chooses to be and that it is immortal and eternal" (Amen, 1990, p. 69). In the second and third emanations, the Universe Soul brings itself out of the Subjective Realm into the Objective Realm (i.e., where energy/matter is differentiated) by separating itself into two. Through the utterance of words, it brings forth its creative faculties: infinite Will and Knowledge (Omniscience, sphere 2) and unlimited Spiritual Power (Omnipotence, sphere 3).

In the fourth through 10 emanations, the Universe Soul goes on to create ruling principles for the existence and oneness of things (e.g., principles of law, order, etc.), along with Universe Helpers[2] to assist in the creation and maintenance of things (sphere 4), and justice or enforcement of the law in the interests of the preservation of the whole (sphere 5). Sphere 6 contains the coordinating and balancing forces between the upper and lower worlds. In sphere 7 are the archetypes or images of the types of things and events to be created, and in sphere 8, are the distinctions between these things. In sphere 9, all of the preceding shaping factors coordinate physical energy/matter into a vehicle. Finally, in sphere 10 is the manifestation

---

[2] According to spiritual traditions, Universe Helpers were created to help God create and keep the universe in order.

of these shaping factors into the physical world. The Tree of Life is shown in *Figure 12.1*.

Figure 12.1
Tree of Life

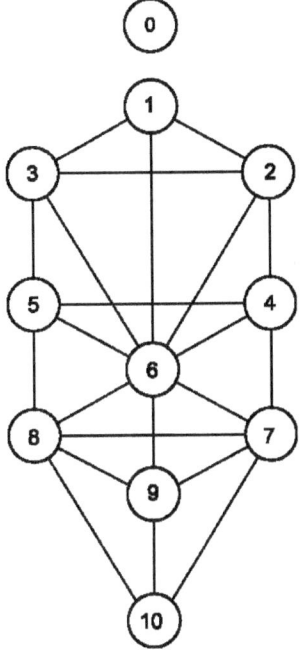

SPHERE

0. Non-being—no-thing, no thought[3]
1. Unity—undifferentiated, unlimited potential; infinity
2. Will and Knowledge—to bring things into manifestation
3. Power—to manifest what is willed
4. Law—ruling principles for things manifested; order and oneness
5. Justice—enforcement of order and oneness for the preservation of the whole
6. Love—the binding force; balance between the upper and lower worlds

---

[3] We do not include sphere zero in our discussion since it is nothing and was before the 10 emanations and the world was created.

7. Imagination—coordination of images that synthesize differences
8. Thought—distinguishes and segregates differences between things
9. Emotion—derived from desire; the driving force and coordinator of all shaping forces in spheres 1-8 used to manifest the physical world
10. Physical—world manifested

Faculties Humans Share with the Tree of Life

Each of us is a mini-universe made of the same substance that the Universe Soul used to layout the universe. There is, therefore, a part of ourselves that corresponds with each sphere of the Tree of Life. Since each sphere corresponds to an aspect of our being, it can be used to determine where we are in our spiritual evolvement and the work that needs to be done. How these aspects of our being or faculties correspond with the sphere in the Tree of Life are briefly outlined below.

Human Faculties

1. **Unity**—the faculty that awakens us to our unity with the Universe Soul, our unlimited potential, and the immortality of our souls.
2. **Wisdom**—the faculty that awakens us to the knowledge of our unlimited potential to be who we want to be and bring things forth.
3. **Power**—the faculty that awakens us to the understanding of our unlimited spiritual power to bring things into manifestation.
4. **Law**—the faculty that awakens our conscience to live in truth, harmony, and balance with the laws of the universe for the benefit of the whole.
5. **Justice**—the faculty that awakens us to be conscientious of what is right and just; be accountable for and judge our actions; and, in turn, gain divine protection.

6. ***Love***—the faculty that awakens us to Universe Love so that we are able to love, share ourselves; show empathy, understanding, and compassion; balance our individual and unified selves (i.e., the aspect of the self that is connected to the world); and awaken to our free will choice to live through our higher selves.

7. ***Imagination***—(i.e., right brain) the faculty of concretive thinking that allows us to synthesize differences between things as well as imagine and create our world.

8. ***Thought*** (i.e., left brain)—the faculty of segregative thinking that allows us to distinguish differences between things so that we are able to make sense out of the world and live in it.

9. ***Emotions***—activated by our desires (including lower physical— to higher spiritual), this faculty allows us to sense the world; stores our emotional memories; and energizes us with the capacity to produce, create, and expand.

10. ***Physical***—the vehicle that allows us to experience the physical world.

If you also recall from Chapter 1, there are seven steps to bliss or heaven on Earth. In Chapter 7, we focused on the tasks necessary for healing and awakening. In this chapter, we focus on the tasks that will help you as a *couple; Soul Partners,* create a world together. The seven steps are:

1. Mastery of your Physical World
2. Mastery of your Emotional World
3. Mastery of your Mental World
4. Awakening to Universe Love
5. Awakening to Universe Consciousness
6. Awakening to Universe Light
7. Unifying with the Universe Soul

A primary task facing humanity is balancing our duality, which is the pull between our subjective (i.e., that part of the self that we share with the Universe Soul) and objective selves (i.e., that part of the self that is differentiated from the Universe Soul). In simple terms, it is balancing between (and rising above) our lower selves and living through our higher selves. If you recall from Chapters 1 and 7, rising to our higher selves entails healing and mastering lower aspects of the self and awakening higher aspects of the self. Chapters 6 and 7 provide guidelines for doing this. However, because we are in physical bodies and in societies that focus more on our physical reality (i.e., materialism), many of us struggle to balance between our lower physical selves and our higher spiritual selves. It takes continuous spiritual work to gain mastery over the lower aspects of ourselves and awaken the higher aspects of ourselves.

Regardless of where you are, a major threshold has been crossed when you come to realize that you are in each other's lives to help each other evolve. Such a realization can lead to being open and willing to learn the lessons that you need to learn through your interaction together as well as learn how to honor and respect each other as you grow together. The 10 guiding principles outlined below are designed to help with this.

TEN GUIDING PRINCIPLES

Just as laws exist that govern all phenomena in the universe, there are principles that guide the soul of man/woman. Although different spiritual systems vary in the number of, and how they describe, such principles, borrowing specifically from Buddhist Noble Eightfold Path, we have devised 10 principles to correspond with the Tree of Life. These ten principles, if followed, will not only assure success and prosperity in your relationships but in life as well. They are briefly described below. How these principles correspond with the seven steps to bliss and the spheres on the Tree of Life are shown in Table 12.2.

10. ***Right Living***—habits, behaviors, and choices around our diets, health, finances, livelihoods, lifestyles, and social connections that are good for ourselves and the world.

9. ***Right Desire***—desires that allow us to produce, reproduce, expand, and create good in the world.

8. ***Right Thoughts***—thoughts and communication that promote good for ourselves and others.

7. ***Right Imagination***—imagining, creating, and bringing into manifestation only those things that are in concert with good and the Divine image of God.

6. ***Right Love***—moving beyond personal experiences with love to love that gives us the ability to share ourselves, show empathy, understand others, have compassion, balance our individual and unified selves (i.e., the self that is connected to the world), and the willpower to live through our higher selves.

5. ***Right Actions***—being right, just, and conscientious of the consequences of our actions, so that we gain divine protection.

4. ***Right Ways***—awakening to and living in harmony with the laws of the universe—MAAT: truth, harmony, and balance.

3. ***Right Understanding***—awakening the understanding we need to tap into our unlimited spiritual power to bring things into manifestation.

2. ***Right Knowing***—awakening to the wisdom that gives us access to our unlimited potential to be who we want to be and bring forth the desires of our hearts.

1. ***Right Being***—self-identifying with nothing other than our unity with the Universe Soul and awakening to our unlimited potential and the eternal nature of our souls.

Table 12.2 Seven Steps and 10 Guiding Principles

Seven Steps	10 Guiding Principles	Sphere on the Tree of Life
1. Mastery of your Physical World	Right Living	10
2. Mastery of your Emotional World	Right Desires	9
3. Mastery of your Mental World	Right Thoughts	8
	Right Imagination	7
4. Awakening to Universe Love	Right Love	6
5. Awakening to Universe Consciousness	Right Actions	5
	Right Ways	4
6. Awakening to Universe Light	Right Understanding	3
	Right Knowing	2
7. Unifying with the Universe Soul	Right Being	1

CLIMBING THE STAIRWAY TO HEAVEN

When you join, you are bringing who you are into the relationship. Your ideas, thoughts, beliefs, experiences, wounds, injuries, moral values and principles, practices, habits, behaviors, personalities, ways of being, etc. are being merged. All of these factors will greatly influence the expectations that you have for yourselves and each other. In some areas, you will complement each other, while, in other areas, you will be completely different. These differences will potentially present great challenges and can be mediated based on the work you did in terms of healing and choosing the right partner. However, it is how you perceive and deal with these differences that will test your strength and the strength of your relationship. Challenges that you encounter can be perceived as obstacles to your happiness or opportunities for growth and spiritual evolvement.

The first few years present the most challenges as you navigate the terrain of getting to know each other and working through your differences. It may take about seven years to get through these challenges. This period has been referred to as "the seven-year itch," which, among many things, means that it is when the challenges come to a head. If you can accept and live with your differences, then the challenges will begin to level off. Many are, however, unable to navigate through their differences and the relationship or marriage ends. Doing the work to heal your physical, emotional, and mental bodies; awakening your spiritual bodies; using good communication skills and using the tools outlined in this chapter, you have the power to get the love you want.

The 10 guiding principles are expanded on below for you to follow as you cultivate your 10 faculties and climb the seven steps of the Tree of Life; the stairway to heaven. The chakras have been added to remind you of the continuous energy (i.e., spiritual) work that needs to be done.

Tree of Life/Faculty: Sphere 10—Physical World
Step: 1—Mastery of Your Physical World
Energetic Correspondence: Root Chakra
Principle: Right Living

Your physical world is the world you are attempting to build together. Your differences in habits, behaviors, and choices around your diets, health, livelihoods, finances, lifestyles, and social connections as well as how you respond to these differences will affect your interaction patterns, your relationship, and the world you are attempting to build together. You can gain mastery over your physical world by controlling your habits and behaviors and making good choices. Right living is practicing restraint and making changes in areas in which they are needed, including eating healthy, taking care of your health, maintaining a clean and organized environment, choosing healthy livelihoods, budgeting, planning for the future, and cultivating and balancing relationships with family and friends.

In most of the early parts of our lives, out of necessity, a great deal of focus is put on acquiring education, tools, and the material things we need to build a world. Unfortunately, in materialistic cultures, many of us get stuck at the physical world level. It is, however, important to remember that our souls were incarnated into our physical bodies to evolve spirituality; therefore, your physical reality is the path to your spiritual evolvement. You must balance the physical and spiritual as you cultivate a spiritual life together, as it is the key to your success and prosperity.

Tree of Life/Faculty: Sphere 9—Emotional
Step: 2—Mastery of Your Emotional World
Energetic Correspondence: Sacral Chakra
Principle: Right Desire

Your emotional world is driven by your senses, which are activated by your desires. When you join, you are transporting your desires into the relationship. Your different desires, what motivates them (e.g., injuries, social pressure), the types of desires (i.e., lower vs. higher levels), and how you respond when your desires are not fulfilled will affect your interaction patterns, your relationship, and the emotional world you create together. Unrealistic desires and unhealthy emotional responses will create an unhealthy emotional world. Mastery of your emotional world can begin with examining your desires, including what they are, what is driving them, whether they are realistic, and what you may need to let go of.

There are, fundamentally, three levels of human desires: 1. physical—to meet our basic needs of food, clothing, shelter, and safety; 2. psychic—to feel safe and secure, belong, give and receive love, and to self-actualize; and 3. spiritual—to transcend our earthly existence. The desire for physical and psychic survival is natural and necessary to ensure that we survive and thrive. However, we do not want to get stuck at these levels.

A great deal of conflict that occurs in relationships has to do with our desires that our partners fail to meet or those desires that we fail to fulfill ourselves. When our desires are unmet or unfulfilled, we feel hurt, disappointed, and, subsequently, bad about ourselves and our partners. Such feelings can lead to repressed feelings or highly charged emotional responses, both of which are unhealthy because they cause a drain or block to the vital force. Expecting our partners to be what we want them to be versus who they are also leads to unhealthy emotional responses. Some people do not have the capacity to be what we want them to be or to do what we expect them to do. We, then, respond emotionally when they do not meet our expectations.

Mastery of your emotional world means gaining mastery over your desires. Right desires are those that are healthy and realistic. Recognizing that you have your own paths, allowing each other to evolve at your own pace, and being patient helps you to gain mastery over the emotional world that you create together. Cultivating your desires and emotions as you cultivate a spiritual life together will, naturally, lead to desires for higher-level things—those things that are transcendent, the Divine. The desire for, and the pursuit of things divine, are truly the keys to happiness.

Tree of Life/Faculty: Sphere 8—Thoughts
Step: 3—Mastery of Your Thoughts
Correspondence: Solar Plexus
Principle: Right Thoughts

Your mental world is based on your thoughts and imagination. You create your thought world from the thoughts that you transport into your relationship from past experiences as well as those thoughts that you form and hold about each other based on your experiences together. Such thoughts greatly affect the thought world you create together, and, subsequently, the type of relationship that you form.

The thoughts that you transport into your relationship are based on social conditioning from your families and the broader society (i.e., group thought) as well as those thoughts that you hold about yourself and others. The health of your thoughts is based on the health of the group thought and the health of the group thought is based upon the health of the culture. Group thought based on materialism, individualism, unhealthy competition, and gender inequality is not a healthy foundation upon which to build a society or a relationship. The thoughts we hold about ourselves shape how we feel about ourselves. Our self-esteem, efficacy, and sense of power are derived from our experiences in our childhood, in previous relationships, and throughout the courses of our lives. In other words, who you think you are is based on the thought forms that you hold about yourself.

Mastery over your thought world begins with gaining mastery over your thoughts. Right thoughts entail letting go of those that are based on unrealistic and unhealthy social conditioning, healing the unhealthy thoughts that you hold about yourselves and others, and letting go of the negative thoughts that you hold about each other. Spiritual cultivation of your thoughts entails focusing your thoughts on the Divine, which is necessary to awaken to higher levels of consciousness.

Tree of Life/Faculty: Sphere 7—Imagination
Step: 3—Mastery of Your Imagination
Energetic Correspondence: Solar Plexus
Principle: Right Imagination

Before you join, you imagine who you are, who you are with each other, and what your world will be like. Differences in who you imagine you are and who you really are, and who you become as you interact together will affect your interaction patterns, your relationship, and the world you imagine and create together. As the relationship unfolds and you learn more about yourselves and each other, you may find that, who you imagined yourselves and each other to be are quite different and, in extreme cases, not at all who you really are.

Many of us also imagine a world for ourselves that, given our skills, talents, and social circumstances, is not realistic. We also do not take into consideration that we incarnated to fulfill a purpose. In addition, many of us are not clear about the amount of work it takes to bring into manifestation what we imagine our worlds to be. When our partners are not who we imagined them to be, and the world we imagined for ourselves appears to be fading, we may respond with hurt and disappointment.

Right imagination means being realistic about yourselves, who you are, and the world you imagine and create together. This may require *re-imaging* yourselves and each other to who you really are. If what you imagine is realistic and some habits or behaviors need to be changed, then you can bring about the necessary changes by first envisioning and meditating on them, and doing the necessary work to bring them into manifestation.

You can also use your imagination to bring into manifestation your aspirations, hopes, wishes, dreams, and the things that bring you pleasure and joy. Since these things might be different for each of you, it is important to explore what they are, whether they are good for both of you and the relationship, and whether you are willing to support each other. Spiritual cultivation of your imagination is necessary to strengthen your imaginative and creative abilities, and imagining and creating things that are Divine is the key to unlimited pleasure and joy.

Tree of Life/Faculty: Sphere 6—Love
Step: 4—Awakening to Universe Love
Energetic Correspondence: Heart Chakra
Principle: Right Love

Our ideas about love are based on societal ideas and our experiences with our caregivers and in previous relationships. When you join together, you transport your ideas about love into the relationship, which forms both the basis of how you express love as well as your expectations for love, which affects your interaction patterns and the relationship.

Our ideas about love are greatly influenced by romantic notions, which are often unrealistic. If we have had challenging experiences with our caregivers and/or partners in past relationships, then it may make it difficult for us to love openly, honestly, and freely and share ourselves in balanced and healthy ways. As we have been hurt and disappointed, many of us have a fear or scarcity approach to love.

We fear opening our hearts because we fear that we will get hurt or we have difficulty sharing ourselves because we fear that we may not have enough, it will not be reciprocated, or, worse, we will be taken advantage of. Such approaches to love stymie intimacy.

Awakening to Universe Love is crossing the bridge from our lower selves to our higher selves. To cross this bridge requires moving beyond personal emotional experiences with love, which can be done by healing your love wounds using the step-by-step guide outlined in Chapter 7. Once you heal your love wounds and remove the energetic blocks that have resulted from such injuries, your heart can open to the currents of Universe Love.

Right love is love that is attuned to Universe Love (i.e., the force that unifies for the benefit of the whole). When we cross the bridge to Universe Love, it awakens our freewill choice to live through our higher selves vs. our lower selves. Approaching love from your higher self means balancing between choices that benefit yourself *only* and those choices that benefit each other. Right love is moving beyond love based on fear and scarcity to sharing yourselves openly, honestly, and freely. It is being kind, compassionate, caring, understanding, and forgiving. Spiritual cultivation of love awakens you to sharing yourselves for the benefit of each other, your relationship, and the world. Sharing yourselves in such a way is the key to the love that Universe Love will return.

Tree of Life/Faculty: Sphere 5—Justice
Step: 5—Awakening to Universe Consciousness
Energetic Correspondence: Throat Chakra
Principle: Right Actions

Our sense of justice is a compass for our moral values and principles. Moral values and principles are based on being right and just and are necessary to keep you and your relationship in balance. When you join, you are transporting your sense of fairness, rightness, and justice into the relationship, which affects your interaction patterns and your relationship. Awakening to Universe Consciousness awakens you to be conscious of being right and just to each other and others;

being conscientious of the law that "you reap what you sow;" understanding the consequences of your actions; and judging yourselves based on your actions while being non-judgmental of each other.

Right actions are necessary for a clear conscience. Spiritual cultivation gives you the courage to do what is right and just, even in the face of adversity, to ensure that you and your relationship are under Divine protection.

Tree of Life/Faculty: Sphere 4—Law
Step: 5—Awakening to Universe Consciousness
Energetic Correspondence: Throat Chakra
Principle: Right Ways

Our moral values and principles are based on our levels of awakening to the fact that laws are governing the universe. When you join, you are bringing your moral values and principles into the relationship and they will affect how you interact together within your relationship. Awakening to Universe Consciousness is awakening to the laws of MAAT—truth, harmony, and balance (i.e., the laws that are necessary to keep things for the good of the whole).

Right ways mean being honest; balanced in your choices and decisions; showing reciprocity; living in harmony; and, ultimately, living through your higher selves. Integrating the laws of MAAT into your ways of being as you cultivate a spiritual life together is necessary to live your lives in truth, harmony, and balance.

Tree of Life/Faculty: Sphere 3—Spiritual Power
Step: 6—Awakening to Universe Light
Energetic Correspondence: Third Eye Chakra
Principle: Right Understanding

Our level of spiritual power is based on right living, right desires, right thoughts, right imagination, right love, right ways, and right actions, all of which awaken you to right understanding. Cultivating a spiritual life together awakens you to Universe Light, which not only helps you understand yourselves and each other as descendants of this light but opens your desires to know the mysteries of the universe. Understanding these mysteries awakens you to your unlimited spiritual power to bring things into manifestation.

Tree of Life/Faculty: Sphere 2—Wisdom
Step: 7—Awakening to Universe Light
Energetic Correspondence: Third Eye Chakra
Principle: Right Knowing
Awakening to Universe Light also awakens the wisdom that comes with knowing the mysteries of the universe. Such wisdom reveals that a will in alignment with Universe Will opens your unlimited potential to bring forth the desires of your hearts. Right knowing that comes with spiritual cultivation gives you the clarity to see yourselves for who you truly are: two souls on a journey to experience, fulfill a purpose, bring good to the world, and live in unity with each other, the world, and the Universe Soul.

Tree of Life/Faculty: Sphere 1—Unity
Step: 7—Awakening to Universe Soul
Energetic Correspondence: Crown Chakra
Principle: Right Being
When you awaken to Universe Soul, your earthly selves awaken you to your eternal nature and you see no separation between your souls, those of others, and the soul of the universe. You renounce attachment to the world of forms, joys, and pleasures and indulge in the pleasures of the Divine. Liberating your souls from the masks of yourselves, your physical bodies and social conditioning reveals to you your souls in their true forms (i.e., your eternal forms). Your souls then, unite with Universe Soul, attaining peace and oneness, and a state of bliss. In unification with each other, you, as soul partners, can become the highest expression of yourselves and vessels for Universe Soul to become the highest expression of itself on Earth.

In conclusion, your soul left the Universe Soul to experience. You and your soul's partner came to Earth to fulfill a purpose and continue evolvement toward reunification with Universe Soul. In this work, we have attempted to provide the tools to help you on your journeys. You are encouraged to use the tools in your religious and spiritual practices as well. In instances in which you find that you need further help, you should seek the assistance of individuals including relationship, marriage, and family counselors/coaches; mental health professionals; and spiritual guides and teachers (e.g., psychic readers, diviners, ministers, priests, energy/reiki healers) who are adept at intuiting and interpreting information from your ancestors, personal cosmic guides and guardians, Universe Helpers, and the Divine. Whether you are single or in a relationship, it is our hope that this work has provided some guidance to help you not only get the love you want, but live a happy, healthy, and fulfilling life of bliss.

Chapter 12 Exercises

> *Stairway to Heaven*

The purpose of these exercises is to use the Tree of Life as a tool to help you explore how you can help each other grow and evolve spiritually.

> **EXERCISE 12.1.** *Tenth Sphere—Physical*

1. Describe how you can help each other heal and grow in matters of diet, health, livelihoods, lifestyles, finances, social connections, etc.

_____
_____
_____
_____
_____

> **EXERCISE 12.2.** *Ninth Sphere—Emotional*

2. Describe and discuss how you can help each other heal, overcome emotional wounds, and how you respond emotionally.

_____
_____
_____
_____
_____

> **EXERCISE 12.3.** *Eight Sphere—Thoughts*

3. Describe and discuss what you need to do and how you can help each other evolve past thoughts that are shaped by unhealthy social

conditioning, and negative thoughts you hold about yourselves, each other, and others.

_____
_____
_____
_____

EXERCISE 12. 4. *Seventh Sphere—Imagination*

4. Describe and discuss how you can help each other be more realistic about how you see each other and the world you want to create and how you can help each other bring into manifestation your aspirations, hopes, wishes, and dreams and the things that bring you pleasure and joy.

_____
_____
_____
_____

EXERCISE 12. 5. *Sixth Sphere—Love*

5. Describe and discuss how you can help each other feel free to open your hearts so that you are able to share yourselves openly, honestly, and freely, balance your individual self-interests with the interests of each other, and live through your higher selves.

_____
_____
_____
_____

EXERCISE 12. 6. *Fifth Sphere—Justice*

6. Describe and discuss how you can help each other stay in line with what is right and just without being judgmental, and to be right and just with each other.

_____
_____
_____
_____
_____

EXERCISE 12.7. *Fourth Sphere—Law*

7. Describe and discuss how you can help each other live in truth, harmony, and balance.

_____
_____
_____
_____
_____

EXERCISE 12. 8. *Third Sphere—Spiritual Power*

8. Describe and discuss how you can help each other engage in spiritual practices to open your understanding so that you can access your spiritual power.

_____
_____
_____
_____
_____

EXERCISE 12.9. *Second—Will*

9. Describe and discuss how you can help each other engage in spiritual practices to gain the wisdom to know how to bring forth the desires of your hearts.

Exercise 12.10. *First—Unity*

10. Describe and discuss how you can help each other engage in spiritual practices so that you attain unity, peace, and oneness with each other, fulfill your purposes for this life, and continue your spiritual journey.

Exercise 12.11. *Narrative*

11. Describe and discuss anything else that is significant and not covered in this and other chapters, as well as the outcomes of all the work you have done/are doing together. You should congratulate yourselves for the progress you have made and then discuss and describe the work that still needs to be done and how you will go about doing it.

300 Soul Partners

Additional Notes

Reference List

Ainsworth, M. D. S., Blehar, M. C., Waters, E., & Wall, S. N. (2015). *Patterns of attachment: A psychological study of the strange situation.* New York, NY: Taylor and Francis.

Amen, R. U. N. (1990). *Metu Neter, Vol. 1: The great oracle of Tehuti and the Egyptian system of spiritual cultivation* (1st Edition). Brooklyn, NY: Khamit Media Trans Visions Inc.

Amen, R. U. N. (2009). *QiGong healing prescriptions.* Brooklyn, NY: Khamit.

Asante, M. (1980). *Afrocentricity.* Trenton, NJ: Africa World Press.

Ba, A. H. (1989). The living tradition. In J. Ki-Zerbo (Ed.), *UNESCO general history of Africa, Vol. I, abridged edition: Methodology and African prehistory* (Abridged edition). Berkeley, California: University of California Press.

Bowlby, J. (1997). *Attachment and Loss: Vol 1.* London: PIMLICO. Chang, S. T. (1986). *The Tao of sexology: The book of infinite wisdom.* San Francisco, California: Tao Publishing.

Chapman, A. B. (2005). *Getting good loving: Seven ways to find love and make it last* (3rd edition). Chicago: Agate Bolden.

Dale, C. (2009). *The subtle body: An encyclopedia of energetic anatomy.* Boulder CO: Sounds True Inc.

Emoto, M. (2001). *The hidden messages in water.* New York, NY: Atria Books.

Fortune, D. (2000). *Mystical Qabalah* (2 edition). York Beach, ME: Weiser Books.

George, C., Kaplan, N., & Main, M. (Unpublished). *The adult attachment interviews.* Berkeley, CA: University of California at Berkeley.

Gray, J. (2012). *Men are from Mars, women are from Venus: The classic guide to understanding the opposite sex.* New York: Harper Paperbacks.

Griaule, M., & Dieterlen, G. (1975). *Conversations with Ogotemmeli: An introduction to Dogon religious ideas.* London: International African Institute.

Holmes, J. (1993). *John Bowlby and attachment theory* (1st edition). London; New York: Routledge.

Johnson, D. R. (2005). *Reaching out: Interpersonal effectiveness and self-actualization* (9th edition). Boston: Allyn & Bacon.

Kaia. (2014). *Reiki masters training manual*. Decatur, GA: Oji Publications.

Karenga, M. (1999). Sources of self in ancient Egyptian autobiographies. In J. L. Conyers (Ed.), *Black American intellectualism and culture: A study of American social and political thought* (pp. 37–57). Stanford, CT: JAI Press.

Karenga, M. (1984). *Selections from the Husia: Sacred wisdom from ancient Egypt* (2 edition). University of Sankore Press.

Love, D. P., & Robinson, J. (2012). *Hot monogamy: Essential steps to more passionate, intimate lovemaking*. CreateSpace Independent Publishing Platform.

Luquet, W. (2006). *Short-Term Couples Therapy: The Imago Model in Action* (2 edition). New York: Routledge.

Minuchin, S. (1974). *Families and family therapy* (1 edition). Cambridge, Mass: Harvard University Press.

Nobles, W. W. (1985). *The Km Ebit Husia*. Oakland, CA: Institute for Advanced Study.

Nobles, W. W. (1976). Extended self: Rethinking the so-called Negro concept. In M. Coleman (Ed.), *Black children just keep growing up* (pp. 160–167). Washington, DC: Black Child Development Institute.

Morris, N, Y. (2008). *Awakening the master feminine*. Powhatan, Virginia: Black River Press.

Orlans, M. & Levy, T. M. (2014). *Attachment, trauma, and healing: Understanding and treating attachment disorder in children, families, and adults* (2nd edition). London ; Philadelphia: Jessica Kingsley Publishers.

Powell, A.E (1978). *The astral body*. Wheaton, Illinois: The Theosophical Publishing House.

Sayin, U. (2011). Altered states of consciousness occurring during the expanded sexual response in the human female: preliminary definitions. *NeuroQuantology*, *9*(4). 882-891. Retrieved from https://www.researchgate.net/publication/260385774_Altered_States_of_Consciousness_Occurring_During_Expanded_Sexual_Response_In_The_Human_Female_Preliminary_Definitions

Six healing sounds: Taoist chant, mantra, and invocations. (n.d.). Retrieved March 24, 2017, from http://baharna.com /chant/ six_healing.htm

Tannen, D. (2007). *You just don't understand: Women and men in conversation* (1st edition). William Morrow Paperbacks.

Teach yourself the six healing sounds Qigong. (n.d.). Retrieved March 24, 2017, from https://theconsciouslife.com/six-healing-sounds htm

What are electromagnetic fields? (n.d.). Retrieved March 24, 2017, from http://www.who.int/peh-emf/about/WhatisEMF/en/

Williams, R., L. (1981). *The collective Black mind: An Afro-centric theory of Black personality.* St. Louis, MO: Williams & Associates.

www.ingramcontent.com/pod-product-compliance
Lightning Source LLC
Chambersburg PA
CBHW071157300426
44113CB00009B/1229